CW01626764

HISTORICAL REMINISCENCES

OF

THE CITY OF LONDON

and Its Livery Companies

Elibron Classics
www.elibron.com

Elibron Classics series.

ISBN 978-0-543-67996-3 (paperback)
ISBN 978-0-543-67995-6 (hardcover)

This Elibron Classics Replica Edition is an unabridged facsimile of the edition published in 1869 by Richard Bentley, London.

THE CITY OF LONDON

AND ITS

LIVERY COMPANIES.

HISTORICAL REMINISCENCES

OF

THE CITY OF LONDON

AND ITS

LIVERY COMPANIES.

BY

THOMAS ARUNDELL, B.D., F.G.S.,

OF ST. JOHN'S COLLEGE, CAMBRIDGE, AND VICAR OF HAYTON.

"Individuals may form communities, but institutions must found a nation."

DISRAELI.

LONDON:
RICHARD BENTLEY, NEW BURLINGTON STREET.
Publisher in Ordinary to Her Majesty.
1869.

TO

THE RIGHT HON. THE LORD MAYOR, M.P.,

MASTER OF ALL THE COMPANIES,

AND TO

THE SHERIFFS OF LONDON AND MIDDLESEX,

This Volume

IS RESPECTFULLY DEDICATED BY

THE AUTHOR.

ADVERTISEMENT.

The following work is founded upon a series of fugitive papers, published weekly in a Yorkshire periodical, during the years 1866-7. The Author's aim is to draw the attention of the general reader to the history and antiquities of the City of London, and to show the dignity and value of many of its ancient corporations.

In an age of restless and rapid movements like the present, the test of utility is ruthlessly applied to every institution, and destruction being the handiest and speediest of all remedies, no institution can be safe which is not manifestly and conspicuously useful. The Author hopes that these pages will leave on the mind of the reader an impression strongly favourable to the preservation of the powers and privileges of the great corporate bodies of the City of London, and their various dignified officials, and that he has indicated satisfactory reasons for many customs and observances which have usually been thought to have only prescription and antiquity on their side. He has also shown that the property of the now wealthy gilds has been created by the contributions and bequests of their own members, has accumulated by their own careful and skilful management, and is employed in a manner accordant with the objects of its donors, greatly to the honour and renown of the Empress City, and to the advantage of her poorer citizens. No property in the land is held by a better title, or is more righteously and beneficially employed.

The Author has much pleasure in acknowledging the kindness of many friends in affording assistance and facilities in the preparation of this work. In particular, he would tender his best thanks to J. J. Howard, LL.D., F.S.A., the learned editor of the "Miscellanea Genealogica et Heraldica;" to the Rev. John Tagg, M.A., Rector of Mellis, formerly a Fellow of Sion College; to the Right Worshipful John Sugden Neale, Esq., Master; to William Bentley, Esq., and Martin Blackmore, Esq., past Masters of the Leathersellers' Company; to the Right Hon. the Lord Mayor; to Colonel Wilson, the senior alderman; and especially to Sir Thomas Gabriel, Bart., past Lord Mayor, for the privilege of searching the treasures of the Corporation Library, the most valuable collection of local antiquarian literature which this country possesses.

HAYTON, YORK,
April, 1869.

CONTENTS.

CHAPTER X.

CHAPTER IX.

CHAPTER XI.

CHAPTER XII.

CHAPTER XIII.

CHAPTER XIV.

CHAPTER XV.

CHAPTER XVI.

CHAPTER XVII.

CHAPTER XVIII.

CHAPTER XIX.

CHAPTER XX.

CHAPTER XXXIII.

CHAPTER XXXIV.

CHAPTER XXXV.

APPENDIX.

HISTORICAL REMINISCENCES

OF

THE CITY OF LONDON

AND ITS

LIVERY COMPANIES.

CHAPTER I.

THE CITY COMPANIES: THEIR ORIGIN AND OBJECTS.

"Towards three or four o'clock
Look for the news that the *guild* hall affords."
SHAKESPEARE'S *Richard III.*

FOR wealth and vastness, London outvies all the cities of Europe. The riches of the Corporation of the City are something marvellous. One of our early kings, when in want of money, "in consideration of his love for his loyal subjects the citizens," and of a sum down in ready cash, grants them by royal charter the village of Southwark, from which one gift alone now arises a revenue sufficient probably to support a peerage. The state observed by the Lord Mayor at his official residence, the Mansion House, is almost regal. Certainly no subject of our Queen maintains an equal amount of courtly ceremony, nor can the state banquets of our greatest nobility surpass in splendour the princely entertainments continually furnished by the sovereign of the City. The frequency, too, of these hospitable gatherings, and the large numbers generally invited—covers being laid, as we sometimes read, for three hundred or four hundred guests, and at the Guildhall for between one thousand and two thousand—lead us to imagine that the cellars of the Mansion House must be as exhaustless as the wealth of the Corporation. If we remember correctly, the present* Lord Mayor has on two different occasions already during his year of office entertained Sovereigns, or Royal Princes, without the necessity, as we understand, of any variation from his usual preparations for his guests. The original sum voted for the present Mansion House was £80,000, besides the site; the supply of plate, the accumulation of centuries, both by purchases and by presents from royal and other personages, is unsurpassed; and no cost is withheld by the City in maintaining the fittings and appointments throughout in a manner worthy of so great a Corporation.

Bearing in mind all these facts, people in the country are frequently rather startled at reading in the London papers, as we did last week,† that the wealthiest city and first county in England had appointed for the ensuing year S. Waterlow, Esq., citizen and stationer, and Francis Lycett, Esq., citizen and spectacle-maker, high sheriffs for London and Middlesex. Not long since the Lord Mayor (Wire)

* Sir B. Phillips (1866).

† Written 1866.

was an innholder; his predecessor a butcher; the under-sheriff a cook; while from the recent lists we extract the names of Alderman Wheelton, sheriff and cordwainer; Mr. Thomas Lott, F.S.A., deputy and baker; Moses Kipling, esquire and blacksmith; E. J. Hutchins and A. S. Ayrton, both members of Parliament and leather sellers; and what is still more curious, the Rev. Markland Barnard, vicar of Rudge and mercer; the Rev. Thomas Lee, vicar of Osset and leather-seller; the Rev. Charlton Lane, rector of Hampstead and mercer; the rector of St. Margaret's, Lothbury, chaplain to the Queen and haberdasher. There is something still more anomalous than all this, namely, that the great and eloquent Earl of Derby is at the same time Prime Minister of England and merchant taylor; while the estimable Prince of Wales, recently the guest of the Lord Mayor and the Archbishop of York, is not only a merchant taylor and goldsmith, but adds to his other professions the lucrative calling of mercer.

Now although many and most of the City gentlemen above named are engaged in trade, probably there is not one of the number connected with the particular trade whose designation is attached to his name; but as it is necessary, in order to be eligible for civic offices, that a candidate shall be a freeman of London and a liveryman of one of the ancient gilds, and as many privileges attach themselves to the office of *liveryman*, all who look for office, or who wish to become participators in the advantages offered by these corporations, connect themselves with one or other of them, whichever offers the greatest attractions, without the slightest regard to its designation. The first cost of admission to the livery varies, in different Companies, from £20 to 100 guineas,* which, in addition to the freedom of the City, and the freedom of the Company and future fines, brings the total cost in some of them to nearly £200. In the early times, none could exercise any craft or calling in the City of London without having first become free of his particular craft or mystery; now, in these days of free-trade, no such restrictions exist, and, consequently, the necessity of these gilds no longer remains. Their vast estates, however, remain, and they, as powerful corporations, will continue as long as society holds together.

Napoleon caught the right idea of the cause of England's greatness when he called us a nation of shopkeepers. Conquest and diplomacy may enrich and extend for a time, but for a nation to live and become increasingly rich and strong, her prosperity must be based upon a sound system of trade. The power of England is felt on every sea, for her merchant ships are there. The wealth of England enables her to maintain her vast influence in every clime, and her wealth is drawn from her rich landed nobles and her prosperous trading communities. The wealth of the nobles, however, has been chiefly obtained from trade. Few of the Norman barons are to be traced through their descendants to the

* The highest we know of is that of the Leathersellers—viz., 100 guineas.

present time; those who now possess our soil are chiefly descended from our great bankers, goldsmiths, and other City traders. Last summer a City man died worth £3,800,000, all of which he had himself accumulated,—Richard Thornton, a Yorkshireman, a native of Burton-in-Lonsdale, in the North Riding, in which parish, during his lifetime, he built and endowed schools at a cost of £40,000. He died at the advanced age of eighty-nine, having been for sixty-six years a liveryman of the Leathersellers' Company of London. We believe that the art of trade cannot be learned in a century, that it must be fostered by a nation, and studied by its disciples, who must understand its history and traditions. England has ever honoured her traders. She knows how much to them she is indebted. The highest offices in Parliament and in Government are open to them, and the Peerage is continually strengthened by admissions from their ranks. It is certainly below the mark to affirm that more than two hundred peerages have been founded by Lord Mayors and other members of the London Livery, since the time of Henry Fitz-Allen (Mayor 1110), each of whom has been in trade. As a curious specimen of the result of an examination of the records of one Company out of the fifty, we subjoin a list of founders of ennobled families from the Mercers :—

1. Sir Adam Francis (Mayor 1354); his daughter and heiress married John, Lord Montacue, Earl of Salisbury.

2. Sir John Coventry (1425); ancestor to the present Earl of Coventry.

3. Sir Geoffrey Bullen; grandfather of Thomas, Earl of Wiltshire, father to Ann Bullen, and grandfather to Queen Elizabeth.

4. Sir William Hollis; ancestor to the Earls of Clare, afterwards the ducal family of Newcastle.

5. Sir Michael Dormer (1542); produced the future Lords Dormer.

6. Sir Thomas Baldry (1523); his daughter married Lord Rich, ancestor of the Lords Kensington, and whose progenitor was Richard Rich, mercer.

7. Sir Thomas Seimour (1527); from him sprung the Seimours, Dukes of Somerset.

8. Sir Baptist Hicks; ancestor of the Viscounts Camden.

9. Sir Rowland Hill; ancestor of Lord Hill, who from 1833 till his death served on the court of this Company.

10. James Butler; ancestors of the Earls of Ormond (reign Henry VIII.)

11. Sir Geoffrey Fielding (1452); ancestor of the Earls of Denbigh.

Sir Baptist Hicks obtained his wealth from the trade of mercer, which he carried on in Cheapside, being mercer to the King (James I.) and the Court. He was first knighted and afterwards created Viscount Camden. This is one of the very few instances on record of a trader being transferred from his shop to the House of Lords. His wealth must have been great, as he not only founded a peerage, but gave each of his daughters £100,000, in those days a vast fortune for an heiress. The present Clerkenwell Sessions' House was built by him for the meetings of the justices for Middlesex, and to this day it is called "Hicks' Hall." He was one of the first citizens who kept a shop after the honour of knighthood, and upon being remonstrated with by some of the aldermen, he laconically replied that "his servants kept the shop, and that he did not live altogether upon the interest of it" (Strype).

A list of founders of ennobled families, equally numerous and distinguished perhaps, might also be selected from the roll of the Drapers' Company, amongst whose lord mayors are such names as Fitz-Allwyn (1190), the Pultneys (1313), the Capells (1303), the Wattons (1415), the Rudstons, of Hayton (1528), the Brydges, Dukes of Chandos (1520), etc.; or from the Grocers' Company, who claim existence as a trading community from the time of the settlement of the Romans in London, and boast of having supplied from their numbers one hundred lord mayors; and from the Goldsmiths' Company might be obtained a list of founders of peerages, which would probably eclipse in numbers and splendour any other of the City gilds, containing, as it would, some of England's greatest names, and many who to Yorkshiremen are especially dear.

Let us look back at the causes of the prosperity of our traders—at the reasons of their unusual success in this country. We must go back for this to Saxon and Norman times, for there we may discern the foundations of the present edifice. The Saxon Gilds were the first nurseries of trade.[1]

Although many other countries have had their gilds and fraternities, nothing like our early gilds has existed. The ancient Romans had their unions of craftsmen and companies of artificers and traders, occupying particular streets to which they gave name, a custom imitated in London soon after the Conquest, as Fitzstephen* tells us: "This city, even

* A monk and secretary to Thomas à Becket.

as Rome, is divided into wards, and all the sellers of wares, all the workmen for hire, are distinguished every morning in their place as well as street."* But what knit these traders together by the strictest bonds was their congregating into fraternities or gilds. They knew that in union is strength, and they hit upon the most happy mode of securing a harmonious brotherhood. They united to the one great object of their desire, namely trade, two accessories, *religion* and *feasting*. There was much knowledge of human nature here. Men are never so amiable and forgiving as when enjoying the pleasures of good cheer, and never so successful as when they feel they are doing their duty. Our old Saxon ancestors did nothing without a good dinner to accompany it; and these traders evinced a deep sense of their dependence upon the Almighty, by the employment of priests to say prayers for their success and for their souls, and to bless the food at their banquets. We frequently find the several gilds quarrelling one with another, but it is most rare to discover any trace of discord between the members of any one particular fraternity.

We occasionally, it is true, meet with differences, but they are generally of the mildest type; one or two we give by way of example. From the Goldsmith records we learn that in 1449 a member was fined for "*revileing a member of the liverie;*" in 1518 a member is fined 2*s.* "*for mysbehaviour in words;*" and another is sent to the Compter "for

* Descriptio Nobilissim. Civit. Lond. "Strype's Stow," ii. p. 4.

many simple and bad words." In 1519 two members, Walter Lambe and Thomas Banister, are sent by the wardens to the Compter, "for that each of them used lewde, revylinge, and slanderous words to the other at the tyme of the eleccon of the new wardens; wher' they abode till they were agreed; that is to say till viii. of the clocke at nyghte; at whiche tyme Mr. Wardens sent for them to the hall, and examyned them whether they were agreed. And they said yea; and also that they were sorry for that they had spokyn. Whervpon they drank to geder and deprted frendly bothe." The minute-book of the Ironmongers' Company contains a similar entry, under date 15th July, 1567: "At this court, Mr. Harvy and Mr. Gamage, olde wardens, complayned against William Penyfather for unkynde words against them and evell order on the feast day in the hall; and it was ordered by this court he shal be sent to prison and pay fyne of xx^{s}, and (at) the request of Mr. Harvy and Mr. Gamage his imprisonment was released."*

Of a very different aspect is a quarrel between two gilds narrated by Northouck. In 1226 so violent a quarrel arose between the goldsmiths and tailors, that each party met on an appointed night to the number of five hundred men, completely armed, and proceeded to decide their difference by blows. Many were killed and wounded on each side; nor could they be parted till the sheriffs, with the City *posse comitatus*, came and apprehended the ringleaders, thirteen of whom were condemned and executed!

* Nicoll's "Hist. Iron Comp." p. 94.

Some of these corporations, by prudent management and the increase in the value of land, have become fabulously rich; and with age, instead of decrepitude, manifest now after many centuries all the vigour of new institutions. The secret of this lies in the social feature which is their distinguishing characteristic. Feeling that their power lay in their union, they banded together for purposes secular, by means of usages religious and social.

There was a time when the occupation of man was confined to agriculture and husbandry, but as the wants of society increased, many detached themselves from these employments, and settling down into some central spot, formed themselves into communities, and founded towns and cities, the marts for all kinds of commodities. Hence sprung municipal governments. Of these communities, one of the earliest in this country was the Frithgild of the seventh century, in which social feastings formed an essential feature, and which partook much of a political character. To this succeeded gilds ecclesiastical, founded for alms-deeds and devotion, not a few of which were established in York and its neighbourhood, consisting both of clergy and laity. When a brother died, a feast was prepared for the day of burial; and in the ecclesiastical laws of King Athelstan we read this declaration: "We have charged all that are admitted into our gildships, that if any one happen to die, every brother of the gild give a loaf." The festivities, however, were not confined to eating merely.

"I found them winding of Marcello's corpse.
And there was such a solemn melody,
'Twixt doleful songs, tears, and sad elegies—
Such as old grandames, watching by the dead,
Are wont to wear the night with.
* * * * * * * *
Ofttimes with wassail bowl refresht
Their grief they drowned in wine."—OLD PLAY.

Even in the Metropolis, as late as the sixteenth century, unseemly banqueting took place at the funerals of the great. The Merchant Taylors' records state it to be an ancient custom of their society "to attend the funerals of worshipful brethren, and on the day of their interment to partake of a dinner at the hall, at which a commendable grace was said for the good brother deceased." In return for this act of respect, the family of the deceased usually presented the Company with a piece of plate. In the ordinances of the Leathersellers' Company, in the times of James I., it is ordered that a cup of £3 value shall be given after the attendance of the livery, by the friends of the deceased member; and it is further ordered that at the funeral of a member "the master and wardens shall attend *in state*." In 1524, Sir Thomas Lovell (of Shakespeare memory) was buried at Holywell Nunnery, Shoreditch, with great ceremony. "The gentlemen of the Inns of Court, forasmuch as Sir Thomas had built their noble gateway at Lincoln's Inn, with certyn *crafts of London*, received the remains at the convent, accompanied by the maior and all the aldermen of London," and during the singing of the dirge, "whyche was solemnly done by all the clerks of London, the maior and aldermen encircled the rails and repeated the *De profundis.*" The mourners, during these services, were suffered to want nothing in the way of refreshments. The libations were most copious, for during the dirge it is stated "there was a drynkynge in all the cloisters, the nones hall, and parlors of the said place," and "every where ells, for as many as would come, as well the *crafts of London,* as gentilmen of the Inns of Court."

This custom of feasting at funerals still prevails universally in the East Riding villages. The entire parish attend the remains of a neighbour to his grave—singing in procession, and in the church, doleful chants to tunes evidently composed at a period anterior to the discovery of music, and the day closes with weeping and festivity. This is an old Saxon usage, unrepealed by the progress of society, but one which seems rather more suited to Saxon times than to the present.

Besides the gilds political and the gilds ecclesiastical, were the Merchant Gilds, or Gildæ Mercatoriæ, of which we especially treat, as the originals of the present livery companies of London. As the name implies, a payment was made to a common fund by every member of each gild. The Saxon word GILDAN—to pay—indicates a tax. Thus, we read in Doomsday Book that "the burgh of Totenais did not geld, but when Exeter gelded, and then it paid twelve pence for geld." * Dr. Johnson

* Firma Burgi, p. 24.

explains the word *guild* as a "society, corporation, fraternity, or company combined together by orders and laws made among themselves by their prince's licence. Hence the common word *gild* or *guildhall* proceeds, being a fraternity or commonalty of men gathered into one combination, supporting their common charge by mutual contribution." Gildam, otherwise Geltum, Geldum, and Geldus, are all derived from the Saxon Gildam and Geldam, whence Gildare is, in Doomsday Book, synonymous with Solvere, Reddere, to pay, to render. Spelman informs us that in like manner Godgildam meant offerings to God, as did Deofulgild, offerings to the devil. Geld, as meaning public taxes, was changed by the Anglo-Normans into Taxum, tax. Gildam, meaning a fine or mulct to the king, occurs in the laws of Ethelbert, Athelstan, and other Saxon princes, as quoted by Granville.

CHAPTER II.

THEIR ANTIQUITY.

"In woollen cloth, it appears, by those ancient gilds that were settled in England for this manufacture, that this kingdom greatly flourished in that art."—HALE'S *Origin of Man*.

OF the three kinds of gilds existing in Anglo-Saxon times, the gilds political (or Frith gilds), the gilds ecclesiastical, and the gilds secular, services, we believe, were required in all cases by the Sovereign. The Frith gilds originated in the country districts in a law requiring every freeman of fourteen years old to find sureties to keep the peace; ten families joined, and became bound to each other to produce him who committed an offence, or to make satisfaction to the injured party. They formed a common fund, and met at stated periods for feasting, which assembly, in the seventh century, was called the "Gebeorscipe," or "Beorscipe," which equals convivium, symposium, a banquet—literally beership, beer-drinking. Tacitus describes these banquets as frequent among the Gothic tribes. It was at such a ge-beership that the poet Cœdmon was called upon to sing, when the harp was handed round to each of the company in turns.* Our ancestors were great patrons of music, both sacred and secular. All festivity was accompanied by minstrelsy and sacred song. Cromwell's people are supposed to have been the most successful psalm-singers this country has produced; but, from a study of Anglo-Saxon times, we should be led to infer that in the days of Edward the Confessor the passion for psalm-singing was at its height; for historians tell us that his royal banquets and great festivals were preluded by no less an effort of lungs and memory than the entire songs bequeathed to us by King David.

In times of war, military services were required of these Frith gilds, and even the ecclesiastical gilds had to appear in battle to intimidate the enemy, and to cheer their own countrymen by all the sanctions of their religion. In William's first and fruitless effort to raise a rebellion in England in his favour, we read that both the Norman Bishop of London and the Norman Archbishop of Canterbury headed the insurgents, armed *cap-à-pie*, with spears in hand, and bravely fought for the Norman. "Red with gore was the spear of the prelate of London; broken to the hilt was the sword militant in the terrible hand of the Archbishop of Canterbury. But the men of London triumphed. The conquered doffed their mail, and crept through the forest to the sea, the two prelates and their attendant priests being the last to gain their boats, and drift across the Channel to the French shores. And thus, in the year of our Lord

* *Vide*, also, Bede iv. 24.

1052, occurred the notable dispersion and ignominious flight of the counts and vavasours of Great William the Duke" (see the Old Chronicles). William again, as well as Harold, made good use of this element in their final battles at Stamford Bridge and Hastings, when a magnificent array of white-robed ecclesiastics accompanied each army. Especially imposing was that of the Normans, who, with pomp theatrical and banners consecrated by the Pope, invoked a curse upon their enemies, and promised certain victory to their own forces. Historians all agree that, but for this accessory to his army, William's success would have been doubtful.

The secular gilds also had to fight when required: and the one of which we know the most particulars in the Anglo-Saxon times was so far military as to owe all their privileges to their prowess in the field. They were called the "Cnighten Gild." Stow, in his "Survaie of London," 1598, gives some interesting details respecting them, whom he calls the "Knighten-gild," and he assigns to them the origin of the Ward of Portsoken, which, he says, means "the franchise at the gate." "In the daies of King Edgar, more than 600 years ago, there were thirteen knights, or soldiers, well-beloved of the King and the realme for services by them done, which requested to have a certaine portion of land on the east part of the Citie, left desolate and forsaken by the inhabitants, by reason of too much servitude. They besought the King to have this land with the liberty of a Guilde for ever: the King granted to their request, with conditions following; that is to say, that each of them should victoriously accomplish three combates—one above ground, one under ground, and the thirde in the water; and after this, at a certaine day, in East Smithfield, they should run with speares against all commers; all of which was gloriously performed, and the same day the King named it Knighten-gild."

It was to this gild Edward the Confessor granted a written charter—the first we hear of granted to any such fraternity; and William Rufus confirmed the same, terming them a *soke*, a *fraternity*, granting them the privileges of a soke "and the land appertaining thereunto, with all *customs* as they had before enjoyed."*

Thus we learn that from very early times the London citizens had been warlike—a propensity remaining with them down to the period of the armed city apprentices and the city trained-bands, and to the present days of volunteer riflemen and artillery. We cannot well understand what King Edgar's conflict underground might be; but that the people were athletic and brave we know, and most expert in contests on the water. That Stow is in error in speaking of them as knights, seems certain. There were no knights in England then, no standing army, no soldiers by profession. The very first mention of any approach to regular soldiers was A.D. 1485, when King Henry VII. appointed fifty yeomen, and this small force was our first "standing army."

* Strype's Stow, i., p. 349.

The order of Knights-Templars was not founded till 1118, centuries after King Edgar's time. Antiquarians are agreed that "Cneughts" signified young men, *i.e.*, young men of the gild, and not knights or soldiers. This gild was undoubtedly "burgensic and secular," and not military. In his beautiful picture of Anglo-Saxon life, given by Bulwer (Lytton) in his "Harold," he uses this word "*cneht*," or "*cnught*," in the same sense; and, in defending himself from the charge of using the word instead of the English word "knight," he says: "I should sadly, indeed, have misled the reader, if I used the word *knight* in an age when knights were wholly unknown to the Anglo-Saxons; and '*cneht*' no more means what we understand by a knight, than a *Templar* in modern times means a man in chain-armour, and vowed to celibacy."

In Strutt's "Sports and Pastimes" (p. 132), we learn some particulars of the water-combats, which were boat-justs, or tiltings, on the water. He was the conqueror, who could parry with his shield the baton of his opponent, and, whilst himself remaining firm, could overturn the latter into the water. The London youths were singularly skilled in these sports.

Stow furnishes many particulars of the bravery and prowess in arms of the young men of London. "The citizens' sons," he says, "issue out through the gates by troops, furnished with lances and warlike shields; the younger sort have their pikes not headed with iron, when they make a representation of battle, and exercise a skirmish. Many courtiers resort to this exercise when the King lies near-hand, and young striplings out of the families of barons and great persons, which have not yet attained to the warlike girdle, meet to train and skirmish. Hope of victory inflames every one. The neighing and fierce horses bestir their joints and chew their bridles; at last they begin their race, and then the young men divide their troops. Some labour to outstrip their leaders, and cannot; others fling down their fellows, and get beyond them."* Of such mettle were the citizens and the youth of early England.†

Records exist of a still earlier gild than the Knighten-gild, called "The Steel-yard Merchants of London," who gave existence to the famous Hanseatic League, first formed on the east shores of the Baltic, in the eighth century, to protect their trade from the incursions of the Norman pirates, and thence called "Easterlings." The Steel-yard Merchants dealt in grain, flax, cloth, and iron; their institution was celibatarian; all were obliged to remain unmarried. Stow informs us that if one "married an English woman, or concubined with one, he lost his *hanse*," or gildship. No one was allowed even a housekeeper, nor to admit a bed-maker. They were obliged to pass the night on the premises, no doubt for the protection of their wares,

* Appendix to Strype's Stow, ii., p. 684.

† Sir John Young (Lord Mayor 1466), with Sir John Crosby, Sir John Stockton, and nine other aldermen of London, were knighted on the field for distinguished bravery in repulsing the bastard Falconbridge in his attack upon the City.

as London abounded with robbers, and the immediate neighbourhood of the city was one dense forest, wild as the Yorkshire Wolds, but wooded, in many parts, as densely as Norwood or Epping Forest, forming good cover for the lawless marauders of that day. We cannot suppose that it was hatred of women that gave rise to these strict laws enforcing their banishment. Their countrymen in particular, and the Anglo-Saxons and Danes generally, were by no means averse to marriage; indeed, so much otherwise, that the early Christian missionaries, especially on the Scandinavian continent, had great difficulty with their converts, who claimed to eat horse-flesh in honour of Odin, and to marry wives *ad libitum*. The puzzled monks, often driven to a choice, yielded the latter point, it is said, but stood firm on the graver matter of the horse-flesh.

This gild having been plundered by the mob in 1493, gradually decayed and finally dissolved itself in 1552. In its prosperity it is said to have exported annually 40,000 pieces of cloth, whilst all the English merchants united exported only 11,000 pieces. The other gilds not only approved of marriage, but admitted females into their societies, who took rank in every way with the men, except only in their being ineligible for offices having the direction of affairs. This admission of females appears not to have been confined to the trade privileges, but they were summoned to the feasts, not as spectators, but as guests at the banquet table. Neither were the invitations restricted to the "female associates," but the wives of the livery were included. In the last charter granted to the Leathersellers by Charles I., in recapitulating the privileges accorded by former charters, especially those of Richard II., certain ordinances are quoted therefrom respecting the presence of females at the banquets; and one day, that on which the election of wardens occurs, is named, upon which heavy fines are inflicted for non-observance of this order; "upon the first Tuesday in August, at the cost of an allowance from the stock of the house, *as formerly and anciently hath been used*, the wardens shall make and keep a dinner or feast in their Common Hall, to which feast all assistants and livery, together *with their wives, as anciently*, shall be called, and then near about the end of the said feast, garlands shall be presented to such of the new wardens as then shall be present; and in default of making the said dinner or feast the wardens shall forfeit £40, that is to say £10 a-piece, to the benefit of the company." A heavy fine in those days. Queen Elizabeth was a Free Sister of the Mercers' Company.

Many of the Companies from the earliest times have not only admitted to their board their "female associates," and "widows," by right, and the wives of the livery upon payment, but if unmarried the liveryman might introduce a "damsel if he pleased." The ordinances of the Grocers' Company, A.D. 1348, contain a quaint and curious decree, that every one of the fraternity, from henceforward, having a wife or companion (compagnon) shall come to the feast, and bring with him a damsel, if he pleases (*ameyne avec luy une demoiselle si luy plest*); if they cannot come from the reason hereafter named (*malade, ou grosse danfant et pres sa deliverance*), they are then, and not otherwise, to be excused. Slovenly composition has given this ordinance an entirely different signification to that which was intended; but the meaning is clear: the contingency named evidently was intended to refer to the wives only.

To the great antiquity of the Easterlings, or Steelyard Merchants, above referred to, all British history attests. They are known to have been settled here before the year 967, for a regulation of King Etheldred's of that date declares that "the Emperor's men or Easterlings, coming with their ships to Belins-gate* shall be accounted worthy of good laws."

A gild of nearly equal antiquity was a wealthy branch of the numerous and powerful craft of leathersellers, viz., the *Gilda Sellariorum* or SADDLERS, of whom we read immediately after the Conquest as possessing "ancient statutes," existing between the Saxon religious foundation of St. Martin-le-Grand and the saddlers, which latter are called "brethren and partakers of all benefits with the Church of St. Martin, both by night and by day, in masses, psalms, prayers, and watches;" moreover that it had been

* A heathen temple once stood here erected to the British Deity, Belin, hence the name of Belinsgate, now Billingsgate.

granted to the gild that "they should all be separately prayed for by name on the Ebdomada (the day preceding the Resurrection) in two masses, one for the living, and one for the deceased brothers of the said gild; and that it had been further granted that for the latter the bell of St. Martin's Church should be tolled and procession made with burial freely and honourably." Herbert says there can be "little doubt of the saddlers being a veritable Anglo-Saxon gild, and consequently one of the oldest on record of all the present Livery Companies."

That these secular gilds were common institutions as early as the reign of Henry II., is evident from Glanville (who prepared a digest of the laws of England, A.D. 1181):—"If a native (*servus*) quit for one year and a day to dwell in a privileged town, so as to become one of the same community (*scilicet gyldum*), he shall be received as a citizen, and liberated from his villeinage" (v. lib., cap. 5). Gildarum nomine continentur non solum minores fraternitates et sodalitia sed ipsa etiam civitatum communitates (Spelm.). And in the same reign we read of eighteen gilds amerced as adulterines, or, set up without the king's licence. This is a proof that the gilds were numerous, for we cannot suppose that any but those of the poorer sort would run so great a risk. Nearly all the companies at present existing may be traced without a break to the period quite as remote as this reign (Henry II.). The Mercers' Company were undoubtedly a trading gild in 1172. Their alderman or master, Robert Searle, was Mayor 1214. From this gild arose, in 1296, the well-known "Company of the Merchant Adventurers," which company, in 1406, obtained from Henry IV. a charter, in which they are designated "Brothers of St. Thomas à-Beckett." The present stately hall of the Mercers occupies the site of the ancient hospital of St. Thomas of Acon, the place of the first settlement of the Mercers in London. Anciently on the spot where is now the entrance to the hall in Cheapside, stood the house of Gilbert Beckett, citizen and mercer. In his youth Gilbert had been fired with religious zeal to rescue the Holy Land from the infidel. He joined the Crusaders, fought well and bravely, was taken prisoner, was released by a "fair Saracen" from his captivity, who, being herself taken captive by love, followed him to London, became a Christian, and eventually the wife of the Crusader. The son born to Gilbert and Matilda the "fair Saracen" was none other than Thomas, in his youth clerk in the sheriff's office, London, and eventually the Archbishop of Canterbury. He was Thomas of Acon, or Acres (the ancient Ptolemais), the birthplace of his mother. Twenty year's after the archbishop's murder, his sister Agnes built a chapel and hospital on the spot where her brother was born; so deep was the reverence of his sanctity that, without waiting for his canonization, the foundation was dedicated "to the worshippe of God Almightie and the blessed Virgin Mary and of the said glorious martyr." Soon afterwards De Helles gave to the master and brethren "alle the lande that was sometime Gilbert Bekkettes, father of the said Thomas the Martyr, and where he was born, which landes be yn in the parishe of St. Mary, of Colechurche, yn London, yn free, pure, and perpetuall almes for evermore," and constituted the company of Mercers patrons. In 1377 Henry III. made a further grant to the master and brethren, at that time twelve in number, "for ynlarging of their said ground." In 1444 they became a body corporate, and in 1456, upon the petition to Parliament of four clergymen of London, power was obtained to found a grammar school "to teach all that will come." The petitioners state that "where there is a great number of learners and few teachers, and all the learners are compelled to go to the few teachers, and to none others, the masters wax rich in money, and the learners poor in learning, against all virtue and order of public weal." The foundation now under the name of the Mercers' School is the result of the aforesaid petition, the prayer of which was regularly granted by Parliament.

The traders of London, even in the days of their greatest prosperity, seem never to have forgotten to express their gratitude to their benefactors, nor were they ashamed to unite in all their ceremonies a due observance of the rites of their religion. Strype describes a most interesting ceremony which used to be observed in old St. Paul's, when the new Lord Mayor, on the occasion of his inauguration, "*after dinner*," was wont to go from his house to the church of St. Thomas of Acon, the aldermen and his livery going with him; thence to the church of St. Paul, where they were wont to pray for the soul of the Bishop of London, William the Norman, who was a great benefactor to the City in obtaining the confirmation of their liberties from William the Conqueror, a priest saying the office of *De profundis* * (called a dirge), and thence they passed to the churchyard where Thomas à-Beckett's parents were buried, and there, near their tomb, they said also for all the faithful departed *De profundis* again."† Dugdale informs us that in the old St. Paul's an inscription existed on a tablet near the prelate's tomb commemorative of this ancient custom, placed there in 1623 by Edward Barkham, Lord Mayor.

"Walkers, whosoere you be
If it prove you chance to see,
Upon a solemne 'scarlet day,'
The City Senate pass this way,
Their grateful memory for to show
Which they the reverend ashes owe
Of Bishop Norman here intum'd,
By whom this city hath assum'd
Large privileges—those obtained
By him when Conqueror William reign'd.
This being by Barkham's thankfull mind renew'd,
Call it the monument of gratitude."

(Dugdale's St. Paul's, (1653) p. 52).

The DRAPERS' COMPANY, again, claims great antiquity. Elkanah Settle, in his elaborate and fulsome preface to his Triumphs of London, or pageant for Sir Thomas Stamp, draper, Lord Mayor in 1691, thus addressed the Company:—

"I dare not pretend in so narrow a paper to

* The words commencing the 130th Psalm.

† *Vide* Liber Albus, lib. i., pt. i., cap. vii.

recount the antiquity and splendour of the Worshipful Company of Drapers. It is enough to say that the honour of your corporation extends as far as trade can reach or canvas wings can carry it, and, from this little island, visits only those nations of the world that there is sea to travel to. As for your first original, drapery is unquestionably so ancient as to have the honour of being the immediate successor of the fig leaves. And, though we are not quite certain that our great first father began it within his fair Eden, yet we are assured that Eve's *spinstrey* and Adam's *spade* set to work together."

The same author thus panegyrizes the CLOTHWORKERS, in his account of the pageant of Sir Thomas Lane, Lord Mayor, 1694:—" The grandeur of England is to be attributed to its golden fleece" (which is the crest of this Company), " the wealth of the loom making England a second Peru, and the back of the sheep, and not the entrails of the earth, being its chief mine of riches. The silkworm is not spinster of ours, and our wheel and web are wholly the clothworkers. Thus, as trade is the soul of the kingdom, so the greatest branch of it lies in the Clothworkers' hands; and, though our naval commerce brings us in both the *or* and the *argent*, and indeed the whole wealth of the world, yet, when thoroughly examined, it will be found 'tis your cloth sends out to fetch them. And thus, while the imperial Britannia is so formidable to her foes and so potent to her friends by her strength and her power, when duly considered, to the Clothworkers' honour, it may justly be said, 'Tis your shuttle nerves her arm, and your woof that enrobes her glory."

Indeed, almost all the principal and most wealthy Livery Companies of London,—the Fishmongers, Ironmongers, Goldsmiths, Leathersellers, Merchant Taylors, and others, may claim an antiquity coeval with the Anglo-Saxon period, they having uninterruptedly cohered as fraternities to the present time throughout the whole period intervening; sometimes, it is true, dwindling into insignificance and ready to collapse, and then, from the mere force of their vitality, springing into vigorous growth, and expanding, through successive ages, into the ample dimensions to which they have now attained.

That in all ages they have taken a high position in the State is evident, from the place awarded them on all royal progresses and pageants, at coronations, royal marriages, and funerals. The master or alderman of each gild ranked as a KNIGHT two centuries prior to the institution of Heralds' College (which was not founded till 1340), when knighthood was the most honourable distinction, at a period anterior to the existence of *social* knighthood; each liveryman ranked as an ESQUIRE, and each freeman as a YEOMAN of the craft. The freemen in all the charters are termed the *yeomanry*. The various sovereigns from Edward III. to the present time have ever paid marked honour to the Livery Companies, nearly all having been enrolled as members of a craft. We might quote innumerable instances of their favour: one will suffice. In the reign of Henry VII., A.D. 1491, on the marriage of Katherine of Spain with Prince Arthur, we read that in the "Banketts and Disguysyngs" which took place at Westminster on the occasion, the principals of the Companies, together with the Lord Mayor, were honoured by being seated next to the King and Queen. At a subsequent period the same king not only became a brother of the Merchant Taylors' Company, but delivered them a new charter from the throne, himself habited in the Company's livery, made of velvet and other rich materials; and in the same dress presided afterwards at the banquet as their master.

Amongst the first to receive armorial bearings from the new college were the leading Livery Companies, and one has only to examine these various grants to discover the high and honourable position which was awarded them. With the exception of the Ironmongers, Mercers, and Vintners, the chief Companies have the privilege of SUPPORTERS.*

* In ancient tournaments the knights caused their shields to be carried by servants or pages, disguised as lions, bears, griffins, blackamoors, etc., who had to support and guard the escutcheons, which the knights were obliged to expose to public view for some time before the lists were opened. Hence these figures were designated supporters, and were introduced into the designs on the banners of the knights banneret. As a rule, none under the degree of baron had the grant of supporters. We learn from Menestrier that, according to the heraldic rules of England, bearing coats-of-arms supported is the prerogative—1st, of Nobiles majores, viz.,

Such was the rank they had attained, and the estimation in which they were held by the monarch of the day, that amidst the royal and courtly personages admitted to the "honours of chivalry," the very highest distinctions, as the archives of Heralds' College amply testify, were accorded by the Sovereign to the great and powerful trading Livery Companies of London.

dukes, marquises, earls, viscounts, and barons; 2nd, of all Knights of the Garter, though they should be under the degree of baron; 3rd, of Knights of the Bath, who receive on their creation a grant of supporters; and, lastly, of such knights as the King chooses to bestow this honour upon. Neither peeresses nor bishops have mottoes or crests; and the latter, though peers of Parliament, have no supporters.

CHAPTER III.

THEIR ALDERMEN.

> But if the trumpets' clangour you abhor,
> And dare not be an alderman of war,
> Take to a shop, behind a counter be."
>
> DRYDEN'S *Juv. Sat.*

NOTHING can more certainly attest the antiquity of the City Gilds than the fact that they first gave the name and created the office of Ealdman, Ealdorman, or Alderman. Alderman equals Senex, whence is derived Senator. The office of alderman of a corporate town is usually considered one of the most ancient which we now possess; but it should be known that before corporate towns existed, and down to the close of the reign of Edward I., the master of each gild was termed alderman, and possessed almost absolute power over the members of his gild. He had the right of search, the power of fine and imprisonment, he and his wardens going their rounds, like juries, to discover spurious articles of their trade, to assay gold and silver,* to decide

* Gold and silver plate, and other luxuries, were more common amongst the Anglo-Saxons than they became in ages much more

on the standard of weights and measures, and on the quality of all articles of merchandise and manufacture; and it was not until towns and cities became incorporated that the name of Alderman became transferred from the mastership of the gilds to the chief magistracy of a ward or district. For this statement we have the authority of the "Judicia Civitatis Londoniæ," compiled by King Athelstan,*

recent. In Anglo-Saxon times, too, the habits of the higher classes were less primitive than they afterwards became. For instance, in Edward the Confessor's time it was customary for the wealthier sort, in retiring to rest for the night, to be enrobed in an ample linen tunic (called *dormitorium*, in the Latin of that period, and *night-rail* in the Saxon tongue); but a few generations later this comfortable and decent fashion of night-gear was abandoned, and our forefathers, Saxon and Norman, went to bed *in puris naturalibus* like the Laplanders. Even the ancient Britons understood the art of working in gold and silver, as is evidenced by specimens of their workmanship discovered in barrows throughout this country, many of which were of a great excellence. The Saxons greatly improved upon their predecessors. When Bishop Wilfred built a church at Ripon, A.D. 628, the columns and porticoes were adorned with gold and silver, and a relic still preserved in the Ashmolean Museum of the time of Alfred the Great proves that in his time workmen in gold and silver and the precious stones were highly skilled. Strutt (vol. i. p. 90) affirms that the Anglo-Normans practised these arts with great success. The list of gold and silver vessels belonging to King Edward I. contains, amongst other things, "a gold ring with a sapphire, of the workmanship of St. Dunstan" ("De fabrica Sti. Dunstani"). In the thirteenth century, such was the simplicity of the times, that one Peter Spileman made fine for his lands to Edward II. to find (among other things) *litter* for the king's bed, and hay for his horse (Pennant, p. 263). We are in error in dating all barbarous customs to the Saxons and their times, or in supposing that they did not possess many things since termed luxuries. Benalt, a monk, invented glass in England as early as A.D. 664. Silk was here A.D. 274, it having been introduced from India in that year, and the manufacture of it about the same time set

* *Vide* Wilkin's "Saxon Laws," 66.

and Madox considers the trade gilds to be so ancient as to have given the origin of gildated towns, and also to have originated the name and office of Alderman. He says that "Alderman was a name for a chief governor of a secular gild, and in time it became also a name for a chief in a gildated city or town."* Still further evidence is furnished by Stow, who in recording the foundation of the Priory of Holy Trinity, Aldgate, by Queen Maude in 1105, says that Cnighten-gild or certain burgesses of London (good proof that they were not knights or soldiers, as he had elsewhere called them) gave to that convent "all the lands and the soke called in English *knighten-gild*," but reserved the right to be a trade corporation, which it is remarkable was not assigned either by this grant, or its confirmations by Henry I., or other sovereigns, and in consequence the prior of Holy Trinity became the territorial lord or alderman of Portsoken Ward; like the other aldermen of London he rendered due account to the Crown; like them he held courts of wardmote; and we are informed further that he was seen by Stow himself

on foot. It is quite true that our ancestors had no chimneys in their houses till A.D. 1200, nor were coals known or used in London until 1357; but it is possible to live very comfortably without either coals or chimneys, as may be seen at the great halls at Oxford and Cambridge Universities to this day. It is true gardening was unknown here prior to 1509, all our vegetables before that time being imported from the Netherlands; nor were pins invented till 1543, the ladies previously using skewers. Silk stockings also were unknown till that same year. Indeed, most of our modern luxuries were unknown two centuries ago.

* "Firma Burgi," p. 30.

riding with the mayor and other aldermen in procession, "only distinguished from them by the colour of his gown, theirs being scarlet, and his ecclesiastical purple."

The ruler of a gild was therefore not then addressed, as he is at present in all official documents, as the "Right Worshipful the Master," but the "Right Worshipful the Alderman;" and his three co-wardens were then, as now, entitled to be addressed individually as "his worship." The Livery have individually no title of honour, but in the aggregate are called the "Worshipful the Livery;" so also "the Worshipful the Court of Assistants." We shall therefore refer to his office as an Aldermanry, and designate him Alderman, as the only title by which in ancient times he was known. We have said that his power over the gild was nearly absolute. To this day such are the traditions of the Companies that it is allowed that for his year of office he cannot do wrong. No one questions any one of his acts. He has no absolute authority by right; no charter has surrounded him with the prerogatives of an absolute ruler; but yet, from the beginning to the present time, he has been allowed almost unlimited power and jurisdiction.

In the early times, if the alderman of a gild had occasion to travel out of London, or if he were prevented by illness from performing the duties of his office, he selected whom he pleased to fill his place. If any member of a gild departed from London without his permission, or in disobedience to his command, the alderman directed a sergeant to fetch him back, and he was kept prisoner during his worship's pleasure. His power, indeed, was supreme, appointing whom he chose to share with him the responsibility of direction, and in other cases retaining all power to himself alone.

The usual course, however, seems to have been for the alderman, who was himself an annual officer, to select three seniors, called wardens, to act as his lieutenants: in procèss of time others were united with them and termed "Assistants," and thus was established a usage, now universal, of having jointly with the master and wardens, a council, called the Court of Assistants. The first authoritative mention of a court occurs in the books of the Grocers' Company under the year 1379, "at ye furst congregacyon of ye wardeyns there shall bee chosin six of ye companie to be helpyng and counsellynge of ye same wardeyns for ye yeere followynge;" and soon after (*temp.* Edward III.) we read of the master, wardens, "and ye fele'ship associed."*

The first legal appointment of a Court of Assistants was made to the Stationers by Philip and Mary, and the members of it nominated in the incorporation charter. It is possible that the masters at times had difficulty in maintaining order at the meet-

* "Herbert," vol. i. p. 420, note, 427—464. This may be taken not as a specimen of the correct orthography of the period, but as a sample of the indifferent scholarship usually prevailing. A hundred years later the Grocers' clerk spells whale oil—wa-loil: 44*s*. is charged for "costs, freight, carriage, wharfage, and piling up of ij shippes of wa-loil, given to the fellowship by Alderman Knolley."

ings of so large a body, and the Grocers' Company have, or lately had, in their possession a curious memorial evidently belonging to those early courts, intended for a purpose similar to that of a chairman's hammer of modern times. It consists of a carved figure of St. Anthony, their patron saint, holding a small bell, which the president struck when he enforced order. In the court-room at Leathersellers' Hall is a handsome ivory hammer, unusually large and heavy, originally intended to quiet disorderly or outspoken members, and bearing an inscription to the effect that the said hammer was presented to the worshipful company, A.D. 1623, by "Francis Barradon, warden of the yeomanry, 1620, and nowe one of the assistants of the yeomanry;" from which date it has been in use uninterruptedly—fortunately, as we are informed, more as an ornamental than a necessary article. From these, and similar relics, it is readily surmised that some amount of tact and much firmness were required in one assuming so responsible an office as president of a gild.

The following extract from the minutes of the Carpenters' Company, shows that some patience was used to be exercised in their councils:—

"1556

"Rsd of master abbott a fyne for that he helde not his peess before the master hade knockyd with the sylence iij tymes vjd."*

In 1487, the Drapers' books record a pay-

* Jupp's "Hist. Acc.," p. 139.

ment for "a hammer to knock upon the table, vj^{s} viii^{d}."

In Heath's "Account of the Grocers' Company," p. 32, we have the following extract from their minutes of the date July 8th, 1670: "Upon complaint and observation of the unseemliness and disturbance, by taking tobacco and having drink and pipes in the court-room, during court's sitting; and for the better order, decorum, and gravity to be observed, and readier despatch and minding of debates and business of the court, and avoiding the occasion of offence and disgust, it is agreed that hereafter there be no taking of tobacco, or drinking used or permitted in the court-room during the sitting of the court; and if any person have a desire to refresh himself with a pipe of tobacco or a cup of drink, at a convenient time or interval of serious business, to withdraw into some retiring room more suitable and fit for the purpose."

As early as A.D. 1512, the Merchant Taylors make mention in their minutes of a "Court of Assistants" by name, when the common clerk (Henry Maynard) is said to have "transacted certain affairs at the commandment and request of the master and wardens, with the advice of the more part of the most substantiall and discreet persons, assistants and counsellers of the said fraternity." The numbers of the court vary in different Companies, but twenty-five is the most usual number. In the early Saxon gilds, where a council was needed, thirteen was the favourite number, in imitation of Christ and his apostles. Du Cange tells of one society (no doubt a religious one), consisting of twelve men and only one woman, who represented the Virgin Mary. Frequently in early times the whole body, as in the case of the Steel-yard Merchants, resided together in one house, after the fashion of a college.

The united council have ever acted in perfect independence of the general body of livery, who have no more authority in the management of the affairs of the company than strangers. At the same time every courtesy is paid to them, and upon request they may examine all documents or accounts of interest, and receive information upon all matters of importance connected with the common weal. The court appointed annually their chaplain, preachers, clerk, steward, bailiff, cook, bargemaster, almsmen, and almswomen, and last, but not least, the most useful of all officers—the beadle—who in some companies was, by the conditions of the charters, to be provided with "a scarlet livery gown each year, and to precede all the processions on horseback, followed by the minstrels, to make way for the master." In addition to his gown, he was to have his "meat found by the master, and to be paid fourpence per week wage." As good land in England let at one shilling an acre in 1554, we do not see that the beadle was much underpaid a century or two earlier at "fourpence a week wage." Even lawyers' bills, and proceedings in Chancery, appear to have been moderate in expense in those days. We copy a bill of costs to the Goldsmiths' Company:—

8 Edw. IV., 1469.

"Costes in the Chauncerie for recoverie of a Counterfete Diamant."

(We modernize the orthography.)

	£	s.	d.
For boat hire to Westminster and home again for the suit in the Chancery began in the old warden's time, for the recovery of a counterfeit diamond set in a ring of gold	£0	0	6
For a breakfast at Westminster, spent on our counsel	0	1	6
To Mr. Catesby, serjeant-at-law, to plead for the same	0	3	4
To another time for boat hire in and out, and a breakfast for two days	0	1	6
Again for boat hire and one breakfast	0	1	0
To the keeper of the Chancery door	0	0	2
To Timothy Fairfax at two times	0	8	4
To Pigott, for attendance at two times	0	6	8
To a breakfast at Westminster 7d., and boat hire 4d.	0	0	11
	£1	3	11

But to return to the master's office, and his early designation of Alderman, to which we have already referred as an evidence of the great antiquity of the gilds. Dr. Johnson seems quite to have overlooked the early origin of this office of alderman, for all we read under the word is, "Alderman, from *ald*, old, and man. The same as senator. A governor or magistrate originally, as the name imports, chosen on account of the experience which his age had given him."

This is rather a meagre explanation of the origin of the office from so erudite a scholar as Dr. Johnson; and although his explanation is precisely correct, as far as it goes, yet those who imagine the office to have been created when towns were first gildated, might doubt whether all the aldermen then, any more than at present, were *old* men. Indeed, it is certain that even in Saxon times men not old have held the office; but if we had been taken back to the Saxon gilds, whence the office originated, we should have perceived that as the presidents are usually chosen in rotation, none but men advanced in years could have been eligible for the office. Thus the name Ealdman, Ealdorman, or old man, was the most appropriate when the office first arose. The influence of these magistrates, not only in the city, but in the state, was great. No national movement occurred without their knowledge, and through them the London lithsmen were represented in the great national Witan or Wittenagemote,* and thus they became concerned not unfrequently in deciding the election even of kings. We must not suppose, however, that none but the highest magistrates were admitted to this council of state. To encourage adventure, a statute was promulgated, that any traders, or sons of traders, who had crossed the seas three times at their own cost and risk, should have a seat at the Witan. This encouragement of trade on the part of the Anglo-Saxons was actuated by a wise and provident policy, and well has it succeeded. But London then, as now, was England, as Paris is

* One of the regulations enforced by King Alfred was that the assembly termed the Wittenagemote should hold a session in London twice a year. The word means literally "an assemblage of wise men." It was evidently of a parliamentary character "nd all the great events of the nation had their sanction here."

France. In the year 1018, a subsidy raised in England reached what was then deemed a stupendous sum—viz., 71,000 Saxon pounds. London contributed 11,000 pounds besides.

In the earlier ages, the Witan had usually assembled wherever it happened the King's Court might be at the time, and the circumstance that King Alfred fixed its meetings to take place periodically in London, may be taken as an evidence of great advancement in the national policy, and of the importance in his day of London as a centre of influence. Although the London lithsmen were represented in this great council, we must bear in mind that they sat there as nobles. *Lithsman*, we acknowledge, means merchant. Northouck translates the word *mariner*. The Saxon word from which it is taken equals *navigare*, which is frequently used by Saxon writers in a mercantile sense. But these merchants, before possessing the high privilege of a seat at the national council, had been elevated to the rank of nobles by a law of King Athelstan, which, for the purpose of encouraging commerce, sets forth in the "agreement" with the citizens of London, that a merchant who had made three voyages across the sea, should be entitled to the quality or degree of a thane or noblemen. Not as a lithsman, therefore, but as a thane, he sat at the national Witan.

CHAPTER IV.

THEIR ALDERMEN, CONTINUED.

In the "Liber Albus," compiled A.D. 1419, by John Carpenter, Town Clerk of London, from the most complete collection of ancient records in the possession of the City, is an interesting paragraph under chapter x., which we extract:—

"If we look to the etymology of the word 'Alderman,' the more aged were so called. For *alde* in Saxon means old, and *alder* is our word for 'older;' and hence, as the judgment is most vigorous in persons of more mature years, the dignitary who among the Romans was known as 'Consul' or 'Senator,' among us is called 'Alderman.' And yet in the case of Aldermen, maturity of mind is to be considered rather than of body, and gravity of manners in preference to length of years; hence it is that in the ancient laws of King Cnut and other kings in Saxon times, the person was styled 'Alderman,' who is now called 'Judge' and 'Justiciar,' as set forth in the 'Liber Custumarum.' Yet in several other laws of Saint Edward, the personages who are now styled 'Justiciars,' were called '*lage-*

manni,' from the Saxon *lage,* which corresponds with the Latin, *lex,* or law; the lagemannus being 'a man of law,' such as we now call 'lawyer,' *juris-peritum,* or more correctly, a 'legislator.'"

These Aldermen, too, in respect of name as well as dignity, it would seem, were anciently called "*Barones.*" For it is matter of experience that ever since the year of our Lord 1350, at the sepulture of aldermen the ancient custom of interment with baronial honours was observed. In the church where the alderman was about to be buried, a person appeared upon a caparisoned horse, bearing a banner in his hand, and arrayed in the armour of the deceased, carrying his shield, helmet, and the rest of his arms, along with the banner, as is still the usage at the sepulture of lords of baronial rank. But by reason of frequent changes of the aldermen, and the repeated occurrence of pestilence, this ceremonial in London gradually disappeared. From this, however, it is evident what high honour was paid to the aldermen in ancient times; indeed, no person was accepted as alderman, unless he was free from deformity in body, wise and discreet in mind, rich, honest, trustworthy, free, and on no account of low or servile condition; lest, perchance, the opprobrium that might be reflected upon him by reason of his birth, might have the additional effect of casting a slur upon the other aldermen, and the whole city as well.*

Than the title of Alderman, the Saxon kings

* "Liber Albus," part i., chap. x.

could have conferred upon the masters of the gilds none more honourable or exalted. Alderman and earl were equal, if not synonymous. Spelman has preserved a monumental inscription, taken from the abbey of Ramsey, which is as follows:—"Hic requiescit D. Alwinus, inclyti regis Eadgari cognatus, totius Angliæ Aldermannus et hujus sacri cænobi miraculosus fundator." Maitland, in his "History of London," p. 565, quotes this inscription, and adds this remark:—"Alderman is the same as earl. Thus Alwin was dignified with the title of Earl of all England, which shows the City of London must have been in very great repute when the noble appellation of alderman was conferred upon her magistrates." It may be interesting to note that this Alwin, or Alwyn, was ancestor of Henry Fitz-Alwyn, the first Mayor of London, from 1189 to 1212.*

Again, we learn from Malmesbury, who wrote in King Stephen's reign, that King Alfred gave London to Ethelred as the marriage portion of his daughter; or, as it is more correctly stated in the Saxon manuscript, "he set London to Alderman Ethelred to hold." As to whether this means that a grant to hold *in demesne* was conferred or not, the learned differ. We refer to the fact here only to show the honourable nature of the title, and that in fact the Saxons could go no higher than alderman when designating the masters of the gilds by that name.

It is difficult now to ascertain the date of the earliest privileges granted to the City of London.

* Pennant, p. 17.

It is usual to praise William I., King of the English,* for his grants to the City, and for his having fostered its infant institutions, but that his charters were not their first enrolment is evident; for when at the instigation of the Bishop of London William, or, as he is usually called, William Norman (surnames not being used in England till A.D. 1220), the Conqueror made the grant, he states therein briefly, "I grant you all to be lawworthy, as ye were in the days of King Edward;" thus implying that he therein only confirmed the previous municipal constitution. But that William or any other king granted a charter without a *quid pro quo*, we cannot believe. A goodly sum was invariably paid if the privileges received were of any worth. For King John's first charter to the City of London, a fee of 3000 marks, or £1000, was paid to the King. Henry III. charged for his sixth charter to the city 1100 marks, 500 to the King and 600 to his brother, the Earl of Cornwall. For his next he charged them 20,000 marks, but this, it states, was "for their great crimes and misdemeanours." Immense sums were paid, we know, for monopolous charters, besides a royalty on all matters sold by the monopolist, but the price of 20,000 marks for a municipal charter in the thirteenth century discovers a large amount of wealth on one side and of appetite for gold on the other.

At the time of the Conquest, the mayor, or port-

* Each of the first Anglo-Norman Kings, till Richard I., styled himself *King of the English;* afterwards, till the time of King John, he styled himself *Basileus.*

reeve, who was chosen from the aldermen of the gilds, exercised jurisdiction over the whole municipality, the privileges of which belonged to the fraternities, and not to the householders, as at present. The gilds, indeed, became the exclusive possessors of all municipal rights; and, in the reign of Edward II., articles were prepared by the citizens, confirmed by the King, and incorporated in a charter, that "no person should be admitted into the freedom of the city unless he were a member of one of the *trades* or *mysteries*." * Here we have the first mention of these Companies under their new name of trades or mysteries, and henceforth, for ages, in all official documents, they are thus designated, and no longer as gilds. No greater proof of the power of the Companies could be given than their compelling all citizens to become connected with them.

For several centuries, not only was the Court of Aldermen composed exclusively of the masters of the gilds, but the Common Council were all, in like manner, the representatives of the same bodies, each Company sending a given number, according to their influence and wealth. The chief sent six, and the smaller Companies two. Herbert has extracted from the city records a list of the "number of per-

* "In England, in regard that there is some mystery in every trade, therefore a trade is called a mystery." (Madox, "Firma Burgi," 32—3.) The same author derives the custom of calling the Companies "mysteries" from the French, who, he says, using the word *mestiere* for a craft, art, or employment, the name came to be used here in a similar sense. No mystery is implied beyond the *secrets of trade.*

sons chosen by the several mysteries to be of the Common Council, 50 Edward III." (A.D. 1368), which list, written in Norman-French, contains 148 names of the representatives from the Companies, at that time forty-eight in number.*

It should be noted, however, that in the reign of the first Edward, all London became divided into wards, each possessing its respective alderman, who gave his name to the ward by right of proprietorship. The Common Council was still returned by the Companies. Who received the purchase-money in the first sale we know not; but, in those days of few taxes, possibly the King may have received it in payment for fines upon the city. In the "Hundred Rolls," first Edward I., is a list of these aldermen proprietors, or, rather, of the wards named after them, viz.:—"Warda Will. Hadestock; Warda de Peter Anger; Warda Roberti de Meldebourne; de Collemannoster; Warda Joh'is de Blakesburn; Warda Wolmer de Essex," etc., etc. Portsoken Ward has already been named as the aldermanry of the prior of Holy Trinity.†

* City Records, lib. lx., fol. 46.

† "1 Richard II., A.D. 1378. Letter Bk. H. fol. 79 (Latin). The Prior of Christ Church, Aldgate, sworn ex-officio as Ald[n]. of Portsoken Ward. On Monday next after the feast of Our Lord's Epiphany (6 Jan.) in the first year &c., in the Mayor's Court holden on that day in the Guildhall of London, in presence of the Mayor, Ald[n]., and Officers, for the same Court summoned, William Rysyng, Prior of Christ Church, in London, was sworn to fill the office of Ald[n]. in the Ward of Portsoken, and faithfully to do all things touching that office, according to the custom of the said City; in manner and form in which the other Aldermen are wont to be charged."—*Riley's Memorials of London*, p. 415.

Farringdon Ward—which was divided into two wards, "Within" and "Without," in Hadley's mayoralty—was originally one aldermanry, purchased by William Faryngdon, goldsmith, A.D. 1279; and remained in his family upwards of eighty years. It was held by the singular tenure of presenting annually, at Easter, a gilliflower (probably for the purpose of church decorations), a flower which was formerly of great rarity.*

Norton is of opinion that, if this proprietary right of aldermen to their wards were ever more than partial in London, it was certainly of short duration, as we find it wrested from them in the succeeding reign of Edward II.; the citizens being then declared to possess the power of annually electing aldermen who shall preside over them.† It probably arose with the introduction of the feudal system, and expired with the grant of those privileges which were secured to the citizens by their early charters, the establishment of a community, and the election of their own magistrates. Norton

* "Faryngdon," says Stow, "purchased of Ralph le Feure all the aldermanrie, and the appurtenances, within the city of London and suburbs of the same, between Ludgate and Newgate, and also within the same gates which Ankerirus de Avene held, during his life, by grant of Thomas Averne. To have and to hold to the said Ralph and his heirs, yielding one clove, or slip of gillyflower, at the feast of Easter, for all secular service and customs which the said Le Feure had warranted unto him by the said Thomas Averne, in consideration of twenty marks, which the said Ralph le Feure did give beforehand, in name of a gersum or fine, to the said Thomas."

† Although the appointment was for life, yet an alderman (of the Ward of *Bredstrete*) was dismissed for deafness (*obtusitatem aurium*). 5 Hen. V. A.D. 1418.—*Riley's Memorials of London*, p. 661.

says that there is no trace to show when the name of "aldermen" was first applied to the presidents of the London wards; the probability is that it was first applied after the Conquest. The denomination was common, in Saxon times, to various judicial dignitaries and officers, from the highest to the lowest rank; but there is no record of it as applied to the heads of particular districts in London during that period: and there is reason to believe that the appellation was not used in that sense until the reign of Henry II., when they are first mentioned as presiding over gilds, some of which were *territorial*, and others *mercantile*. In the reign of Henry III., *aldermanries* had become a common term for a civic district comprised within a leet jurisdiction, as well in London as in other cities.*

Honourable as was the office at all times it has never been without its disadvantages to the possessor. In days when liberty had not been secured and developed, and when the King was absolute, he must be very yielding who could escape penalties. It is true the alderman was himself occasionally despotic in his gild,† but he had in his turn to bow the neck to authority. Henry VIII., found the gilds a mine of wealth to his extortions, having in 1545 compelled them by a forced

* "Comment. Lond.," p. 436.

† "W. Hulot, Esq., then dwelling with the Bp. of Bath, and an official of the Receipts of his Lordship the King, was adjudged to have his hand struck off in the Guildhall, for an assault upon John Rote, an alderman, in the Mayoralty of Nicholas Exton (1387), the 10th year, that is to say, of King Richard."—*Riley's Liber Albus*, p. 32.

loan to advance him £21,263 6*s*. 8*d*. towards the expenses of his wars with Scotland, determined to raise a further sum by a benevolence, and sent into the City to demand the same. One sturdy alderman, Richard Read, objected to this arbitrary proceeding, and positively refused to pay the sum demanded of him; for which the strong-willed King enrolled the unruly alderman as a foot soldier, and sent him in person with the army into Scotland, where (says Northouck), after great hardships, he was taken prisoner and obliged to pay a considerable sum for his ransom. Queen Elizabeth had studied politics in the same school, and was not much behind her royal father in the severity of the measures to which she resorted to enforce obedience to her demands. Strype, in his edition of Stow, gives several instances of most arbitrary acts of this nature, especially in her granting monopolies to the injury of the various crafts. In 1590, Edward Darcey, "one about the court," purchased for a large sum a patent from the Queen, against the Leathersellers' Company, empowering him to search and seal all the leather throughout England, and our author says "he found it a very gainful business to him; for on the skins he sealed, he sometimes received the tenth part, the ninth part, . . . and sometimes even the fourth or third part of the commodity." His profits lasted, however, little longer than a year. Even leathersellers can be roused to indignation if the cause be sufficient, and in 1592 the mighty host of manufacturers in the trade of leather, fellmongers, glovers, point* makers, purse makers, saddlers, girdlers, coffer makers, badget makers, white tawyers,† jerkin‡ makers, leather dyers, makers of sconces, baggs, bellowes, bottles, lanthorns, pouches, barchides, or coverings for chariots, poles, standards, trimets,§ buckets, and many others, rose as one man to resist this inroad upon their prerogatives. The Queen knew how, and when, to yield; no one ever knew this better; she bowed before these warlike workers in leather, and a breach was prevented by her timely concession. The wardens of the leathersellers are highly praised by Strype for their firmness, for upon being imprisoned for their stubbornness, they defended themselves by pleading that at their first incorporation (*temp.* Edward III.) they were charged with a precise oath to "be obesiant and obedient unto the mayor and ministers of the city, the franchises and customs thereof to maintain, and this city to keep harmless in that that in them was." "Judge," they said to the aldermen who were sent to mediate, "if to admit Mr. Darcey's ministers to search and seal our leather is not to run into the horrible sin of perjury, which

* A string with a tag. "For a silken point I'll give my barony." —*Shakespeare.*

"I am resolved on two points;
That if one break, the other will hold;
Or if both break, your gaskins fall."—*Shakespeare.*

† Dressers of coney (rabbit) skins.

‡ A short coat; a waistcoat.

§ Qy.? *trimmer.* A piece of wood or leather, used in uniting the joists and girders in staircases. (*Vide* Moxon's "Mech. Exerc.")

the Queen's Majesty could never abide, nor ever yet left unpunished." Thus stout and hardy were these leathersellers.* Old is the proverb, wherever originating, "There's nothing like leather."

The Governments of the day have usually kept a careful oversight of the rich citizens, and when in want of supplies, have not always been very scrupulous as to the means made use of to obtain them. Three years prior to the execution of King Charles I., the party who had wrested the Government from him having placed their "committee of safety" at Haberdashers' Hall, sent to the master of the Grocers' Company a most remarkable message. It was to the effect that they had learned that one Richard Greenough, who "was found to be a delinquent to the Parliament," was their creditor to the amount of £500, for which the company had given their bond, and they (the Parliament) therefore demanded a speedy payment of the same to them. This, in A.D. 1645. The master and wardens were naturally amazed at so novel an application, and craved for time for consultation; but all was vain, they had to borrow the amount on their company's seal and to pay to the Parliament the debt due to Greenough.

These aldermen or masters of the mysteries appear themselves not to have been immaculate. Bribery at elections is not much charged against them, but that they sometimes carried elections by violence is certain, for in 1385 the Grocers' Company having returned two years successively their alderman,

* Strype's Stow, ii. 293.

Sir Nicholl Brembre, mayor, against the general voice of the City, an inquiry into the circumstances of the election took place. The historian of the day informs us that "this yere, Sir Nicholl Brembre, was chosen maire *be certayne crafts and not be fre eleccion of the cetee of London as it owith to be*: and the oolde halle was stuff'd with men of armes overe nighte, be ordinannce and assente of Sir Nicholl Brembre, for to chose hym maire on the morrowe; and so hee was." (Chronicle of London.) A petition is sent up to Parliament, 10 Richard II., 1386, complaining that the said "Sir N. Brembre, wyth his upberers had through debate and stronger partye, by carrying a grete quantity armure to the Guyld-hall" to overcome the citizens, procured his own election. The result was, it was determined that henceforth four Common Council men should be elected annually from each ward, instead of as aforetime from the crafts; and inasmuch as Brembre's Company had sixteen aldermen at the time, which gave it a preponderance, it was decreed that no Company should have at the same time more than six aldermen.

CHAPTER V.

THEIR MAYOR.

"There was a sharp prosecution against Sir William Capel for misgovernment in his mayoralty."—BACON'S *Henry VII.*

AMONGST the other privileges attaching themselves to the office of liverymen, that of appointing their Mayor has ever been considered one of the most important. They only, we have seen, have had the right of returning sheriffs, aldermen, and Common Councillors; and with them also exclusively rested the privilege of returning from the aldermen the Mayor. In early times this official held sway over the City in style right royal; his power was almost unlimited; what the alderman was in the gild, the Mayor was in the City; the Londoners yielded unmurmuringly to each and every order or exaction issued in his name.

The City was *imperium in imperio*, and within the walls the Mayor was considered supreme sovereign. The monarch of the day, upon all royal visits to the City, has ever appeared to humour this fancy, and to recognize the existence of this rival throne. Temple Bar alone, of all the many gates of entrance, has been preserved from destruction, no doubt because, being the entrance from the royal residences, it has been necessary on all occasions of royal visits, for the purpose of keeping up one of the most ancient of civic customs, that of closing the gate against the sovereign, and requiring him before entrance to ask the Mayor's permission to enter within his domain.

The ceremony is interesting because of its antiquity, and its origin cannot now be traced. The Mayor, upon receiving the King's request, is usually sufficiently complaisant to accede most readily, and with all respect to hand to the King on bended knee the key which will admit him within the precinct. He also gives up his sword and mace, in token that he is not a rival, but a loyal subject, and the King as readily returns the same, in token that he has confidence in the Mayor's integrity, and is willing to retain his services as his lieutenant. On all such occasions, the Mayor, if he had not previously won his spurs, had conferred upon him the honour of knighthood. This formerly was a high distinction, especially at a period anterior to the institution of a *social* knighthood. As aldermen of London claim rank above a *social* knight, they will never accept a civic knighthood.*

Upon James I. instituting the hereditary order of knighthood, termed Baronets, for the purpose of

* A few weeks after the above was written, this rule, for the first time, was broken by two ex-Lord Mayors (Aldermen Rose and Phillips) accepting knighthood. Hitherto aldermen who were knights had received the title previously to their election as aldermen; but no prior case is on record of the acceptance by a past Lord Mayor of a civic knighthood, which is in truth an *advancement-retrograde!*

raising funds for his Government, he made it for the time a purchasable rank, and to any subject, whatever his position, if he could only produce the sum named (£1095), letters patent were immediately granted, and he became a baronet.* A large sum was realized by the King from this source, many merchants of wealth and aldermen of London and other towns being purchasers, and very many of the present baronetages go back to the years 1610 to 1620, not one of which titles, we believe, was granted but by purchase.

We believe that Charles I. did not follow his father's example in making merchandise of this honourable and hereditary order; but in the first year of his reign he commenced trading in an equally objectionable manner with the order of knighthood. Rushworth copies from the Government records certain writs to sheriffs of counties upon this matter, and adds, "Writs were directed to all sheriffs, commanding all such as possessed £40 a year of lands, or revenues, for their own use for three years, and are not yet knights, that they do at their peril prepare to present themselves in his Majesty's presence by the 31st Jan., to receive the order of knighthood."†

From all that we can discover respecting this injunction, we are led to believe that its monstrosity

* Hallam says that "James I. sold several peerages for considerable sums. The sale of baronetages was notorious. They were offered for £1095 a-piece, and in six years 93 patents were sold, raising £101,835."—"Constitutional History," vol. i., p. 461.

† Rushworth, vol. i., p. 190, A.D. 1625.

defeated its end; that none were found ready to comply, and that the whole affair was covered with contempt, and forgotten in the sad tragedies which succeeded so soon and in such quick succession. We know, however, that the aldermen of London would not accept the title as a gift, nor to this day will they accept a title below that of baronet.* It is true we may now, and at all times, find aldermen who are but knights, but in every instance the knighthood was anterior to the becoming an alderman. The Sovereign now, on all occasions of a royal visit to the City, confers upon the Lord Mayor a baronetcy. That Charles had a precedent for this injunction we admit, for by a statute of Edward II., all who possessed land of £20 a year in fee or for life were to take the order of knighthood.† In Maitland's "History of London" will likewise be found a copy of a writ addressed to the sheriffs (18 Edward III., 1344), requiring all citizens who possessed £40 a year in fee to become knights. This was to assist the King in his French wars. To such an extent did these extortions affect the citizens, that many refused the knighthood, and had to submit to fines; and at length the Commons petitioned that it might be enacted that no man should be fined twice for not receiving knighthood, but the bill never received the royal assent.‡ Carpenter, the founder of the City of London School, and one of the executors

* See note, p. 55.

† Fosbroke's "Encyclopædia of Antiquities," vol. ii., p. 748.

‡ Nicolas's "Proceedings, etc., of the Privy Council," 5 preface, pp. 23, 24.

of Richard Whittington, upon retiring from public life obtained, in 1439, letters patent from the King, dated 3rd Dec., 18 Henry VI., exempting him for life from all military and civil duties, among which are included serving in Parliament and receiving the honour of knighthood. The original of this patent is still extant among the Cottonian MSS. in the British Museum, and is referred to by Brewer, in his valuable Life of Carpenter.*

By the earliest ordinances, the Mayor is the King's lieutenant, and, with the Aldermen and Common Council, can make by-laws for the government of the City. He has also the authority of a kind of judge. When Alfred divided England into counties, and counties into hundreds, and hundreds into tythings, he constituted the portreeve, or bailiff, or sheriff, the chief governor of the City. William the Conqueror's first charter, which is still preserved at Guildhall, is addressed to William the Bishop and Godfrey the Portreeve. "Portreeve" is governor of the port,† as "sheriff" (from "sher," or "shire," a county, and "riff," or "reeve," a bailiff), signifies the King's bailiff of a county. After the conquest,

* *Vide* "Proc. and Ord. of the Privy Council," edited by Sir Harris Nicolas, 8vo, 1835, vol. v., p. 3.

† Port, in the Saxon and Teutonic languages, is of the same meaning as *Civitas*, city. Ever since England was a kingdom, the honour due to an earl, as well in the King's presence as elsewhere, has belonged to the chief officer of London: hence it is, too, that the sword is borne before him as before an earl, and not behind him.—("Liber Albus," Bk. I., part i., ch. ii.)

the name usually assigned to the chief magistrate of London—which by charter is both city and county—was bailiff until the reign of Richard I. when, in the year 1189, it was changed into that of mayor. This King, in order to maintain the expenses incurred in the Crusades, levied large subsidies upon the City, and, in return, granted to the citizens the privilege of electing their own chief magistrate, who was designated "Mayor," a title taken from the Norman *Maire*. The first elected to this high office was Henry Fitz-Alwyn, whose ancestor, Allwin, cousin of King Edgar, was entitled "Alderman of all England," as before mentioned.

Within the City, the Mayor of London has ever been recognized as the King's representative; "and though elective, this office may be said to be perpetual—for his authority ceaseth not, neither on the demise or abdication of the King, as that of all commissioned officers do; wherefore, in such cases, the Lord Mayor of London is said to be the principal officer of the kingdom, as he appears to have been upon the demise of Queen Elizabeth and the accession of King James I. to the throne."* As early as A.D. 1354, King Edward III., by royal charter, granted permission to the mayor to have gold and silver maces carried before him; and, in referring to this privilege, Maitland remarks that "this great favour of having gold and silver maces carried before the chief magistrate was peculiar to London, for all the other cities and towns in the kingdom were, by a

* Maitland's "History of London," p. 559.

royal precept, expressly commanded not to use maces of any other metal than copper" (p. 85, bk. i.). They might be used, moreover, in the absence of the mayor, "and as often as it shall happen any of the said sergeants to be sent to foreign places, and without the City, to do their offices, at the command of us, or of the mayor and sheriffs aforesaid, they may lawfully carry, going and coming, publicly, as our own sergeants do carry their maces, any ordinance or commandment made to the contrary notwithstanding."*

When the title of "Lord" was first added to that of "Mayor," cannot now be distinctly traced. All charters and history are silent upon the point. Possibly it is merely a complimentary addition from immemorial usage. Maitland, one of our best-informed annalists, confesses himself unable to ascertain this. He says: "Our historians being silent in respect to the time when the appellation of 'Lord' was added to that of 'Mayor,' I imagine that no time bids so fair as the present, when the chief magistrate of the city had the honour conferred upon him to have maces, in all respects the same as royal, carried before him. But, as the several charters to the city are likewise silent on this head, the origin thereof may probably be owing to a compliment instead of a grant" (p. 85, bk. i.). The same doubt exists as to the origin of the title "Right Honourable." The author just quoted places it at this same period. But we do know that, shortly

* Royal Charter to London, A.D. 1354; King Edward III.

after Jack Cade's rebellion, so pleased was the King (Henry VI.) with the conduct of the London aldermen on that occasion, that he called the then Lord Mayor, Godfrey Fielding (A.D. 1452), to be a member of his Privy Council, and consequently to the degree of "Right Honourable."

About the same period, an interesting instance occurred, as recorded in Maitland (p. 117), of the scrupulous regard observed by the Lord Mayor in respect to the question of precedence.* It appears that, on a call of new serjeants-at-law, A.D. 1464, a great entertainment was given by them at Ely House, Holborn, to which they invited the Lord Mayor, Aldermen, Sheriffs, and other principal citizens, who, upon entering the place of entertainment, perceived that "the Lord High Treasurer (Baron Ruthen) had assumed the most honourable seat at table, in derogation of the dignity of the Lord Mayor, who, at all times and on all occasions, as the King's representative, in honour of his principal and sovereign, assumes the pre-eminence, or most honourable place, of all subjects within the City and liberties. However, the imperious treasurer, though in detraction of his master's honour, kept possession of the place. This misdutiful behaviour was by the mayor and citizens no otherwise resented than by their withdrawing from the hall and returning to the City, where they were by the mayor entertained in a very

* "Hen. V. gave the seat of honour to the Lord Mayor (Nicolas Watton), 1415, before the Archbishop of Canterbury and the King's brothers."—*Riley's Memorials of London*, p. 60.3.

elegant manner, whilst the lords of the feast were left to bewail the rude and insolent deportment of their guest, Ruthen."

The same historian mentions another fact, occurring about the same time (A.D. 1467), not quite so creditable to the good taste of the chief actor. "This year, John Derbyan, an alderman, for opprobrious language given to the mayor, and his obstinacy in refusing to remove, or pay for removing, the noisome carcase of a dog from before his door, was by the Court of Aldermen fined in the sum of *fifty pounds*."

CHAPTER VI.

THEIR MAYOR, CONTINUED.

IN Nicoll's very able and elaborate "History of the Ironmongers' Company," printed in 1866, for private circulation, is a minute of the court of that Company, dated Dec. 3, 1619, which brings to light another privilege pertaining to the office of Lord Mayor, with which we remember nowhere else to have met, namely, that of making "*three persons free of the cittie.*" This right seems to have been exercised in this particular case with some eccentricity, for "An order of court before the Lord Maior in ye tyme of Sir Sebastian Harvey, dated ye 5 daye of October last, was now read, wherein it was declared that ye Lord Maior, by his prerogative of making three p'sons free of ye cittie, had obtained ye freedome of Mr. Stapleton as ye first of ye said three, and yt he should be admitted into ye freedom of ye company by redemption; upon wch order ye court being willing to gratify Sir Sebastian Harvey, ye said Stapleton being his gardener, are contended to admit him into this company, soe as he doe once a quarter take care to keep the company's garden in order and repair, and to trym ye same, wch he very thankfully accepted of, promising to p'forme ye same, and therefore took his oath appertayning, and paid for his oath xijd." (p. 116). A similar entry occurs in 1610, when "it is ordered that Robert Key shall be made free, as the first of the three yearly made by the Lord Mayor" (p. 144); and in October, 1610, the still more curious claim is made by the Lady Mayoress, who requests Rob Dawkes, "her ladishippe's coachman," may be admitted, which request was allowed (p. 145).

Curious speculations have been propounded respecting the origin of the use in procession by the Right Hon. the Lord Mayor, of the *sword and cap of maintenance.* In the very early times when the sword was always in request, we can easily understand that the great earls or aldermen would at all times parade this emblem of authority, especially on occasions of administering justice, but the *cap of maintenance* is of far more recent origin. Pope Leo X., we read, to pay honour to that dutiful son of the church, King Henry VIII.—as he was at that time—presented, with great form and ceremony, a consecrated sword and cap of maintenance.* The

* In Drake's Eboracum (page 181) we read that as early as the year 1393, when King Richard II. presented Robert Savage, then Lord Mayor of York, with a gilt mace, he also gave a cap of maintenance to the sword-bearer; but this story is entirely traditional, and no authority for it can be found in the archives of that city. Richard, Duke of Buckingham, informs us that he witnessed at Rome (A.D. 1828) the procession of St. Peter, and that "before the Pope was borne the sword and ducal cap, which, according to annual custom, he had blessed in the morning." He adds that this sword and cap the Pope used in olden time to send, after the mass of the day, to

sword, as an offensive weapon, was to destroy the enemies of the church; the cap of maintenance was a piece of armour to defend the head in time of conflict. We remember to have met with no earlier mention of a cap of maintenance in England, and no doubt the King would esteem its presentation by the Pope as a great and distinguished favour; and being at all times a great benefactor to the trade companies of London, and to the City generally, it is not improbable that he might have conferred upon the metropolis of his kingdom, as Maitland surmises, these further emblems of royalty, and granted the right and privilege to use, in addition to the gold and silver maces, both the sword and cap of maintenance.

At a very remote period the honourable distinction was conferred upon the mayor, of his being appointed cup-bearer to the King at the coronation. Among the City records * is still preserved at the town clerk's office a list of the heads of the great Livery Companies, chosen by the Common Council to attend the Mayor of London to Westminster, as cup-bearer at the coronation of Richard III., which privilege has continued to the present time unrepealed. It is evident that marked honour was, and is, connected with this ancient office,

some Christian Crusader Prince. "It is now sometimes sent to some Catholic monarch as a mark of the Pope's especial favour. The first instance of this benediction is read in the Councils of Constance, when Pope John XXII. sent it to the Emperor Sigismond." (Diary, vol. iii., p. 50; London, 1862.)

* Lib. L. fol. 19, a and b., *vide* Herbert.

from the fact that so many as twelve eminent citizens, masters of companies, were required to be present at the ceremonies, as attendants upon the chief cup-bearer; all of whom went in great state, the most prominent places being formerly, if they are not still, awarded to them in the pageants. The mayor, by virtue of this office of King's cup-bearer, formerly exercised the prerogative of appointing the coroner for the City, which right, however, was taken from him by the fourth charter to the City of King Edward IV., and conferred upon the Livery Companies.

We are not to suppose that because the mayor and aldermen, in many cases, were shopkeepers, and in all cases traders or merchants, they were necessarily unused to feats of arms or country sports and pastimes. The citizens generally were a brave and manly race, and the pursuit of trade seemed in no way opposed to the development of a military spirit. We have shown how even a crusader, one imprisoned in the Holy Land, and redeemed by "Matilda, the fair Saracen," upon his return to London, married his deliverer, and with the "fair Saracen," opened shop in Cheapside as mercer. How to this Gilbert Becket, and "Mrs." Becket, was born Thomas, afterwards Archbishop of Canterbury, the immortal martyr. Mention has also been made of the twelve warlike aldermen, knighted on the field of battle, on the occasion of Thomas Nevil, natural son of Lord Falconbridge, and therefore called the bastard Falconbridge, attempting to force the City; when, with 17,000 men, he took possession of Southwark, caused 3000 to cross the river while he attacked London Bridge. We read in Maitland that Alderman Basset, the commanding officer at the bridge, sallied out to meet the invader; Earl Rivers, with a strong force, likewise took the field, but Falconbridge was repulsed "by that gallant citizen, Ralph Joscelin, late Lord Mayor, and pursued with great slaughter as far as Redriff (Rotherhithe). The King (Edward IV.) hurried off to the City in pursuit of the rebels, staying no longer than while he knighted the twelve following aldermen for their gallant behaviour on the field:"—Sirs John Stockton, Ralph Varney, John Young, Will. Taylor, Rich. Lee, Matt. Philips, Geo. Ireland, Will. Stoker, Wm. Hampton, Thomas Stallbrooke, John Crosby (of Crosby Hall), and Bartholomew James.*

The entire second charter of King Edward II. is occupied in reciting the military services of the citizens in besieging the Castle of Leeds, in Kent, and in divers other parts of the kingdom, and grants that such military service shall not be drawn into precedent. That they should not go to war out of the City was one of their most ancient privileges. Judge Foster, in his discourse on Crown laws, shows that the King, in all cases, had a prerogative *right* to impress. This exemption, therefore, to the citizens in a warlike age must have been felt to have been a great boon, although the real origin of their exemption was, no doubt, that by the condition of their

* Fabian and Hall's Chronicles; Maitland, p. 120.

tenure, according to the feudal system, they were bound only to defend their own walls.

Not only have the citizens generally been characterized by a warlike spirit, but manly games and rustic pastimes have ever held a prominent place amongst them. No doubt the origin of many of these customs is earlier than the Saxon era. An able antiquary (John Bagford) ascribes even our prize-fighting to nothing else but the same sort of exercise practised by *Roman Gladiators*. "Our bull and bear-baiting are the remains of the same people, as are our May-games, mumming, morice-dancing, etc., which happened about the same time of the year as they do now amongst us."*

We might enumerate many instances of their love of English rural sports. Several Lord Mayors have been so ardent in their love of the chase, that even in their civic pageants they have made reference to them. On the arrival of King Henry VI. at Dover, after being crowned King of France in 1432, "the mayor and aldermen rode against him on horseback; the aldermen with robes of scarlet with sanguine hoods, the mayor in crimson velvet, with a great velvet hat furred, a girdle of gold about his middle, and a jewel of gold about his neck, trailing down behind him; he was followed by his three huntsmen on great coursers, in entire suits of red, all spangled with silver. The liverymen brought up the rear clothed in white gowns and scarlet hoods."†

* Leland's "Collectanea." † Stow.

Lydgate has a poem written on the occasion, from which we extract a stanza or two :—

> "Their clothying was of colour full covenable;
> —— The noble mair clad in red velvet,
> The Shrieves, the Aldermen, full notable,
> In furryd clokes, the colour of scarlett;
> In stately wyse whaune they were met,
> Ech one were wel horsyd, and made no delay,
> But with their maire rood forth on their way.
>
> The citizens ech on of the citee,
> In their entent that they were pure and clene;
> Ches them of *whit* a ful fair livere
> In every craft, as it was well sene;
> To shewe the trowthe that they dede mene,
> Toward the King hadde mad them feithfully
> In sundry devyses embrowdyd richely."

The Lord Mayor anciently claimed the privilege of nominating sheriffs * by drinking to persons deemed qualified. Dr. Hughson, in his "History of London," says that in the month of July, 1583, Sir Edward Osborne, the then Lord Mayor, ancestor of the present Duke of Leeds, with several of the Aldermen and the Recorder, dined at the Haberdashers' Hall; after the second course had been served, the chief magistrate took the great cup, which being filled with hippocras, he stood up, and in a speech drank to Mr. Alderman Massam, as the sheriff for the year ensuing. The sword-bearer † thereupon

* "The Lord Mayor had the appointment of aldermen in every case in which the vacancy had not been filled up within 15 days."—*Riley's Liber Albus*, p. 35.

† "He shall have 2 other sergeants at least, and an esquire, a man well bred (one who knows how in all places, in that which unto such service pertains, to support the honour of his lord and of the City) to bear his sword before him."—*Riley's Liber Albus*, p. 44.

repaired to Grocers' Hall, where the alderman was dining, and acquainted him with his elevation to the shrievalty, upon which he thanked God, "who, through his great goodness, had called him from a very poor and mean degree to this worshipful state. Secondly, he thanked her Majesty for her gracious goodness in allowing to us these great and ample franchises. And thirdly, he thanked my Lord Mayor for having so honourable an opinion of his company of grocers as to make choice of one being a poor member of the same."

This right was called in question, but enforced, in the reign of Charles I., by the Mayor, who claimed it as a privilege of three hundred years' standing. From Thomson's "Chronicles of London Bridge," we learn an instance of this ceremony being abused, in 1489, when Sir Henry Colet, the Mayor, father of Dean Colet, drank to his carver, John Percival,* and nominated him sheriff for the year ensuing. The carver not only served the office of sheriff with the celebrated Hugh Clapton, but also became Sir John Percival, Knight, and Lord Mayor 1499.

This right, it appears, was strongly opposed in 1682. Bishop Burnet, in the history of his own times, describes the occasion: "When the day came in which the mayor used to drink to one and to mark him out for sheriff, he drank to (Dudley) North, a merchant, that was brother to the chief justice. Upon that, it was pretended that this ceremony was

* Sir John Percival was knighted on the field by Henry VII. He was the first Merchant Taylor Lord Mayor.

but a bare nomination, which the Common Hall might receive or refuse, as they had a mind to it." The citizens put up Papillon, but the mayor declared North elected. The former brought an action for false return against the mayor, which was tried before the infamous and execrable Judge Jeffreys, who fined Papillon £10,000 for his "presumption" in opposing the Court candidate. The defeated candidate and unsuccessful plaintiff escaped to the continent, and thus evaded payment of so heavy a fine.

Upon an investigation in 1682 into the usages and practices of the City, in respect to the election of sheriffs, a report was prepared and printed, to the effect that "this privilege of the Lord Mayor, according to the City records, is perfectly conformable with ancient custom, rules, and ordinances of the City." Since 1748 the appointment of the sheriffs has been exclusively in the hands of the Livery. The mayor, however, had no power to appoint as sheriff the keeper either of a brewery, a bakery, or a tavern. The sheriff was sworn to be obedient to the mayor, and the "Liber Albus" names one who had to pay to the chief magistrate "ten tuns of wine for disobedience committed towards him." In the same book the sheriffs are styled "the eyes of the mayor."*

All charters to the City Companies subject the members to the control of the mayor. It seems but reasonable that, as they had power over their own

* Lib. i., part i., chap. 14.

craft, there should be somewhere a sort of visiting jurisdiction over all the trade societies of the metropolis. This rested with the mayor, who was viewed by all as a most powerful official, whose anger must be appeased, and good opinion courted. In some cases the measures adopted were not the most scrupulous or proper. Unblushing bribery seems to have been the order of the day.

Subjection to this high personage is curiously acknowledged by the Brewers' Company, who, in a very humble petition, dated 1435, address the chief magistrate as their "right worshipfull and gracious lord and sovereign, the maior of London." He is styled in after times "master of all the companies;" sometimes, the "warden of all the companies." He had power to fine and imprison the wardens of companies at pleasure; and they, to propitiate his favour, were not slack in their benevolences.

The brewers were especially unfortunate. From their records we learn that, on July 30, 1422, Robert Chickley, the mayor, sent for the master and twelve assistants, and fined them £20 for selling *dear ale.* Their objections were vain, and they were all sent off to prison until the fine was paid. In 1422-3 occurs a note (in Latin) that "William Walderne (mayor that year) behaved well to the company until two or three weeks before his retirement from office;" when, beginning to annoy them, they "assuaged his displeasure" by presenting to him "a boar, price 20*s.*; and an ox, price 17*s.*"

Even Whittington himself does not come out with quite clean hands, for he is stated to have been bribed through his servants. £7 3*s.* 4*d.* is charged for "ij pipes of red wine to Richard Whetyngton's butler." In a succeeding mayoralty, £13 6*s.* 8*d.* is entered "for gyfts to the lord maior." Other entries show such complimentary gifts to be customary to obtain favour. Thus, in 1423 is an entry of "money given to divers serjeants of the maior, for to be good friends to our craft;" or, as it is in another place more carefully expressed, "for thair labour to the profit of the craft." Mention is also made of £16 "given to a tasker of the kings, to suffer our carpenters still in our work."

Some of these entries are exceedingly expressive, "short and sweet." Thus—"A.D. 1424. A record in praise of John Mitchelle. He was a good man, and meek, and soft to speak with." Upon his inauguration, a present was made to him of "an ox that cost 21*s.* 2*d.*, and a wild boar, price 30*s.* 1*d.*; so that he did no harm to the brewers, and advised them to make good ale, that he might not have any complaint against them."

One instance occurs, singularly, of a mayor who was indeed impervious to bribes. An entry for the year 1423, the year preceding John Mitchell's mayoralty, is thus expressed *in hisce verbis*:—"William Crowmere, mayor this year, was a good man, and well pleased all the citizens, especially the brewers; when the masters offered gifts to him, he thanked them, but would not receive any."

The interesting custom of presenting an offering to the Lord Mayor is still retained by one or two of the Companies, although, of course, instead of a gross bribe to purchase favours, it is now a graceful act of respect for the office of chief magistrate. The "Fruiterers," to the present day, annually present to the Lord Mayor, with great ceremony, a handsome present of all the choicest and most rare fruits of the season. The continuance of this ancient custom speaks much for the good taste of the court of that Worshipful Company.

We are not to suppose that the exercise of the mayor's authority has been always confined to the citizens and the gilds. His authority has been recognized far beyond the limits of the City, or even of the county of Middlesex. A curious instance of his interference occurred in 1440, shortly after Sir Richard Wick,* Vicar of Hermetsworth, in Essex, was burnt on Tower Hill, for religion, and being by the people reputed a holy and pious man, the Vicar of Barking, a fraudulent and covetous priest, embraced the opportunity to impose upon the credulous multitude, by mixing ashes with the powder of odoriferous spices, which he secretly strewed upon the place where the vicar was burnt, and industriously published the pretended miracle of the "Fragrance of the Ashes," which was no sooner known than it produced the desired effect; for the people, in great

* Clergymen who were literates were entitled "Sir," while graduates were designated according to their degree, "Doctor" or "Master."

numbers from all parts, hurried to the place of execution, where, finding the ashes answerable to the report, they began to arraign the justice of the judges for condemning that holy man; and by the address and management of that crafty vicar, the people were inadvertently drawn into idolatry, for numbers invoked him as a god, and offered at his shrine large sums of money; in return for which they were plentifully supplied with odoriferous ashes, as sacred relics, which were carefully reinstated before the next morning. This practice continued about a week, when it was opposed by the Lord Mayor, who apprehended the vicar, whereby the imposture was discovered by his own confession.*

Neither have his sentences at all times been of the mildest character. Life or death have been not unfrequently at his sole disposal. Some startling instances of absolute authority occur in civic history, such as the case of Hammond Chickwell, or as his name is spelled in the early records and the "Liber Albus," Hamö de Chiggewelle, Mayor 1319 to 1327 (*temp.* Edward III.), who took Dr. Stapleton (Bishop of Exeter) prisoner, and beheaded him, for demanding the keys of the City gates. So in the mayoralty of Sir Andrew Aubrey, 1339—51 (*temp.* Richard II.), in a quarrel between the Fishmongers and Skinners, the mayor being assaulted and struck, he, without any hesitation, ordered two persons to be beheaded, a sentence which was carried out with great form in Cheapside.

* Maitland, p. 108.

In Wilson's "Life of King James the First," a circumstance is recorded of some importance as showing the boldness of a Lord Mayor in that servile period. The King had written a work entitled "The Book of Sports," enforcing the lawfulness of games and sports on the Sabbath-day, which by proclamation he ordered to be read in all churches. This work gave great offence to the citizens, and the Lord Mayor ventured to stop the King's carriages while travelling through the City during the time of divine service. The hot-tempered King was in great wrath, and sent post haste a warrant to the Lord Mayor, to permit them to pass. The summons was obeyed, his lordship observing that "while he possessed his power he had done his duty; but that *being taken away* by a higher power, he had done his duty in obeying."

CHAPTER VII.

THEIR MAYOR, CONTINUED.

On Friday, Nov. 9, 1866, at one of those magnificent banquets given by the Lord Mayor of London with more than regal splendour, the Chancellor of the Exchequer,* in glancing at the advantages conferred upon the nation by the great corporations of this country, gave utterance to this elegant truism: "Individuals may form communities, but institutions must found a nation." Our Saxon ancestors evidently duly appreciated this truth, and gave a fostering oversight to infant fraternities and gilds of commerce, and planted deep in a good soil the roots from which the great companies of the present day originally sprang. Some few may advocate a life of isolation and asceticism, but the mass of mankind are fully alive to the great fact, that in matters either religious or secular, *union is strength.* The mayors of our great cities would be powerless if unsupported by the suffrages of the large corporations they represent; their influence in the nation will always be found to correspond, in a very great degree, with the numerical strength and wealth of

* The Right Hon. B. Disraeli.

those who form their constituency. The various sovereigns of this country have seen this, and have ever been forward to confer distinguished honours and benefits upon the chief magistrates of the two metropolitan cities, York in the north, and London in the south, because they were the centres of influence of their respective provinces. Long may this state of things continue, in which the people possess so large a share of self-government, not the liberty of licence, but subject to due control. We can compare, with patriotic pride, our Old York with New York, and boast that we prefer the constitution of the old city to that of the new, and that we can give the honest preference to the principle of local self-government prevailing in the capital of England to the system obtaining in the gay and beautiful capital of France.

Before closing our remarks on the Mayor of London, we would wish to add a few notes supplemental to what has been already stated. By the charter of King John, of May 19th, in the sixteenth year of his reign (1215), "to the City was granted and confirmed the appointment of a Mayor," as follows:—"Know ye that we have granted, and by this our present writing *confirm*, to our barons of our City of London, that they may choose to themselves every year a Mayor, who to us may be faithful, discreet, and fit to govern the city, so as, when he shall be chosen, to be presented unto us, or our justices, if we shall not be present, and he shall swear to be faithful to us; and that it shall be lawful to them, at the end of the year, to remove him, and substitute another, if they will, or the same to remain, so as he be presented to us, or our justices, if we shall not be present." We have supposed that the aldermen were formerly styled barons, but it is quite clear that they are not in this charter so designated, as with them never rested the choice of mayor, but with the Livery. In legal phraseology, *baron* and *femme* have ever stood for *man and wife*. The word baron means, in its original signification, nothing more than man. In the "Liber Albus" we read, that a woman *coverte de baron* may follow a trade. A note explains this as *protected by a husband*.*

The Lord Mayor of London, by charter of Edw. III., *anno primo*, is one of the Judges of Oyer and Terminer and jail-delivery for the jail of Newgate, and is still always placed at the head of the commissions which create criminal jurisdiction in London.† During the King's absence in France, we are informed by Maitland, the Lord Mayor, together with the aldermen, were commissioned to discover and punish certain rioters, an authority which the mayor exercised with undue severity, having tried in a summary manner and immediately executed two, whom he deemed most culpable. This was considered a stretch of power, and to keep the mayor harmless the King had to grant an indemnity from the consequences. The charters of Richard II., so liberal to the ancient city of York, were equally favourable to London. By them we learn the con-

* Bk. iii., p. 1.

† Norton, Commentaries, 351.

sideration in which the citizens were held, from the circumstance that in the famous Poll Tax, which gave rise to the rebellion of Wat Tyler, the Lord Mayor ranked as an earl, and the aldermen as barons.* The wealth of individual aldermen may be surmised from such acts as those of Whittington and Philpot; the latter, at his own private expense, having fitted out a fleet of ships, containing 1000 men, and himself sailed with them, for the purpose of attacking some pirates who had long been the scourge of British merchants. This noble alderman returned successful, having destroyed the whole of the enemies' ships.† Sir Richard Whittington, at a banquet given in 1431 to Henry V. and his queen, on the successful termination of his campaign in France, is said to have gratified and astonished his royal guests by throwing into the fire bonds for which the king was indebted to the citizens to the amount of £60,000.

We extract two or three curious notices from Stow's "Survey of London," illustrative of the civic worthies.

How Fitzwalter did Service as Bannerer, 1303. —"The said Robert and his heirs ought to be and are chief bannerers of London, in fee of the Chastilarie which he and his ancestors had by Castle Baynard in the said city," etc. "The said Robert ought to come on horseback, covered with cloth or armour unto the great west door of St. Paul," etc.

* Cotton's "Abridgment of the Records."

† "Thos. Wals. Hist. Angl."

"The Mayor, with his Aldermen and Sheriffs, armed in their arms, shall come out of the said church of St. Paul with a banner in his hand, all on foot, which banner shall be gules with the image of St. Paul, etc. Fitzwalter then salutes the Mayor:—'Sir Mayor, I am come to do my service which I owe to the city,' and the Mayor and Aldermen shall answer, 'We give to you as our bannerer of fee in this city this banner of this city to bear,'" etc. "And the said Robert shall receive the banner in his hands," etc.

How Henry Picard, Mayor, Feasted Four Kings, in 1363.—"Henry Picard, Vintner, Mayor 1357, in the year 1363 did in one day sumptuously feast Edward III., King of England, John King of France, David King of Scots, and the King of Cyprus, then all in England," etc.

How Thos. Knoles, Mayor, First Builded Guildhall, 1400.—"Thos. Knoles, Grocer, Mayor, 1400, with his brethren and Aldermen, began to new build the Guildhall in London, and instead of an old little cottage in Aldermanberie-street, made a fair and goodly house more near unto St. Lawrence church in the Jurie," etc.

How William Walworth, Mayor, Slew Wat Tyler, 1381, at the head of 30,000 rebels.—"The Mayor (William Walworth) arrested him (Tyler) on the head with a sound blow, whereupon Wat Tyler furiously strooke the Mayor with his dagger, but hurt him not by reason he was well armed. The Mayor having received his stroke *drew his basiliard*, and grievously wounded Wat in the neck, and withal gave him a great blow on the head," etc.

So fond was King Charles II. of the society of Lord Mayors that no less than nine times he feasted with them at the Guildhall. It was on one of these occasions that the incident occurred so graphically recorded in the *Spectator* (No. 462). "The Lord Mayor was Sir Robert Viner, who was a very loyal man, and if you will allow the expression, very fond of his sovereign; but what with the joy he felt at heart for the honour done him by his Prince and through the warmth he was in with continual toasting Health to the Royal Family, his Lordship grew a little too fond of his majesty and entered into a familiarity, not altogether so graceful in so public a place. The King knew very well how to extricate himself on all kinds of difficulties, and with an hint to the company to avoid ceremony, stole off, and made towards his Coach which stood ready for him in the Guildhall yard: But the Mayor liked his company so well, and was grown so intimate, that he pursued him hastily; and catching him fast by the hand cried out with a vehement oath and accent, '*Sir, you shall stay and take t'other bottle.*' The airy monarch looked kindly at him over his shoulder, and with a smile and graceful air (for I saw him at the time, and I do now) repeated this line of the old song, '*He that's drunk is as great as a King,*' and immediately returned and complied with his landlord."*

The first Lord Mayor's Feast given in the present

* Vide also Pennant, p. 457.

Guildhall was by Sir John Shaw, Goldsmith, says Pennant, knighted on the field of Bosworth. These gorgeous and extravagant banquets became at length so costly that in the reign of Philip and Mary a sumptuary law was made to restrain the expense both of provisions and liveries; but the mayors it seems did not regard it, for in 1544 an order of Council was issued to remind the citizens of their relapse into luxury. The Lord Mayor's feast given to the King and Queen and Royal Family in 1727 cost no less than £4390. That given in 1761 to George III. and Queen Charlotte cost £6898.

Adjacent to Guildhall was formerly Guildhall Chapel, or College, a Gothic building, founded by Peter Fanlove, Adam Francis, and Henry Frowick, citizens, about the year 1299. The establishment was a warden, seven priests, three clerks, and four choristers. Edward VI. granted it to the Mayor and commonalty of the City of London. Here used to be service once a week, and also at the election of the mayor, and before the mayor's feast, to deprecate *indigestions* and all *plethoric* evils.

A London paper, recently, after quoting a list of items of expenditure of Sir James Sanderson, Lord Mayor 1792, which shows an outlay during the year of £6055 14*s.* 7*d.* out of his own purse beyond the splendid sum allowed by the City, has the following: "A positive expenditure to this extent proves that Sir James Sanderson, however carefully his accounts were kept, spent his own money with a liberal hand —for the pleasure or benefit of his fellow-citizens.

Lord Mayors of a more recent date have been accused of making a profit out of the receipts of office; and there is no difficulty in believing this. A chief magistrate of a super-economical tendency might be able to do this, by dispensing with the costly accessories of the mayoralty, giving common dinners instead of princely banquets. During the last twenty-five years there have been many examples of public-spirited lord mayors, who made their labour and large outlay a delight, and were never so well satisfied as when supporting, by their unbounded munificence and untiring hospitality, the high character of the vast metropolis they represented. Certainly none of these have exceeded the late Alderman Cubitt and the present Alderman Phillips, nor can we soon cease to recollect at the brilliant City ceremonial or gorgeous banquet, those truly noble representatives of the highest qualities and virtues of first-class London merchants."

Lord Derby, in a recent speech at the Guildhall, said that he had never witnessed more magnificence by a Lord Mayor than that which had been displayed by the late Lord Mayor (Phillips), and in a lecture recently delivered by Charles Reed, Esq., F.S.A., on "The Ward of Farringdon," similar testimony was awarded, when the lecturer concluded by saying:—"The life of a late Alderman, Mr. Kelly, has been written to show what energy and business talent, combined with integrity and piety, might and did achieve. Another history might still be published, and it would show the career of one, springing from the people, and from a class once subjected to grievous religious disabilities, who had, by the blessing of Almighty God, by earnestness of purpose, force of character, and great natural abilities, worked his own way from narrow means up to affluence and wealth, realizing the day dream of his early life, and the ambition of riper years, in the unanimous election of his fellow-citizens to the office of chief magistrate. It is great honour to him (Mr. Alderman Phillips) and no small honour to us, that he has been permitted to entertain royalty at his private table, and that, in turn, he has been received as a distinguished private guest at the Court of Brussels, and honoured with the highest style of meritorious decoration. It is honour to us that twice during the year the heir-apparent of these realms has visited the Mansion House, on one occasion with the Princess and his Royal brother. He leaves for his successor an admirable example, and for himself a noble name."

It is a curious coincidence that the cities both of York and London should in the same year each be served by men as first magistrates alike eminently distinguished by all the excellences which should adorn the high office of Lord Mayor.

From the following royal writ it would appear that in early times the functions of the Lord Mayor were not entirely either civil or military:—13 Ed. III. 1345, 8th July—"To the Dean, etc., of St. Paul, London, the Mayor, etc."—"Whereas divers citizens have devised tenements and rents to found divers chantries in your church, and to offer prayers for their souls; and whereas when we pass by said church, which we hold to be our Mother Church, we see daily with our own eyes there are but few chaplains to sing, in proportion to the endowments, we pray you, to the honour of God, for the profit of the Church, and salvation of your own souls, that such defects be amended, to the end that the pious may have the greater feeling of devotion."*

An ordinance of the thirteenth century, preserved in the *Liber Albus*, gives an insight into the sharp practice prevalent among certain City corn merchants in those days, adding not a little to the labour of the mayor in administering justice. We quote it *in extenso:*—"And whereas some buyers and brokers of corn do buy corn in the City of country folks who bring it to the City to sell, and give, on the bargain being made, a penny or half-penny by way of earnest; and tell the peasants to take the corn to their house, and that there they shall receive their pay. And when they come there and think to have their payment directly, the buyer says that his wife has gone out and has taken the key of the room, so that he cannot get at his money; but that the other must go away, and come again soon and receive his pay; And when he comes back a second time, then the buyer is not to be found; or else, if he is found, he feigns something else, by reason whereof the poor men cannot have their pay, and sometimes while the poor men are waiting for their pay, the buyer causes the corn to be wetted,†

* Riley's "Memorials of London."

† For malting.

and then when they come to ask for their pay which was agreed upon [they are told] to wait until such a day as the buyer shall choose to name, or else to take off a part of the price; which, if they will not do, they may take their corn and carry it away, a thing which they cannot do, because it is wetted [and] in another state than it was when they sold it. And by such evil delays on part of the buyer, the poor men lose half of their pay in expenses before they are fully settled with.—It is provided that the persons towards whom such knavishness shall be committed, shall make complaint unto the mayor; and if he shall be able to make proof and convict the buyer before the mayor of the wrong so done to him, the buyer shall pay unto the vendor double the value and full damages as well, in case that the mayor shall see that the value aforesaid does not suffice for the damage which he has received; and, nevertheless, let him be heavily amerced unto the King if he have the means, and if he have not the means of paying, then he shall be put in the pillory, and remain there one hour in the day at least, a serjeant of the City standing by the side of the pillory with good hue and cry as to the reason why" [he is punished].*

This curious item is followed by one concerning butchers:—"And whereas some butchers do buy beasts of country folks, and as soon as they have the beasts in their houses kill them, and then at their own pleasure delay the peasants of their pay; or else

* Riley, p. 229.

tell them that they may take their beasts.—It is provided that the penalty which in such case is as to buyers and brokers of corn ordained, shall be incurred by such butchers, as shall thereof be attainted."*

From the frequent mention of the bakers in these ancient records, it would appear that the mayor had considerable trouble with that indispensable fraternity, against whom it is but fair to admit certain severe restrictions and penalties were enforced. For instance, they were compelled to make "two loaves for one penny, and four loaves for one penny, and no loaf shall be baked of bran." "No baker shall be allowed to sell bread before his own oven but only in the market of his lordship the King. And if any one is found selling in his house he shall be amerced in the sum of 40*s.*; and that no baker shall buy corn to sell again."† "According to ancient manner he shall give 13 articles of bread for 12."‡ "That no baker presume to enter upon the calling of a baker unless he have moveable goods to the value of 40*s.*"§ "That he shall bake pies for one half-penny," and charge no more for making paste for a capon than one penny. And lastly, bakers shall not carry a sword or club for making affray."‖ "And if any default shall be found in the bread of a baker in the City, the first time let him be drawn upon a hurdle from the Guildhall to his own house, through the great streets where there may be most people assembled, and through the great parts that are most dirty, with the faulty

* Riley, p. 230. † Ibid., p. 231. ‡ Ibid., p. 232.
§ Ibid., p. 295. ‖ Ibid., p. 611.

loaf hanging from his neck. If a second time he shall be found committing the same offence, let him be drawn from the Guildhall through the great Street of Chepe in manner aforesaid, to the pillory; and let him be put upon the pillory, and remain there at least one hour in the day. And the third [time that such] default shall be found, he shall be drawn, and the oven shall be pulled down, and the baker [made to] forswear trade within the City for ever."*

The butchers and bakers were not the only trades troublesome to the Mayor, for we find an ordinance (viii. Ed. I.) to the effect that the fishmongers shall so ordain that the baskets in which they bring their fish from the sea be more convenient and of larger size; and that from henceforth each basket contain in itself but one manner of fish. And that no one of the fishmongers as aforesaid, or of their partners, be so daring as falsely to dub their baskets, that is to say, to make a show at the top of the basket of desirable fish, and beneath, in such baskets, to put undesirable fish of little value. And if any person be attainted of so doing, such fish is to be forfeited, and the dubber to be imprisoned, and from henceforth let him be held a cheat.†

The Mayor was moreover responsible for dogs and their behaviour out of doors: for "to avoid the noise, damage, and strife, that used to arise therefrom, it is forbidden that any person shall keep a dog accustomed to go at large without guard thereof, by day or night within the franchise of the City,

* Riley, p. 232. † Ibid., p. 327.

genteel ['gentilx'] dogs excepted, under pain of paying 40*d*. to the use of the Chamber.*

Again, "if any woman shall be found to be a common receiver of courtezans, and if the same shall be attainted, let her be openly brought, with minstrels, from prison unto the thew (pillory), and set thereon for a certain time at the direction of the Mayor, and then let her hair be cut round about the head."†

Such were some of the arduous duties of the Lord Mayors in the olden time.

* Riley, p. 389. † Ibid., p. 395.

CHAPTER VIII.

THEIR SHERIFFS.

"Concerning ministers of justice, the high Sheriffs of the Counties have been very ancient in this kingdom."—BACON.

THE office of Sheriff, or *Shire-reve*, is, with the exception of that of Alderman, the most ancient existing in this country. Its origin is coeval with that of counties in the time of Alfred, and consequently is far more early than the office of mayor. Fitz-Stephen tells us in his *Descriptio Nobilissimæ Civitatis Londoniæ*, that London had its annual Sheriffs instead of consuls, with senators and other inferior magistrates. In some counties, from a very distant period, the Shrievalty was hereditary, as Blackstone surmises it to have been in Scotland till the statute of George II. 43, and as it still continues in the county of Westmoreland to this day. No doubt this claim was founded originally upon a purchase of the office. We know that in 1195, Geoffrey Plantagenet, Archbishop of York, purchased that of York for the enormous sum, paid to the King, Richard I., of 3000 marks (or £2000).* Sheriffs of counties,

* Lcl. Coll. vol. ii., p. 210; Stow's Chron., p. 157.

although now in the election of the Crown, were formerly chosen by the inhabitants. This right is recognized, 28 Edward I. c. 8, which directs that in every shire where the Shrievalty is not of inheritance the people shall elect, etc. The City of London has also the inheritance of the Shrievalty of Middlesex vested in their body by charter (undated) of Henry I., in which they are empowered to hold Middlesex to farm, for £300 (this, according to the value of present money, was £12,000, a rather large sum to be paid yearly for a privilege, which, however, has turned out to be an important and honourable one for London), "upon accompt to them and their heirs so that the said citizens shall place as Sheriff whom they will of themselves, and shall place whomsoever, or such one as they will of themselves (as Justiciar) for keeping the pleas of the Crown and of the pleading of the same." It appears, says Norton (p. 80), by Madox's extracts in the Firma Burgi, p. 165, that notwithstanding this charter, both Stephen and Henry II. appointed the Sheriffs quite at their own will and pleasure, sometimes three, four, and five at a time.

The term "to hold Middlesex to farm," means that the citizens are to exercise their custody and power over Middlesex, and to have the collection of the King's demesne revenues arising within it, but this right is not to be confounded with the tenure by which the City held their private landed possessions in the county. That it was anciently very remunerative, as well as honourable, is certain from the fact that the records speak of large sums having been paid by persons for the office of custos or farmer. The franchise bestowed on the citizens of farming the Sheriffwick of the county of Middlesex, at a stipulated rent, must therefore be considered as a very distinguished mark of the Royal favour, and to have obtained it, no doubt the citizens had at a certain period greatly assisted the Crown. In enumerating the many privileges granted to the citizens by his predecessors, no mention is made of the Sheriffwick. Thus it would appear that both Stephen and Henry II. had usurped the appointment to that office, and Richard was not disposed to restore it. John's first Charter makes no mention of it, but his second granted expressly for that purpose confirms the Charter of Henry I., and further states that the "ferm" rent of £300 of "blank sterling money" (silver melted down or blanched in order to ascertain its goodness) is to be paid twice a-year into the Exchequer, £150 at Easter, and £150 at Michaelmas. This is the first dated Charter recognizing or granting to the City the county of Middlesex, and in the body of the Charter itself, it is expressly stated, that the citizens are granted it "because it was in ancient times fermed (to them) for £300." Henry III. by his Charter, dated February 18th, 1227, fully confirmed all the former grants respecting the Sheriffwick of London and Middlesex, and *Liber Albus* states that no Sheriff is to let to farm the county of Middlesex, for it is to remain alone in their keeping, "so that the people in the said county may be treated and governed in due manner as the law demands, without extortion committed to any one.*

The livery, it would seem, were not at all times particular enough as to the status of the favoured ones whom they appointed to the high office, for in the *Liber Albus*, lib. iii., p. 2, Edward I., it is thus recorded:—"Also, it is forbidden that the Mayor, Sheriffs, Aldermen, or their clerks, serjeants, or bedels shall from henceforth brew, themselves or by others, for sale, or shall keep oven or wine tavern or shall trade in any other thing to which a low estimate is attached. And he who shall contravene this ordinance shall be ousted from his office."

The duty of the Sheriffs of counties is to preside at elections of knights of the shire and for the city, and at the elections of Lord Mayor. As the keeper of the King's peace, both by common law and special commission, he is the first man in the county and superior in rank to any nobleman therein for his year of office. He is bound *ex-officio* to pursue all traitors and misdoers. He is to defend his county against all enemies, and may raise the *posse comitatus*. In the City of London proper, some of these duties devolve upon the Mayor, to whom alone the Sheriff yields precedence. In olden times all the freeholders of the county, of every rank, were obliged to give their personal attendance to add to the magnificence of his train, so that his retinue must almost have equalled that of his Sovereign. At the coronation of Charles II. the procession is said to have exceeded

* Lib. 1, pt. 1, cap. 17.

in splendour any which had previously been seen in this country. Maitland, in his description of the pageant, says—"Then came the Sheriffs' men in red cloaks richly laced with silver to the number of *fourscore*, then followed 600 of the several Companies of London on horseback, in black velvet coats and gold chains, each Company having footmen in liveries, etc. Then his Majesty's Lifeguard and the various City officers; then the two Sheriffs and all the Aldermen, with footmen in liveries, red coats laid with silver and cloth of gold; the heralds and maces in rich coats; then the Lord Mayor, carrying the sword bare, with his Excellency (the General) and the Duke of Buckingham, bare also; and then as the lustre to all this splendid triumph rode the King himself between his royal brothers, the Dukes of York and Gloucester." We perceive from this account that the Sheriffs made a brilliant display with their fourscore footmen in their splendid liveries; indeed, from the records of the City we learn that at all times they have made a very magnificent appearance.

In the learned "Account of the Carpenters' Company," by E. B. Jupp, we have some interesting particulars of the ancient civic custom of setting out the midsummer watch, compiled from Stow, in which we read that the Mayor himself came well mounted, with his sword-bearer in fair armour on horseback, preceded by the minstrels and the Mayor's officers in liveries. The Sheriffs' watches came one after the other in like order but not so numerous; for the Mayor had besides his giant three pageants, whereas the Sheriffs had only two besides their giants, each with their morris-dancer and one henchman. King Henry VIII., says Stow, came privily in this the first year of his reign to view the setting of the watch, "being clothed in one of the coats of his guard;" and with the next muster, "The King and Queen came roially riding to the signe of the King's Head, in Cheape, and there beheld the watch of the cities which was set with divers goodly shows as had been accustomed." The Sheriffs here seem not to have been behind even the Lord Mayor, for while he had three pageants, and they had but two, they had two giants and the Mayor but one; and Mr. Jupp quotes the account merely to confirm its accuracy by extracts from the books of the Company, from which it appears they sent archers and arrows to take part in the pageant.

Giants in those days were rather formidable monsters. In his "Sports and Pastimes," Strutt quotes from the Harl. MSS. particulars relative to setting the watch at Chester, A.D. 1564, when it was ordained that the pageant, "according to ancient custome," should consist of four giants, one unicorn, one dromedary, one luce, one camel, one ass, one dragon, six hobby-horses, and sixteen naked boys." He calculates the large cost incurred in reviving these pageants at the Restoration, all things having to be made new "by reason the ould modells were all broken." The materials of each giant at the least would be five pounds, and four men to carry them, two shillings and sixpence each. The items for the constitution of a giant are curious, "hoops of various magnitudes, deal boards, nails, pasteboards, scaleboards, buckram, size, cloth, old sheets for their bodies, sleeves, and shirts." The last particular is ludicrously significant, it is "for arsnick to put into the paste to save the giants from being eaten by the rats."* The Sheriffs were sometimes attended in state by the various companies, for in the year 1460, 39th Henry VI., the Carpenters "Payde for the hyre of the Barge to Westminster with the Shrieves, iiij's."†

The present regulations of London require that henceforth the two Sheriffs ‡ should be elected by the Livery only; that the election be held on June 24th, but if that falls on a Sunday, then the day following; that the sheriffs shall be sworn in on the vigil of St. Michael the Archangel next ensuing, for one year; that all the Aldermen who have not already served the office "shall be publicly put in nomination, according to their seniority, before any Commoner;" that the Lord Mayor, between April 14th and June 14th, may nominate in the Court of Aldermen any number

* Herbert, vol. i. p. 198.

† Jupp's "Carpenters' Company," p. 31.

‡ The following legal fact is curious:—"The Lord Mayor and citizens of London have the shrievalty of London and Middlesex in fee by charter, and two Sheriffs are annually elected by them, for whom they have to be answerable. If one of these Sheriffs die, the other cannot act till another is made, and there must be *two* Sheriffs of London, which is a *City and County;* though *together they make but one Sheriff* of Middlesex, they are several as to plaints in their respective courts."—3 *Rep.* 72. *Show Rep.* 289.

of persons, "not exceeding nine," being free of the City, to be put in nomination for the office, to the Livery, in open hallmote; and that if any so nominated, within six days after notice thereof, pay £400 to the Chamberlain, and 20 marks (£13 6*s*. 8*d*.) for the prison ministers, together with the usual fees, he shall be exempt from the office so long as he does not become Alderman. That no freeman shall be sworn in if he swears himself worth less than £20,000, the same assertion to be attested by six witnesses. That every person so elected shall at the next Court of Aldermen give £1000 to the Chamberlain, that he will take upon himself the office on September 29th next, and that if he does not give a bond he shall, if an Alderman or Commoner of the City of the Lord Mayor's nomination, forfeit and pay £600; but if nominated otherwise, he shall pay £400. The fines paid within the present century we believe to have amounted to a very large sum. At the present time it is usual for the duties of Sheriff to be performed chiefly by the Under-Sheriff, who, in return for his services, receives all the fees of office, amounting to about £1500 per annum, for which he holds the Sheriff harmless against any actions which may arise against the Sheriff. The expenses to the Sheriff range from £3000 to £4000 for the year.

The duties are not in every case now the same as formerly. In 1188, Henry de Cornhille, the Sheriff, was commanded to provide the King with a certain number of military accoutrements, and ten years after the Sheriffs were ordered to provide weights and measures for standards for the several counties. Madox tells us that Henry III. descended so low as to make the Sheriffs provide a muzzle, iron chain, and cord for the white bear in the Tower, while Edward II. ordered them to pay the leopard keeper 6*d.* a day for the sustenance of them. In 1254 the Sheriffs were imprisoned for the non-payment of "*aurum reginæ*," or queen's gold, a tax levied on them; while in 1262 the Exchequer Court decided that the Sheriffs of London might distrain anywhere in Westminster, even to the Abbey Gates. On September 1st, 1439, a prisoner was seized from a Sheriff's officer, and conveyed for safety into St. Martin's-le-Grand College. The Sheriffs thereupon entered the college, seized the prisoner and his rescuers, and chained them all up together in Newgate. In 1478 Sheriff Byfield was fined £50 for resenting the Lord Mayor's rebuke of his kneeling too close to him while before St. Erkenwald's* shrine, Old St. Paul's. When Lord Stafford was condemned to the block for his supposed share in the Titus Oates plot, the King thinking that property ought to mitigate the penalty from hanging to beheading, the Sheriffs sent to Parliament to inquire by what right the King showed his power of

* Ethelbert, King of Kent, the first Christian monarch of the Saxon race, at the instance of St. Augustine, appointed Mellitus the first Bishop of London. Erkenwald, the son of King Offa, fourth in succession from Mellitus, ornamented the cathedral (St. Paul's), and improved the revenues with his own patrimony. "He was most deservedly canonized, the very litter in which he was carried in his last illness," says Pennant, humorously, "continued many centuries, to cure fevers by the touch; and the very chips carried to the sick restored them to health." (Pennant's London, p. 357.)

mitigation, when the Commons returned answer that they "would be content with his head in whatever way the sentence was carried out."

The most disagreeable duty which the Sheriffs have to perform is to attend the execution of a criminal at the Old Bailey. It has been generally admitted that if an executioner cannot be found to perform the duty which Calcraft has now to carry out, one of the Sheriffs must do it. It is stated that during the shrievalty of Sir Richard Phillips, 1808, there was no execution in London, but, when some culprits were ordered to be whipped, Jack Ketch told the Sheriff to do it himself. The reason of this appears to have been a difference as to wages, which Sir Richard agreed to raise from a guinea to a guinea and a half per week.

In a former chapter, we showed from the "Liber Albus" how a Sheriff was fined by the Mayor "ten tuns of wine for disobedience committed towards him." In the same book (lib. i. part II. chap. xii.) we read—"Also as concerning the Sheriffs and Aldermen, provision must be made as follows:—The Sheriffs are to have their serjeants and the Aldermen their bedels becomingly and fairly arrayed and shod, prompt and ready to obey the commands of the Mayor. And, if perchance any of them should be an aged man, weak or infirm, or have sore eyes, then another person must be substituted in his place to perform such duties."

By tampering with the privileges of the citizens not of London only, but of other ancient corporations of this country, the Stuarts lost their throne. The celebrated *Quo Warranto* was one of the worst blunders ever monarch made. Evelyn, in his Diary, tells us that through it Sir George Treby, the Recorder, was displaced, "eight of the richest and chiefe aldermen were removed, and all the rest made only justices of the peace, and no more wearing of gownes or chains of golde, the Lord Mayor and two Sheriffs holding their places by new grants as Custodes, at the King's pleasure." Evelyn thus sighingly exclaims, "The pompe and grandeur of the most august city in the worlde thus changed face in a moment, which gave greate occasion for discourse and thoughts of hearts, what all this would end in. Prudent men were for the old foundations."

So in our days "prudent men are for the old foundations," and in these times of unquiet, restless seeking after change, we look back upon the time-honoured institutions of our forefathers and rejoice that we have not yet been deprived of all our cherished "old foundations."

It was necessary that the Sheriffs should be men of substance, as the office involved great responsibility. For every fatal accident the King demanded a heavy fine, and the Sheriffs were held answerable for its recovery. Thus we read in the "Liber Albus," 13th Henry III., A.D. 1229—"It happened that a certain boy, Adam de Norfolk by name, fell from a horse into the Thames, being dragged in by another horse, which he was holding by the band while watering it, and was drownd. No one was held suspected therein. Judgment, 'Misadventure.' The value of the horses was four marks, for which sum the Sheriffs were to make answer; who afterwards answered for the same" (to the King).*

The Common Serjeant-at-Arms of the City, otherwise called the Common Crier, also had certain heavy claims upon the Sheriffs, for we read in the "Early Ordinances—"He shall further receive from the Sheriffs twelve pence for every cry that he makes throughout the City; to enable him to do which, they shall find him a sufficient horse for the honour of the City."†

They had also to summon the Aldermen to the hustings in great state, for it was ordained "that they (the Aldermen) ought, by usage of the said City, to be summoned by an officer of the Sheriff, mounted upon a horse of the value of one hundred shillings at least."‡

Neither must they keep taverns, for in Riley's "Liber Albus" is the following:—"Also, it was forbidden that the Mayor, Sheriffs, or Aldermen, shall brew or keep for sale, or keep oven or wine tavern, or shall trade in any other thing to which a low estimate is attached."¶

To meet the numerous fines and penalties for which the Sheriffs were liable, they had certain emoluments, some of which appear curious. For instance, in the Charter of King Edward III. we read—"Also, that the Sheriffs of London shall have wholly the forfeitures of victuals, and of other articles

* Riley, p. 79.
† Ibid., p. 43.
‡ Ibid., p. 170.
¶ Ibid., p. 237.

and merchandise, according to the tenor of the charters," * etc.

All kinds of spurious manufactures were to be seized by the Sheriffs, entries occurring in the records of various items, such as "false breeches and purses" seized, "putrid meat," "stinking capons," "a stinking rabbit," "malt and corn sold in secret," "putrid pigeon," "a peck of stinking eels," "hides forfeited for being badly tanned," "shoes of Basil † sold as tawed ‡ leather," "a stinking pig," "false dice," "stinking partridge," "rotten fish called conger," "rotten and stinking pike and eel," and the like. Some were of a less disagreeable character, such as a "penalty upon an Alderman because his mantle, or cloak, was single, and not trimmed with fur." Also, seizure of dorsers [baskets] of fish not of a size. "Burning of the dorsers and forfeiture of the fish." The Sheriffs, moreover, took toll of fish, viz., from each dorser one lamprey.

We thus find that whatever the responsibilities of office, they were sweetened by the daily participation in the fines, good and bad, inflicted by the Sheriffs upon their erring fellow-citizens.

* Riley, p. 131.

† Prepared sheep-skin.

‡ Tanned leather. Tawyer, currier; white tawyer, dresser of white leather with alum.

CHAPTER IX.

THEIR NAME LIVERY.

"On St Dunstan's Eve all the hoole Companye of the Lyverye shall assemble at the Hall in their second lyverye, and shall have iiij Chapelynes to wayte and goo before them to Pawll's" (St Paul's).—Goldsmith's Warden's Accounts, 1 Edward IV.

It was once wittily said of a late Bishop of London that in bestowing his preferment "he cared more for the cut of a man's coat than for his degree." This of course was a joke, but it was not without a basis of truth. There can be no doubt that in making selection from his clergy for appointments to town livings, that learned prelate did consider as a very important matter the question of dress and address, and invariably, other things—the candidate's moral and religious character—being equal, thought more of his bearing and deportment than of his former University distinction. This he did in deference to the popular taste. The motto of mankind, he well knew, is not always "*Mentem hominis spectato, non frontem,*" nor was he ignorant that "*Optima sæpè despecta.*" We may justly ridicule the Turveydrops of the age, but there can be but one opinion upon the point that deportment and address are of the greatest value to an aspirant for public favour of any kind, and it is as unwise, as the world goes, to sneer at these qualities because they are sometimes possessed by a Turveydrop, as it would be for a barrister or clergyman to despise oratory because it is occasionally to be met with in a Robespierre or a John Bright. Many great men have been overlooked by the age from the mere accident that they were not presentable : while others, to use a commercial phrase, have done a large amount of business with a remarkably small capital. In studying the ancient historic records, it is curious to remark at how very early a date we may discover evidence of the fact that our forefathers were even greater believers than we are in the importance of dress and appearance. Indeed, to such an extent had the love of dress progressed in the reign of Elizabeth, not a little encouraged by her own royal example (for we are told by Pennant so fond was she of her attire that three thousand different habits were found in her wardrobe after her death), that sumptuary laws were enforced, some of them greatly ridiculous, against vulgar wenches and persons of low degree. The Queen required the masters of the Companies to read her proclamations respecting the "caps, gownes, kirtles, and petticoates," which were to be unmingled with silk; and the Ironmongers' books, as quoted by Malcolm, inform us that "two members of that Company were in 1579 chosen to attend, with two men free of the Grocers, at Bishopsgate, from seven o'clock in the morning till six in the afternoon, who were to examine the habits of all persons passing through the gate."

In all ancient mandates to the mayors and governors to provide a given number of horsemen and footmen to meet and escort the Sovereign in his pageants and progresses, mention is always made that they shall be "proper" and "presentable" persons. In 1559, the Ironmongers were required to send to Greenwich, to meet Queen Elizabeth, "28 *hanssome men* well and handsomely arrayed." The Grocers were required to send "190 *personnes, apte and picked men*, for the *shewe* at Greenwich." From this it would seem that the Queen had a higher opinion of the good looks of the Grocers than of the Ironmongers, 28 hanssome men only being hoped for of the latter, while 190 "picked men were expected from the former." Very especial regard too is to be had to their uniformity in dress. Indeed, this clearly has been a national feeling from a very early period. The original ordinances of the several London Companies specify that on all occasions of their members attendance at the hall, whether at feasts, obits, funerals, or otherwise, they shall come suitably attired.

So ceremonious were the rulers of the City of London that even the horses upon which the Sheriffs' officers rode were to be of a certain value. In the "Liber Albus," compiled in A.D. 1419, amongst the ancient orders stands the following. "Item: the Aldermen of London shall be summoned to come to the hustings; and they ought by usage of the said City, to be summoned by an officer of the Sheriff, mounted upon a horse of the value of one hundred shillings at least."* Great care also was taken,

* Lib. iii. p. 1, "Of the Aldermen."

where the dress was altered every year, that no official should wear a second-hand costume: each garment was to be made new for its wearer. In "Liber Albus"* it is thus recorded—"Also the Mayor, Sheriffs, and Aldermen were all accustomed to array themselves in a like suite on two occasions in the year; when the Mayor rode to have the oath administered at Westminster on the morrow of the Apostles Simon and Jude; such vestments being trimmed with proper furs." Again, it was the usage for them to be arrayed in a like suit against the feast of Pentecost, the linings being then of silk. Hence it was that the Monday next after the feast of our Lord's Epiphany, in the thirty-first year of the reign of Edward III. (A.D. 1358), an ordinance was made by the Mayor and Aldermen that "whenever it should so happen that the Mayor and Aldermen should be arrayed in such like suit, no one of them should give or part with his robe within that year, under pain of forfeiting one hundred shillings. And if it should so happen that any one of them shall depart this life within that year, his executors, under the penalties aforesaid, were not to alienate or give to any one such robe within that year." In the same book (cap. xviii.) we read that the "Common Serjeant-at-Arms shall (besides his salary) receive from each of the Aldermen for his fee the entire robes or cloaks in which they are sworn upon the day on which they receive charge of their office."

In the final ordinance confirmed by King Charles

* Lib. i. p. 1, cap. x.

I. to the Leathersellers' Company, in which are recapitulated various former charters granted to that Company from "21 Rich. II. and long before," it is declared that upon the master's summons to the feasts, the livery shall attend in a "sad suit," and not "in russet boots." From Jupp's historical account of the Carpenters' Company, (pp. 139-140), we learn that the same scrupulous attention to dress prevailed amongst that honourable craft. We extract the following entries:—

1556.

"Rsd of John gryffen a fyne for that he came to the hall in his coote and his lether aprone - - vjd.

"Rsd of Richard hutton a fyne for comyng wyth - oute his hode to wayte apone my lorde mayer on all allon daye, at powlls (St. Paul's) - - - - xijd.

"Rsd of John gryffen a fyne for pullyng of his gowne at dynner at the beryall of John snelling and for yll wordes geven to the wardyns - - - - iij's."

It would appear that the said John Gryffen was unusually careless of the observances which he had sworn to maintain. There could be no possible harm in his wearing his coat and leather apron on suitable occasions—but to appear in them at the hall was, to say the least, out of taste. He deserved, we doubt not, the fine inflicted on him then, and also at the subsequent funeral of John Snelling, when his conduct must have been exceedingly bad for a fine of three shillings to have been inflicted. However, stern discipline answered in his case; at any rate his name does not again occur amongst the offenders. In 1567 (p. 141) the wardens "received of Thomas Harper for comyng in a wronge lyverie gowne at the buryall of Mr. Trull, xiid." It is possible this might have been a mere oversight, but the law must be maintained, and the fine accordingly was paid. From the same source (p. 142) we discover a lack of observance creeping into the court itself; for under the date of "1603, Septemr 12th," we read—"It is this daye ordered yf anye one of the assistaunts shall come to sitt in this courte without a capp, or any the assistaunts or lyverie to come at anye solempnitye without a capp, to doe his attendance, for everye tyme so offending he shall foreit xijd." Before closing this curious volume we extract one entry (p. 208), which indicates the great appreciation of this worshipful court of the niceties of costume even in the person of an official: "1668, 1 Sept.: Item paid wch was given and allowed to Will Levett, Cooke of this Company, for a laissed capp with the Companies armes, to be worn and vsed by him vpon all publique dinners of the said Companie xls."

The Companies have ever been scrupulous in the observance of the laws of heraldry in their ceremonies, pageants, and funerals. Each fraternity possessed costly hearse-cloths of cloth of gold and of exquisite workmanship, to be used at the funerals of the livery, the designs for the devices of which were executed under the direction of the Lancaster Herald. The cost of one of these palls is entered in the Carpenters' records, date 1513, 5 Hen. VIII., at £15 12*s.* 9*d.* One item is as follows: "Pd. to the brotherar [embroiderer] for hyss workmanschyppe viii£, spent apon mastyr lankestyr the herrad at armys for the oversyght of your cloth 2s. viiid."*

This particularity in dress in the olden time, and study of uniformity, must not be supposed to have arisen from the mere love of show. The nobility and large proprietors from the time of the Conquest, claimed by universal usage the privilege of assuming liveries or distinctive dresses to their followers and dependants. The providing them for the households of the King, for his judges, officers, servants, and retainers, was a usual subject of the rent of farmers of demesnes and cities and the farm of sheriffs. The nobility and the most powerful subjects used to clothe so many of their followers about the time of Richard II., for the purpose of maintaining their state and their quarrels, that they began then to be denounced by statute under the name of *maintenances*.† As the citizens of London ever held the highest rank amongst territorial lords, the privileges which the nobles enjoyed of course were claimed by themselves, and liveries were granted by the Mayor and Aldermen to the great gilds of the City.

As civil feuds were of frequent occurrence, it was necessary that the retainers of each nobleman should be easily recognized from those of another by some distinguishing badge, and thus a particular dress or livery was introduced. In the hope of appeasing these frequent feuds a petition was forwarded to Parliament in the 13th of Richard II., "that no

* Jupp, p. 21.

† *Vide* Anderson's "Hist. Com." vol. i. p. 365; vol. ii. p. 17.

spiritual or temporal Lord or other of less estate should give livery except to his household or relatives." In the same reign, it was ordained that no "varlets, called yeomen, nor none other of less estate than esquire, shall use or bear any sign of livery, called livery of company, of any Lord within the realm, unless he be menial, and familiar or continual officer of the said Lord." Nicholl, in his history of the Ironmongers' Company, says that "in every act for the suppression of liveries, from 1 Richard II. to the 12 Edward IV., whenever mention is made of the gilds, a special clause of exemption is made."

Stow, who is a great authority on all such matters, informs us that in 1270, on the marriage of Edward I., at Canterbury, with his second Queen, Margaret, the fraternities rode, to the number of 600, "in one livery of red and white, with the connuzances of their mysteries embroidered on their sleeves."* In Fabian's Chronicles, under the year 1446, in the account given of the reception of Queen Margaret in London, the dress of the livery is thus described:—"She was met with the mayre, aldermen, and sherifes of the cytee, and the craftes of the same, in blewe, with browderyd slevys; that is to meane, everye mysterye or crafte wyth conysaunce of his mysterye, and rede hodes upon eyther of their heddes." Herbert,† states that the earliest dress of the gilds consisted of an upper and under garment, called a "coat and surcote," the cloak or gown, and the hood, being reserved for cere-

* Strype's Stow, 1247.

† Vol. i. p. 59.

monials, and completing what was termed "*the full suit.*" There was also an undress, or part dress, called "*the hooding,*" perhaps allowed to freemen, who were not esteemed "full brothers," like the livery, and who ranked as yeomen only, and not as esquires, as the livery.

As far as we can learn the fashion of the livery gowns has not altered since the reign of Henry VI. From a choice design in the illuminated charter, granted by that monarch to the Leathersellers' Company, we discover that the robe and hood were precisely the same then as those worn to this day on occasions of ceremony and in attendance at divine worship. Stow mentions the hood (evidently copied from the monk's cowl, and somewhat like the university hood) as an indispensable appendage to the ancient civic liveries. He says the coverture of men's heads in these times was hoods, for neither hat nor cap is spoken of, except in the case of John Wells, mayor; and he refers to the liveries of Thomas of Lancaster, in the reign of Edward II., who allowed to every garment of his liveries fur, to fur their *hoods;* and to the pictures of Aldermen in the reigns of Henry IV. and Henry VI., who wore scarlet gowns on their backs, and hoods on their heads. He considers square caps, afterwards used, to have had their rise not earlier than Henry VII. He sneers at Sir John White, amongst the "young aldermen," as the first that wore the flat round cap. He speaks also of the Spanish felt hats just then coming in, but adds, "in London, amongst the graver sort, I mean the *livery of Companies*, remaineth a memory of the hoods of old, worn by their predecessors." "These hoods were worn, the roundlet upon their heads, the skirts to hang behind in their necks, the tippet to be on the shoulder or about their necks." We must not suppose that it is any special beauty of design or pattern which has caused the companies to cling so tenaciously to the ancient style in the fashion of their costume. It possesses to them the charm of antiquity, the sanction of many monarchs who have been the firmest friends of the mysteries, and who themselves have been pleased, as livery-men-kings, to wear the same; and, above all, it is the identical livery to wear which the various charters have conferred a royal licence.

Although, as we have shown, the gilds at a very early period had their distinctive dress or livery, it was not until the reign of Edward III. that these great and numerous companies obtained a royal warrant granting to the brotherhoods this privilege, and thus henceforth they were known by the designation of the LIVERY COMPANIES. They were no longer in their subsequent charters called gilds, but crafts and mysteries; their Alderman no longer bore that name, but was called "Master," or "Prince Warden." The heads of the several wards were alone termed Aldermen. The King at the same time confirmed by royal charter all their privileges, which had been held in some cases only by sufferance or by permissive sanction. King Edward, however, did not grant them such powers as later monarchs have yielded to them. He gave no grant of a common seal, nor did he generally empower them to purchase or accept lands, neither did he confer various other liberties necessary to establish them in their present greatness. He was fully aware of the vast influence upon commerce of these trading communities in a trading city like London, and to foster their growth and to augment their power, he became himself a member of a craft which he deemed specially valuable to the State, the *Linen Armourers*, since better known as the *Merchant Taylors*, celebrated at that time for their large importations of woollen cloth, which he desired to make the staple manufacture of England. He was the first livery-man-king. Richard II. became a brother of the same company. The nobility and clergy imitated such examples, and henceforward the chief companies of the City presented at their banquets a most imposing array of affluence and beauty. The vast wealth they possessed in plate, attracting as it did the cupidity of future monarchs in the hour of need, was not the result of purchase so much as complimentary presentations from the royal and noble members. In the lists of great and eminent brethren of the Merchant Taylors' Company, in the reign of Richard II., are the names of no less than four royal dukes, ten earls, ten barons, and five bishops. The Mercers and Skinners were at this time the next in favour with the great, and each presented a splendid display of distinguished and noble names upon its roll.

After so many descriptions of pageantry, parade, and self-adornment, it may be asked, if for such purposes man has been sent into this world? Is it prudent or wise to waste life's brief moments in the practice of "that outward adorning of wearing of gold, or putting on of apparel?" We say that if these are the only adornments of a man, he must indeed be ill furnished for a future life. But to him are permitted pleasures, as well as duties; life is not all toil, "*Otiare, quo labores*" has been truly said. We are to have the sweets with the bitters. "There is a time to work, and a time to laugh." Neither is there anything culpable in a careful study of the proprieties of dress, so that, with all the advantages of grace and dignity, a man possesses what is of still higher value, "the ornament of a meek and quiet spirit, which is in the sight of God of great price." Let us not attempt to sit in judgment upon a past generation, neither upon the present. A day is approaching when this shall be done for us and upon us; in which of each individual it may be said, in the beautiful and modest language inscribed on the tomb of a great man in Westminster Abbey, "*Qualis erat, iste dies indicabit.*" Our next chapter, on the "Religious observances of our forefathers," will tend to show that they were no mere idlers on the stage of existence, but earnest-minded men, working with a will both works of charity and devotion, being not in name only, but in reality, Christian men.

CHAPTER X.

THEIR RELIGIOUS OBSERVANCES.

"He that is void of fear may soon be just;
And no religion binds men to be traitors."—Ben Jonson.

That there was much superstition prevalent amongst the Anglo-Saxon Christians, and indeed their successors also up to the time of the Reformation, there can be no doubt, but that there was a deep current of sound religious feeling beneath it all, especially in the early ages, is equally credible. Our forefathers had no tendency to that species of unbelief which so characterizes the present age—the habit of doubting and even denying the truth and inspiration of the sacred writings, and of treating lightly the mysteries of our holy religion. They were not merely nominal Christians, but they had a firm faith in the Founder of Christianity, or as He is so beautifully designated in their earliest form of institution to office, "Him Crucified."*

* "The Feast of the Apostles Simon and Jude being now come, about the tenth hour by the clock (*de campana*, properly by the bell, the hours in these times being announced by bells), it was the custom for the Mayor and all the Aldermen—arrayed in cloaks of violet—to meet at the Guildhall. Silence and attention being then enjoined by the Common Crier, in other words the Sergeant-at-Arms, the Recorder, seated at the right hand of the Mayor, announced to the

These simple Christians believed in the sacred books of the old dispensation, and in those also of the new, which record the sayings and teachings, the miracles and sufferings, of Him who was born of the Virgin. It is true there was much of darkness in those days, but there was the "true light" shining amidst the gloom. They were child-like, earnest, willing to learn, desirous to be taught. Though citizens here, they remembered that they were but pilgrims journeying to that "land which is very far off." Thus it was that a sense of their dependence upon a good Providence, and the knowledge that no object could permanently succeed without the blessing of God, pervaded all their doings. Especially was the religious principle of these early merchants manifested in the rules which bound them in their trade fraternities. They looked beyond the present, and neither prosperity nor adversity moved them from the right. Their motto seems to have been "*In secundis time, in adversis spera,*" or, notwithstanding their love of show and parade, "*Fructu non foliis, arborem æstima.*" The secret of the abiding character of these civic gilds has been already indicated as lying in the deep religious principle avowed in all their regulations, and the social element equally

people that he who was to be Mayor for the then ensuing year was to take the oath. This done, the out-going Mayor vacated his seat, and the Mayor-elect took his place; the past Mayor, however, sitting next to him, on his left hand. Then the Common Sergeant-at-Arms, holding before him the book (the Gospels), with the effigy of Him crucified on the outside thereof, and he placing his hand upon the book," etc.—(Riley's "Liber Albus," p. 21.)

prominent in their foundation. Nothing was ever done, no work entered upon by them, without *prayer and feasting*. No distinct records are extant of the rules of any of the Anglo-Saxon trade gilds, but those of a similar fraternity for mutual protection in case of loss by fire or death remain, and no doubt they were similar to those adopted by the others. We quote the following from "A Treatise on Friendly Societies," by Chas. Ansell, F.R.S., who obtained it from Dr. Hicks's "Dissertatio Epistolaris De Ling. Vett. Septentrional. usu," pp. 21, 22.* These rules are translated from the Saxon :—

"Society at Exeter.—This meeting is held in the city of Exeter for the sake of God and our own souls, that we may make such ordinances as tend to our welfare and security as well in this life as in that future state we wish to enjoy in the presence of God our Judge. Three stated meetings to be held every year,—at each meeting every member to contribute two sextaria of barley meal, and every knight (*cnut*, young man) one, together with his quota of honey. At each of these meetings a priest shall sing two masses (the one for the living, the other for the departed members). Every one shall, moreover, in his turn, procure six masses and six psalms to be sung at his own proper expense. That when any member is about to go abroad, each of his fellow-members shall contribute 5d.; and if any member's house shall have been burnt, 1d."

Another is taken from the rules of a society at

* Thesaurus, iii.

Cambridge. "When any member shall die, he shall be carried by the whole society to whatever place of interment he shall have chosen; and whoever shall not come to assist in bearing him shall forfeit a sextarium of honey, the society making up the rest of the expense and furnishing each his quota towards the funeral entertainment."

In a former paper mention was made of the great antiquity of the Steelyard Merchants and also of that of the *Gilda Sellariorum*, or saddlers, both undoubtedly of Anglo-Saxon origin. The *Tellarii*, or woollen cloth weavers, are spoken of by Madox as possessing a charter as early as Henry II., in which all their liberties and customs are confirmed as having been enjoyed by them in the reign of Henry I. The fact also is established of some of the gilds having been chartered long before Edward I., and possessing immunities immediately after the Conquest. In the *Quo Warranto*, quoted by Madox, the weavers are required to show by what authority they claimed to have their gild in the City, and after the specifying of several other privileges, which they had claimed, occurs the passage which has occasioned in this place a reference to the proceeding, viz., "And lastly, why none (*i.e.*, workmen) were allowed to work between Christmas and the Purification, or at night by candle-light at other times proscribed."* The defence of the weavers was based upon their charter from Edward I., confirming the charter of "The Lord Henry, of good memory, our progenitor, late King of

* Firma Burgi, pp. 283, 284.

England," made to the weavers of London, etc., dated at London, April 8th, 27 Edward I. (A.D. 1300). The strictness with which the Christmas festival was observed by this ancient brotherhood will be the more apparent when we bear in mind that Christmas-day falls on December 25th, and the Feast of the Purification on February 2nd, giving a period of forty days of cessation from labour. Other instances of a regard for the observances of religion frequently occur. It has been truly observed that "the maintenance of their 'arts and mysteries' during so many ages was blended with so many religious customs and observances that it was not till the times subsequent to the Reformation that the fraternities could be regarded as strictly secular."

The ordinances of nearly all the companies contain directions for the brethren on stated seasons assembling in their liveries on election and quarter days, and proceeding *en masse* to church. Especially formal was the attendance on the anniversary of their patron saint. In 1346 the Grocers are said to have agreed by "Com'on assente, yat everie man of the brotherhood, hee being yn the cytie the daie of St. Antoyne, yn the monyth of Maye, shall comen to the cherche of St. Antoyne aforesaid, yf they bee in London, for to here the High Masse, and there to abyde from the begynnyne unto the endyng of the masse, and eche of them shall offre a peny in the worshype of God, his blessed moder Marye, Saint Antoyne, and All Seyntes."* The Fishmongers

* Quoted by Herbert, vol. i. p. 67.

in 1426, direct that every year on the festival of St. Peter, "Alle the brethren and sustern of the same fraternite shall come in their new lyvre to the chirche of Seint Peter, and there here a solemyne masse in the worshippe of God and Seint Peter, and offir atte offering tyme of the same masse what at is her devocion." *

Stow gives a glowing description of the procession of the Skinners' Company on Corpus Christi day. They were accompanied by the religious orders in their rich costumes, bearing wax torches, and singing. There were "borne before them more than 200 priests in surplices and copes, singing, and then the torches of wax burning bright, and above 200 clerks and skinners in their best liveries."

At this distance of time we know very little of the internal history of the various gilds, although we do know that they existed in large numbers, and were greatly prosperous. None of the present companies possess records anterior to the reign of Edward III., but from that time to the present unbroken records exist. Many of the fraternities date to that reign their re-formation. Interesting particulars are extant respecting the re-establishment of the Grocers' Company; and as the account may be quoted as a fair specimen of what occurred on the establishment of all the companies, a few extracts are subjoined from Heath's unpublished "Account of the Grocers' Company," 8vo, 1830, from which we learn that the books of that Company

* Herbert, vol. i. p. 68.

present an unbroken series of minutes of proceedings from the beginning of the reign of Edward III. to the present time. On the occasion of refounding their society, we are told that twenty-two persons, carrying on business as pepperers, in Sopers' Lane, Cheapside, agree to meet together at dinner, at the Abbot of Bury's, St. Mary Axe. There they elect after dinner two wardens or governors, and appoint a priest or chaplain to celebrate masses daily, and perform the other pious duties devolving upon his office. Every member paid twelve pence to the common fund. It was resolved that the brotherhood should adopt a *livery*, for which each was to pay "even on the day of the feast;" that the priest should begin his duty by singing and praying on the festival of St. John, or Midsummer-day, then next ensuing, for the same brotherhood, and for all Christian people; and to the support of the said priest, every one was to pay at the rate of one penny per week in advance of the ensuing year, or four shillings and fourpence each one's share. Then follow the names of eighteen persons, who then and there paid down one year's share of the priest's wages, making £3 18*s.* towards the same. The date of the curious entry is "xij daie of Juyn, in the yere of owre Lord Jhu' m.llecccxlv., and in the xix yere of Kyng Edward the thredde."*

More than two centuries and a half after the circumstances above recorded transpired, the first man of his day as an architect of genius, Inigo Jones,

* Heath, p. 46.

received from James I., as surveyor of the works done about the king's houses (Whitehall and elsewhere) no more than 8*s.* 4*d.* per diem, and £46 per annum for a house.* We, therefore, must not deem these "Pepperers" penurious in fixing their priest's stipend at the sum named. It was a liberal payment considering the value of money at the time. The chaplains selected by the craft, in addition to all other qualifications, were to be "able of cunnyng, that is to say, redying and syngyng and of covenable understandyng (not soft) and honest of convrsation." These twenty Pepperers, founders of the present powerful and wealthy Grocers' Company, must have been undoubtedly men of enterprise and riches, or so great results could not have followed,

> "Haud facile emergunt, quorum virtutibus obstat
> Res angusta domi."

And again,

> "Quantum quisque sua nummorum servat in arca,
> Tantum habet et fidei."

It appears from Heath's "Account" that in 1401 the Grocers raised the chaplain's salary; for this entry occurs—"Sir Roger, the chaplain, his salary from Easter to Easter £6 13*s.* 4*d.*, beside his yearly charge for bread and wine and candle, for singing mass, 2*s.*"

The religious character of these corporations is not only exhibited in the mode of their foundation, in appointing chaplains to pray for each member by name, to sing mass daily, and to say grace at feasts,

* Pennant, p. 105.

but also in choosing patron saints, and founding altars to such saints in the churches, the advowsons of which they held. We know of no trade company of the kind which was not at its origin ranged under the protection of some patron saint. The Drapers claimed the Virgin Mary, mother of the "Holy Lamb," and worshipped at St. Mary Bethlem Church, Bishopsgate; the Fishmongers adopted St. Peter (who was himself a fisherman), and attended at St. Peter's Church; the Goldsmiths' patron saint was St. Dunstan, supposed to have been a brother of the craft.* The Merchant Taylors, a branch of the Drapers, chose St. John the Baptist, the harbinger of the Holy Lamb, so adopted by the Drapers; the Leathersellers claimed the Holy Virgin, and the figure of the mother of our Lord formed the company's common seal until the Reformation, when, the emblem being deemed Papistical, the seal was destroyed, and a new one, still in use, was executed with the device of the arms of the said company. In some case the gilds were called after the name of their patron saint, as the Grocers, who designated themselves "the fraternity of St. Anthony," and had their altar in St. Anthony Church; the Fruiterers, "the fraternity of St. Martin," their altar being at

* The legends of the Romish Church ascribe to St. Dunstan the invention of the Æolian harp, and for this he was represented to King Athelstan as a conjuror. He worked cunningly in gold, silver, and brass. Tradition, moreover, affirms, that once, when employed at his forge, Satan visited him in a female form, but knowing the tempter, he seized him by the nose with the red-hot tongs till he roared again.

St. Martin's Church; and the Salters and the Skinners, both "Societies of Corpus Christi," from assembling at the altar of churches bearing that name, situate in Laurence Pountney Lane and Bread Street.

CHAPTER XI.

THEIR RELIGIOUS OBSERVANCES, CONTINUED.

The veneration paid by the early merchants to the memory of their patron saints was not only superstitious but idolatrous. In admiring their reverence for the good, we must not shut our eyes to their errors, nor may we visit their observances with a severity of criticism, remembering that the puerilities of their worship, and the sensuous character of their rites, were characteristic of the age, and not a peculiarity exclusively their own. When the leaders of the Reformation propounded great truths, and maintained the necessity of the religious observances of men being such as men, and not children, might approve, they received no opposition from the mercantile community; and when the alterations proposed became law, these great companies were the first to comply with the rubrics of the Reformed and Protestant Church of England, in their adherence to which they have ever continued staunch and consistent.

In taking an historical glance at these ancient gilds, their reverence for their patrons appears to us remarkable. The Goldsmiths paid to St. Dunstan's memory honours without end. Their gorgeous hall was adorned with his image of silver gilt, set with gems and precious stones of fabulous price; much of their plate bore his effigy; they had their "St. Dunstan light" in St. John Zachary's Church, the cost of maintaining which formed an annual item in their warden's accounts. In 1369 (42 Edward III.) an agreement, still extant, was entered into between them and the Dean and Chapter of St. Paul's, for maintaining a chantry in the chapel of St. Dunstan, in that cathedral, for the soul of John Hyltoft, goldsmith of London, in which the Dean and Chapter allow that such chantry shall be kept in "the Chapel of St. Dunstan, in the south part of the new work in St. Paul's Cathedral, next to the Chapel of the glorious Virgin Mary." The date at which the Goldsmiths founded this chapel in the cathedral we know not, but that they maintained its altar in great splendour is evident from mention in the accounts of items of expenditure connected therewith, such as that of 1 Edward IV., as following:—"Memorandum.—Payed for a Riddel and scowing of the Blew Buckram for the Tabernacle and Ymage of St. Dunstan at St. Paul's, £6 16*s.* 10*d.*"* In the Ordinances of the Company we read—"That on Seynt Dunston's eve, allways hytherto the Aldermen of thys Fellyshipp hath bene used to assemble in theyr vyellett gownes and cloakys; and all the hoole companye of the lyvery to assemble at the hall in their second lyverye, and to have iiij chapelynes to

* Warden's Accounts.

wayte and goo before them to Pawll's." Thence after service to St. John Zachary, and attend service there. The next day services were to be similarly attended at St. Paul's and St. John's, and after dinner at "Seynt Maryelebowe," also their "almesmen, beadel, and other officers to accompany them." In addition to all this certain services were held in their own private chapel at the hall (2 Henry VIII.).

On its being debated whether St. Dunstan's day should be kept by shutting up their shops, the company agreed that they should "shut their shops and keep holiday." He is even designated in their books "Seynt Dunstan, our blessed patron, protector, and founder," and on particular occasions, if not at all their feasts, they drank to his memory from a great and costly cup, called "St. Dunstan's cup." That the good saint had been a brother of their craft they had no doubt. Indeed, some of his works were extant in 1280, for in the wardrobe accounts of Edward I. is an item of "a gold ring with a sapphire of the workmanship of St. Dunstan" *(de fabrica Sti Dunstani)*.

Goldsmith or no goldsmith, however, all this hero worship ceased at the Reformation. Alas for the vanity of human applause! Under the date 1550, "the company change their election day (and the accompanying religious observances and festivities) from the feast of St. Dunstan to that of the Holy Trinity." Still more cruel to the memory of the sainted goldsmith who had never turned his back upon the brethren, was their treatment of his effigy at an earlier date, for in their minutes it is thus recorded:—1547. October 4. "At the assembly on this day, Mr. Wardens desired to know the pleasure of the assystents for the Ymage of Seynt Dunstan, bycause of the Injunctyons." And they agreed that "Mr. Alderman Bowes (Sir Martin) and the wardens, with iiij other, soche as they sholde appoynte, should take the same ymage and breke yt, and to turn yt to the moste profett of the house. Also that the gret standying cup with St. Dunston on the topp, sholde be lykewyse by thym broken and turned into other plate."

"O tempora! O mores!"

From the records of the various companies we learn that it was usual with the fraternity to pay particular attention to their religious observances on the occasion of elections, funerals, and obits of deceased members. The obit was the anniversary of the death of an individual; and to observe such a day with prayer, alms-giving, or other commemorations, was "keeping an obit." When the common belief was in favour of prayers for the dead, these services were highly prized, and large sums were left by the rich in order that their obits should be kept with becoming splendour. For the same reason mural tablets and other monumental works were originally introduced into the churches, not so much from a vain desire that the deceased should be remembered by future generations, as from the hope that all who beheld them might offer a silent prayer on behalf of the departed, and thus shorten the period of

9

their purgatorial probation. These futile hopes have now vanished; faith in the efficacy of prayers for the dead has almost ceased amongst us, nor may endowments any longer be made for the celebration of obits, or for prayers for the dead. Herbert extracts from the accounts of the Drapers' Company the following ordinances:*—

At elections it was ordained that every year on Lady-day "the whole body of the feljschip in their newest livry" should go to Bow Church there to hear the Lady Mass, "abide till it was done," offer a silver penny on the altar, and attend again in like manner at "even song," to hear the dirge for deceased members. They were to repeat their attendance on the following day to hear the mass of requiem, and were to offer another silver penny; and on the same day, or another day, as the wardens might assign, were to walk two-and-two in their livery to the place "ordained for the feast." From the next extract we discover that the custom still prevailing in many parts of the north of England, and especially in the East Riding of Yorkshire, of the most honoured friends carrying the deceased at funerals, prevailed in the gilds; "funeral of Mrs. Peke, August 14th, 1518, buried this day, Mrs. Elizabeth Peke, widow. There were named to bere her unto St. Michael's Church—Mr. Cornhill, Mr. Burton, Mr. Carter, Mr. Rudston, Mr. Gerard, *alias* Brereter, Mr. Brothers, and Mr. Perpoint: and upon the morrow there dined all our Aldermen; and of the company twelve persons, and

* Vol. i. p. 441.

our two chaplains and the clerk. She had our best beryall clothe (very costly, the gift of Sir John Milborn), and every of the vj berers had a sylvr spoone for his labor." Four of the names mentioned as bearers of Mrs. Peke became very distinguished. Mr. Rudston, who was son of the Lord of the Manor of Hayton, near York, became Sheriff in 1522, and Lord Mayor in 1528, having been knighted by King Henry VIII. In 1522 an entry occurs in the Drapers' books, that the King of Denmark being here, it was agreed that Mr. Rudston, the Sheriff, should have two pageants at Midsummer, namely, one of the assumption and one of St. Ursula, "but to be no precedent hereafter." Some of the charges are as follows:—"Child's eldest daughter for Saynt Ursula, and the vj virgen, wth hyrr bothe nyghts;" together with "xiiij porters that bare the assompcion," 16*s.* 8*d.*; two harpers and two luters, in Albes, with wings and crowns, 5*s.* 4*d.*; wax-lights, 30*s.* 4*d.* The bill concludes with the following ludicrous items:—"For mending of the apparell of all the virgens, ijd.; for a fyn smok of Gally's daughter, that was hurt by the cresset light, viijd."* Sir John Rudston died 1531, and founded a "yerlye obit," to be kept by the drapers of London, of which company he was a member, at the church of St. Michael, Cornhill, where he was buried. To the master was to be paid for ever, 3*s.* 4*d.*; each warden, 20*d.*; the clerk, 12*d.*; the renter, 12*d.*; for potations at Drapers' Hall, 10*d.*; besides almes to poor.

* Herbert, p. 456.

The historian, Pennant, in speaking of the antiquity of the church of St. Michael, says that before the fire of London, "This church had its pulpit-cross, like that of St. Paul's, built by Sir John Rudston, mayor, in 1528, who was interred in a vault beneath in 1531."* In the year 1642, Walter Rudston, a descendant of Sir John, entertained King Charles I. with great hospitality at Hayton Hall, and for his loyalty was that year created a baronet.

We regret to say that sometimes, no doubt, evidence creeps into light which would lead one to think that the appearance was manifested of bargaining for the prayers of the faithful, and if it were not uncharitable to say so, we might express a fear that too often those most anxious to found masses for their soul's salvation, were not most careful to live as if in preparation for a future world. At any rate, the belief in the efficacy of such intercessions evidences want of acquaintance with Holy Scripture, and must tend to the encouragement of a careless life. That negociations of a rather commercial character sometimes occurred, may be proved from the records of the Companies. Those of the Goldsmiths contain this entry, under the date 1 Henry VIII., January 16th (1509): "At this meeting was shewed Mrs. Jonys's offer, which was, that she offered to geve to the feliship, for to have a preste founde for euer to syng for Robert Johnson's soule, her late husband; and for her sowle; and also to have an obite kept yerely for euer of xxjs, viijd, cccc

* "History of London," p. 426.

markes. To the which the c'mpany would not agree, but said that she should pay vc (500) marks and no lesse. And if she would not do so, then she to be spoken withall, to bring in to Mr. Wardens c marks, which her husband did bequeth vnto the feliship; or els ther shold none of the lyurey come to the obite of her late husband." The Drapers' books contain the following:—"1514. 15th August. It was represented to the Court of the Company that Sir William Capell had sent in a bill of divers parcels of lande, and other things, which he was minded to give to the fraternite, for them to cause certain services to be done for his soul for ever, and wishing to know what ready money they would demand therefore, in case they refused such lande." The Court on debate answered "that they would accept the trust offered for 1000 marks immediate payment, and £14 yearly, and would add any other services he might wish further at that rate." They further stipulated that the chantry priests to be provided should, when required, "wait on the company at divine service for the worship of the same," and threw out the following not very delicate hint:—"Moreover, we trust to have a specyall and a kynde brotherlye tokyn of remembraunce of plate—as basins, potts, cuppis, or other things of pleasure for a dailye memorye when yt shal be sene, to the intent that his soule may be thereafter remembered and prayed for, which we submytt unto that honourable lady his wife and to his worshipful executors."

Sir William departed this life at Capel Court,

Bartholomew Lane, almost immediately upon the settlement of these affairs, and was interred in great state by the Livery at St. Bartholomew's, Royal Exchange. This good citizen, highly honoured by his generation, was Lord Mayor from 1503 to 1509, and was knighted by King Henry VII. His descendant, the first Lord Capel, for supporting the royal cause, was beheaded; but his heir, at the Restoration, was raised to the rank of Earl of Essex, the line of the Devereuxs having become extinct.

These obits, so prudently purchased and liberally provided for by the dying knight, continued to be scrupulously and religiously kept and observed until the Reformation, when they and all others were declared illegal, and the endowments for the same seized by the King. All the Companies, rather than separate themselves from the endowments and trusts imposed upon them by their deceased members, came to terms with the King, and purchased the whole at the rate of twenty years' purchase. Much of their present charity funds flows from these sources, and, as land chiefly formed the legacies, in consequence of the vast increase in the value of real property, the increase in many cases has been more than a hundredfold. These obits were invariably observed with religious strictness, as all other trusts are to this day by the Livery Companies. The Goldsmiths kept no fewer than twenty-five obits on twenty-five different days in each year. The utmost regard to honourable and upright conduct may be said to have been ever a distinguishing characteristic, not only of the rulers of these gilds, but of British merchants everywhere. To show the attention paid to the dying injunctions of their brethren, we would add that the "keeping of obits" became so frequent, and the duty so burdensome, that it was impossible for many of the Livery to give their attendance at them all, and in process of time much of this labour was deputed to the almsmen and women of the Companies, and at length, even they wearied in their work, as may be seen in a curious entry in the books of the Goldsmiths :—"Memorandum.—That Adam Shadewell, in contempt of St. Dunstan and of all the good folk of the Goldsmiths of London assembled, refused the alms of St. Dunstan, and did the same in the time of the last wardens." The reason of Adam refusing to become an almsman is not stated, but Herbert surmises that it arose from a dislike to the constant attendance which the almspeople were obliged to give at obits and other mortuary services, and which, "in the Goldsmiths' Company," he adds, "was exacted with much strictness."

In addition to these numerous religious observances maintained by the several companies, there were many others of a more general character in which they took part. In "Liber Albus" it is stated that on the Feast of All Saints (1st November) the Mayor and his household and the Aldermen were to meet at the church of St. Thomas, the substantial men of the several mysteries arrayed in their respective suits, and thence proceed to the church of St. Paul, and there hear vespers. In like manner, also, upon the day of our Lord's nativity, they should proceed to St. Paul's, where the Mayor and Aldermen would stand on the right side of the choir, the former in the stall next to that of the Dean, while vespers and complines (the last two of the canonical services) were read. The same to be observed upon St. Stephen's Day (26th December), as also upon the day of St. John the Evangelist (6th May). Again, upon the Feast of the Innocents (or Childermas Day, 28th December), when they were wont to hear vespers in the church of St. Thomas de Acon, and on the morrow to hear mass there and vespers as well. The former ceremony was observed also upon the Feast of the Circumcision (1st January), the Feast of the Epiphany (6th January), and the Feast of the Purification (2nd February). In addition to all this, they, with vast multitudes of the city people, went in grand array "to the Hospital of the Blessed Mary without Bysshopesgate on Easter Monday, Tuesday, and Wednesday to hear a sermon."*

The Reformation made little difference to the Livery Companies beyond the alteration in the religious services, but here the change was great indeed. The chaplain now had comparatively few duties to perform. The liturgy and sermons took the place of daily mass, but these occasions of divine service were not so numerous as under the old system. We must not, however, suppose that religion was set aside. The services, though less

* Lib. i., pt. i., ca. viii.

frequent, were more intelligible. On public days, the chaplain's duty was to pray for the prosperity of the fraternity. In some companies a very solemn custom prevailed of calling over the names of the members one by one, and praying for each individually, and by name. In 1645 the Merchant Taylors' books have this entry:—"The names of the Livery being called over, according to ancient custom, after which, in reverent manner, prayer was made by the chaplain; then some of the ordinances of the hall being openly read, preparation was made for dinner." His duty was also to preach before the Company at their various churches, in each of which special pews were set apart; as we find to have been the case at St. Martin's Church, where a gallery was expressly erected for themselves. In like manner the Fishmongers had an aisle reserved for themselves in the church of St. Michael, Crooked Lane.

Besides these occasions of public worship, prayers were said in the Common Hall, as we learn from an entry in 1566 of "Common Prayer on Court days, according to the laudable custom of this lande." Herbert gives a copy of this prayer, the conclusion of which, for its excellence, we subjoin:—"Good Lord, keep this noble city of London, and defend it from grievous plagues and contagious sickness, that we may often in brotherly and true love assemble and meet together, to Thy glory and our mutual comfort in Christ Jesus; and, Merciful Father, bless this society and brotherhood, and be present with us in all our assemblies and councils, that we may use them to Thy glory and the discharge of our duties. Bless and direct by thy Holy Spirit all our actions and endeavours, and give us grace faithfully and honestly to discharge the trust reposed in us, as well for our good friends and brethren deceased, as any other way belonging to us, to the glory of thy Holy name, and peaceful comforts of our own souls, and good example and incitement of others."*

Even the plate belonging to the Companies was frequently executed in "accordance with their ecclesiastical character, being ornamented," as Mr. Jupp remarks of the Carpenters' plate, "with the figure of a saint, or some other religious device." The same writer adds: "In the early part of Henry VIII.'s reign, we find in an inventory of plate the following articles enumerated:—'ij. great massers, with I. H. S. yn the bosses; a masser of Wyllyam preste, wt. a ymagge of sent thomas yn the bosse; John Ruddockk gave a masser of sylvr. gylte, wt. a picture of Jhus; Rs. of Rychard togoode, a syllvr. spone wt. peter; Rs. of Roger Coke a sellwer spon wt. powll (Paul);' and many others, embracing nearly all the Apostles."†

* Herbert, vol. i. p. 192, from Merchant Taylors' Records, A.D. 1566.

† "Carpenters' Company," p. 25.

CHAPTER XII.

THEIR RELIGIOUS OBSERVANCES, CONTINUED.

How highly the English monarchs in the early days have valued the prayers of the faithful, and especially those of the good London citizens, may be surmised from the fact, that in some cases valuable privileges have been conferred by charter upon the "Mysteries," upon the condition that the members of the said crafts or mysteries should pray for the souls of their sovereign and his relatives, whether living or dead; and we think that this fact, and the number of endowments bequeathed by the wealthy in order to found obits in the various companies, tend to show that the merchant princes and traders, of whom they were composed, had merited, or, at any rate, had secured, the respect and reverence of their generation.

To illustrate this, we quote from King Edward IV.'s charter to the Drapers' Company, or "The Master, Wardens, Brethren, and Sisters of the Gild or Fraternity of the Blessed Mary the Virgin, of the Mystery of Drapers," whereby many privileges are conferred, for which in return the "company engage to establish and maintain two chaplains to pray for the good estate of the said King Edward and Elizabeth his Queen, for the wholesome government of the said fraternity of drapers, and the brothers and sisters thereof, whilst living, and for their souls when dead; as also for the souls of the King's late father, Richard Duke of York; Edward Earl of Rutland, brother to the said King Edward; the Earl of Salisbury, the King's kinsman; and Sir Jno. Neville, Knight, son of the said earl." This same Company of Drapers, not only founded several churches, and had their own chapel and altar at various of them, but in common with nearly all the gilds, had also we believe their own private chapel at their hall. In addition to these religious works, they founded, early in the reign of Edward III., the fraternity of St. Mary Bethlem, or Bethlem Hospital. We subjoin a description of its character from the beautiful preamble of the deed:—

"To the honor of our Lord Jhu Crist, and his swete moder, Seint Marie, our Ladie of Bethlem, in which most holie place, our seid Lord Jhu Crist was chosen to be born in hys salvacion of al his people, in which place of Bethlem the starre appeared to the shepherds, and gave and shewed lyght to the Kyngs of Coleyne, who offered in the same place of Bethlem their gyftes, golde, myrrhe, and insense; one fraternite is begone for the same honor, in amendment of their lives, by the assent of the fryar, William Tytte, fryar of the Hospital of our Ladie of Bethlem, and for other good people, drapers of Cornhill, and other good men and women, which will be broders and sisters, and maintain the same fraternite for the term of their lives and the points that follow."*

This institute exists to the present day, under the altered name and character of Bethlem (or Bedlam) Hospital. They also maintained priests and altars, and observed anniversaries at St. Michael's, Cornhill, St. Thomas of Acon (where they had a chapel), Austin Friars, and the Priory of St. Bartholomew. Amongst the Lord Mayors belonging to the company, no fewer than seven, at their individual charges, have been founders of churches. This, by no means the wealthiest of the gilds, is introduced as affording a specimen of the religious works which the City companies have performed in the olden times, and to the continuation and upholding of which good works, a large proportion of their present revenues is still religiously devoted.

The Skinners' Company, at their incorporation as a brotherhood, A.D. 1327, 1 Edward III., are quaintly designated as the "Master and Wardens, brothers and sisters, of the gild or fraternity of the skinners of London, to the honour of God, and the precious body of our Lord Jesus Christ."† They were, moreover, under the patronage of the Virgin Mary; and have enrolled amongst their numbers six kings, five queens, one prince, nine dukes, two earls, and a baron. Their motto being "To God only be all glory."

The Haberdashers were enrolled as a brother-

* Strype's Stow, i. p. 460. † Ibid, ii. p. 273.

hood, A.D. 1447, by letters patent, by the style of "The fraternity of St. Catherine, the Virgin, of the Haberdashers of the City of London." Possibly the blessed Catherine had been a zealous devotee at the stalls of this brotherhood, and thus obtained the honour for ever of being recognized as the haberdashers' patron saint. The motto to their arms is most excellent, "Serve and obey," suitable alike for haberdashers and all men, in this and in every age.

The Ironmongers' Company seems to be almost the only one of the great gilds not under saintly patronage, nor do the kings appear to have asked for the prayers of these workers in iron. Possibly blacksmiths, and all other successors of Vulcan, have had the character of hard-heartedness: nevertheless, the Ironmongers have conducted their vast affairs as a company with consummate ability, probity, and success, and have been throughout their lengthened career, no doubt, God-fearing men, notwithstanding that they have professed but little of saintship, even in days when such professions were almost universal. Their motto is as good as it could be: "God is our strength."

People are apt to attribute to the Puritans the first introduction of the custom of doing all things in the name of God, and of making even our daily concerns a matter of prayer and thanksgiving. It is quite possible on public occasions to overdo this, and to make sacred subjects common, and to use the Great Name irreverently; but it is also possible to forget God altogether, and not to have Him in all our thoughts.

To show how early this religious element was observable even on occasions of pageantry, we would refer to a scarce and curious tract in the Bodleian Library, entitled, "The Passage of our Most Dred Sovereign Lady Queene Elizabeth, through the Citie of London to Westminster, the day before her Coronation, anno 1558-9. Imprinted at London, in Flete Street, within Temple Barre, at the sign of the Hand and Starre, by Richard Follett, the xxiii. day of January; *cum privilegio.*"

This pamphlet describes in quaint terms the procession and its accessories, and shows how ably Queen Elizabeth (young as she was) had read the character of her people, and how peculiarly she adapted herself to the national mind. Saturday, January 14th, 1558, at two o'clock in the afternoon, we learn that the "most noble Christian Princess, our most dred Sovereigne, marched from the Tower, richly furnished and accompanied with barons, nobles, and a notable train of beautiful ladies. Entering the City, she was marvellously received with prayers, wishes, welcomings, cryes, tender words, and all other signs, which argue a wonderful earnest of love, and her Grace, by holding up her hands and merrie face to such as were afar off, and by tender language to those that stood nigh, showed herself thankful for the people's goodwill; when they said 'God save your Grace,' she answered agayne, 'God save you all.'"

So there was nothing but gladness and comfort. The people were ravished with her earnest expressions of love, and they conceived a wonderful hope as to her worthy government. Even when the baser sort offered her flowers, or other signification of good-will, or had any suit to her, she most gently stopped her chariot, and heard their requests.

Thus, passing from the Tower, she came to Fenchurch Street; and when a child, speaking in a pageant, said—

"Welcome, therefore, O Queene, as much as heart can think;
Welcome agayne, O Queene, as much as tongue can tell;
Welcome to joyous tongues, and hearts that will not shrink,
God thee preserve, we pray, and wish thee ever well."

there was a wonderful shout from the whole people, and her Grace thanked them in most touching, friendly terms, "which drew tears from many." A pageant in "Gracious Street" represented all her Majesty's ancestors, Kings and Queens of England, personated by certain children, who all pronounced a blessing upon her; orations were delivered, as part of the ceremony, at each pageant, and they were very numerous; and Elizabeth made answer to them all (in Latin, when that language was used).

At Soper Lane was a Scripture pageant, "The eight beatitudes, expressed in the 5th chapter of St. Matthew, applyed to our Soveraigne Lady, Queene Elizabeth." When at the Standard, in Chepe, her Grace was told that there was placed Tyme. "Tyme," quoth she, "and Tyme hath brought me hither!"

Then the Holy Bible, in English, was presented to her, and she said, "she should ofttimes reade over that book." Then Mr. Recorder gave unto her 1000 golden marks, in a beautiful purse, which she took with both hands, and made answer, thus :—

"I thank my Lord Mayor, his brethren, and you all. You aske that I should continue your good Ladye and Queene. Be ye ensured that I will be as good unto you as ever Queene was to her people. No will in me can lack; neither doe I trust shall ther lacke any power. Persuade yourselues that for the safetie and quietness of you all, I will not spare, if need be, to spend my blood. God thank you all."

The journey to Westminster occupied several hours, for there was a fresh pageant at every available corner, and all the speeches, some of them very long, were in Latin, or rhymed stanzas, which now have a strangely prosaic sound.

According to the pamphlet, before Elizabeth quitted the Tower, on entering her chariot, she raised her eyes heavenward, and said :—" O Lord, Almighty and Everlasting God, I give Thee most hearty thanks that Thou hast been so mercifull as to spare me to beholde this joyfull day. And I acknowledge that Thou hast dealt as wonderfully and as mercifully with me as Thou didst with thy true servant Daniel, the prophet, whom Thou deliveredst out of the denne from the cruelty of the gredy and raging lyons; even so I was overwhelmed, and only by Thee delivered. To Thee, therefore, onely be thankes, honour, and prayse, for ever. Amen."

Well had this great monarch studied human nature. She was naturally haughty, vain, overbearing, and tyrannical, but, in this instance, she forgot not the motto, "*Humanitas et gratior et tutior.*"

At the time of the Reformation, all "Papistical emblems" were ordered to be destroyed; and such were the narrow views and the ignorant zeal of the times, that some of the finest works of art possessed by this or any other country, fell a sacrifice to puritanical fanaticism. Many specimens of painted glass, such as modern times have never surpassed, if they have equalled, were destroyed. Sculptures of priceless worth were dashed to pieces; pictures of surpassing excellence were cut with knives and committed to the flames; and all this Vandalism in the name of religion and of Christianity! whilst, in some instances, even pagan deities were set up in preference to the Virgin or Apostles.

London was peculiarly rich in all the gems of art, and consequently lost the more in this crusade. Pennant informs us that in the middle of Cheapside stood a beautiful cross, placed there in pious memory of Elinor, his Queen, by Edward I., on the spot on which her body rested in its way to its place of burial in 1290. This ancient relic having fallen into decay, was rebuilt in 1441 by John Hatherby, mayor, by public subscription. It was ornamented with various images, such as that illustrative of the Resurrection, of the Virgin, of Edward the Confessor, and the like. It was kept in exquisite order, being regilt on all occasions of public entry.

After the Reformation, these images gave great offence; they were mutilated and then pulled down, and instead of the effigy of the Virgin was put up that of Diana. Queen Elizabeth objected to these acts of the fanatics, and offered a reward to discover the offenders, and directed a plain cross to be placed on the summit and gilt. In 1643, however, Parliament voted the taking down of all crosses and the demolishing of all Popish paintings, and to Sir Robert Harlow they entrusted the work of destruction of this cross. Accompanied by a troop of horse and two companies of foot, the enlightened knight commenced his work.

"This most *pious* and *religious noble* knight," adds Pennant ironically, "did also attack and demolish 'the abominable and most blasphemous crucifix' in Christ's Hospital, and broke it into a thousand pieces" (p. 400).

In 1645 the Parliament came to the following resolutions respecting the King's collection in York House:—

"Ordered, that all such pictures there as have the representation of the second Person in Trinity upon them shall be forthwith burnt.

"Ordered, that all such pictures there as have the representation of the Virgin upon them shall be forthwith burnt."*

* "Anecdotes of Painting," vii. p. 106.

The City halls, so rich in works of art, and especially those connected with religion, felt the full force of the Puritans' dislike to them, and as early as 1643 many of them had been compelled to dismantle their venerable edifices, and strip them of relics which to the members of the gilds were invaluable. The Merchant Taylors possessed some tapestry hangings, most choice and rare, containing incidents in the life of St. John the Baptist, their patron saint. In their minutes, under the head of July 3, 1643, a complaint is stated to have been made, "that in the Company's hangings for the hall there are offensive and superstitious pictures." The court desired the master and wardens to "view the same, and to take order for reform, if there was any excess;" but they either would not see, or were loath to alter, for another order occurs nearly a twelvemonth afterwards as "to defacing some of the superstitious pictures in the hangings in the upper end of the hall, and such other things as concern the same." They were eventually noticed as being "defaced."*

* Herbert, i. p. 180.

CHAPTER XIII.

THEIR RELIGIOUS OBSERVANCES, CONTINUED.

THE *Perfect Diurnall* for June 7th, 1649, affords us an insight into the changes which the revolution had produced in reference to the religious observances on occasions of festivity: "This day, according to an invitation from the Lord Mayor and City of London, the Speaker of the House of Commons, with the representative members now sitting in Parliament, his Excellency (Fairfax) and the officers of the army now in town above the degree of lieutenant, the Lord President and Counsel of State, after hearing two sermons at Christ's Church preached by the reverend divines Mr. Goodwin and Dr. Owen, went to Grocers' Hall, where a sumptuous feast was prepared for them. Mr. Speaker, the lord general, the lord president, Earl of Pembroke, Earl of Salisbury, Lieut.-General Cromwell, and other members of the Parliament and Council of State, sat at the upper board; the other members of the house at two tables on each side of the hall. Major-General Lambert and other officers at the middle table. The Lords Cheefe Justices and Lords Cheefe Barons, and other judges of both Benches, dined in a spacious room over the parlour, and the Lord Mayor, Aldermen, and Councilmen at another table in the same roome. No drinking of healths nor other uncivil concomitants, nor any other music but of the drum and trumpet. A feast, indeed, of Christians and cheefetains, whereas others were rather of *Chretians* and *Cormorants*."

The same paper of the next day adds that " Sir John Woollaston and other aldermen came to his Excellency the Lord General Fairfax, at his house in Queen Street, and in the name of the City presented him with a large and weighty basin and ewer of *beaten gold*, and sent to General Cromwell a great present of plate, value £300, and 200 pieces in gold."

The sermons of these two reverend divines are well known to this generation, and if Dr. Owen and Mr. Goodwin preached at the same length on this occasion as was usual with them, the day's business must have involved considerable fatigue to all the notorious individuals for whose benefit they were delivered.

It is observable that singing formed no part of the festival. In this, as in other things, the Parliament men knew no middle course. Is it wise, if one be ill, to say he shall be killed, not cured ? If music and singing sometimes were abused to purposes of licentiousness, they required amending, not abolishing. Nothing was more likely than that during the enjoyment so richly provided for the guests at these festive boards, an occasion might arise in which a song should be heard neither virtuous nor moral; but the whole brotherhood should not suffer for one brother's error; more stringent rules should have been enforced and the evil remedied. It is clear, however, that the leading spirits in those days of blood had no better ear for music than they had taste for high art. How much more wise the proceedings of the Company of Ironmongers only nine years after the event above recorded. From their records we learn that strong disapproval had been expressed at certain unhandsome songs at a feast, and the Court, in haste, determined to have no more music at their entertainments, but upon time for reflection at the following Court appears as follows :—

"1658, it is recited that at a Court on the 3rd July, it was ordered that, 'the choice of master and wardens, with the ceremony thereunto belonging, should be performed in future without musicke, by reason of some unhandsome songs which were sung in the Hall that day, which did give distaste unto several strangers and members of this Company.' This Court having taken the same into consideration, and considering that the musick in itself was not badd, ordered that musick should be provided for this election day and others that should follow, with a charge unto the present wardens and their successors that they take an espetiall care to give notice unto the musitioners that they sing noe offensive, wicked, unhandsome songs before the company that day, and if any member of ye company shall call for any songs which shall be adjudged by the next Court to be unhandsome he shall pay for a fine for the use of the poor of this Company tenn shillings for every such song called for by him."*

* Nichol's "Ironmongers' Company," p. 273.

From a careful perusal of the records of the several companies it is beyond all doubt that as a rule no profane language from a member was tolerated. The books of the Drapers' Company contain an entry that in "1482, William Spark owyth for a fyn for vngodly language spoken to Richard Stakeley."

The Carpenters have similar entries, two or three of which may be selected as examples :—

"1549, 3rd Edward 6th, Lycens was geven to edmond lugg to have home his prnyts tyll he can speke better eynglys." In other words, he was sent home until his English was that to which a moral person could listen.

From the next extract we discover that two of the brethren had rather troublesome wives.

"1556, Received of francs steleerag a fyne for yll words yt his wyffe gave to John dorant ij's."

"Received of John dorant a fyne for yll words yt he gave to mystris francs, xvj'd."

"Received of Wyllm mortymr a fyne for calling of mystris francs beste ij's.*

Had William Mortimer called Master Franks a beast, such conduct would have been unworthy of a Livery member, and deserving of a fine ; but to call Mistress Franks by such a name was utterly inexcusable. We do not learn what particular kind of beast he designated her, but it must have been one to which woman most strongly objects to be likened, by the Court inflicting so heavy a fine as that of ij's. John Dorant was fined xvj'd (see the next entry above)

* Jupp, p. 139.

for ill words given to the same lady; of what those ill words consisted we, at so great a distance of time, cannot tell; but that they were not so intensely offensive as the words of Mortimer, we doubt not, by the fine being of less severity.

It would seem from the records that the use of profane oaths was not a common vice in the early period, nor indeed until the Restoration. Such wicked language would not have passed unpunished; but few such entries occur. From the same sources we find that very rarely are the apprentices charged with the crime of unchastity. The only one instance with which we have met is narrated by Herbert,* in which a most severe punishment is inflicted upon John Rolls, apprentice of John Hends, draper, for this crime (an offence which the Drapers' Company viewed as of a very heinous character) "to the entent that all other apprentices that heard thereof, and of his said unthrifty deeds, should take ensample by him, and should be afraid to fall into like unthriftiness for fear of the like or worse punishments."

That great regard to morality has been ever manifested by the livery may be deduced from the fines inflicted upon the least infringement of decorum. They were not a lawless people. The fishmongers had a rule that "members falsely withdrawing themselves from their creditors, or going into *Sanctuary* or keeping-house for debt, are to be ineligible to be called to any court, council, or assembly, unless they can find security for their paying and better conduct in future." For perjury, instant expulsion was the rule

* Vol. i. pp. 423, 424, note.

of all. Any man of the craft brawling or fighting openly in the street was to forfeit 6*s.* 8*d.* For unseemly words there was no palliation. "*Quid enim non excitet vox blanda et nequam?*" Severe, too, was the fine against all who neglected when summoned to attend "dirge, anniversary, or masse burying of a brother."

The minutes of the Merchant Taylors' Company contain some interesting entries, indicating the terms of amity upon which they conducted their proceedings, and may be quoted as illustrative of the spirit of all the gilds. Under date 1583 is the following:—

"This day a court was held, at which it was ordained that George Sotherton and Howell Sotherton, two *loving brethren* and assistants of this company, should talk with the King of Harolds (Heralds) concerning the crest of the Company's arms, for the altering of the same, as may stand in good form of heraldry." The result of which was the granting, December 19th, 1586, a royal warrant of supporters and the other alteration desired.

The next extract reflects great credit upon the court:—

"1610, May 23.—John Churchman, an ancient brother and had served master fifteen years before, but now brought to decay, became suitor for a vacant almshouse. Whereupon, by 'general consent he was elected an almsman, and over and above his pension, an annuity which had been formerly granted him of £20 per annum was continued;' and, with praiseworthy delicacy, they agreed that his gown should be made without *conuzance* [badge], and that he need not attend at the hall with the other almsmen but at his own pleasure. All that was asked of him was that he should attend divine service at the church, and pray for the prosperity of the company, which he readily promised to do."

"1638, May 29.—The sum of £10 and half a tun of French wine were voted to Thomas Gardiner, Esq., Recorder of London and Counsellor to this Company, to keep his reading at the Inner Temple, to which he was appointed Reader. 'The £10 as a token of their love, and for his pains in the company's affairs,' and the wine 'as an extraordinary love to him.'" A vote creditable alike to Counsellor and Court.

These were the kind of men to rule a great corporation, and such has been the opinion entertained of the Merchant Taylors by the nobles of the land that they have numbered upon their rolls as loving brethren 10 kings, 3 princes, 27 bishops, 26 dukes, 47 earls, 81 lords, and 16 lord mayors. May their shadow never be less!

The strictness with which the rules of the crafts were enforced may be seen from the following entries in the Merchant Taylors' Records, as quoted in the "History of the Merchant Taylors' School":—

"John Swinnerton (afterwards Sir John Swinnerton, Lord Mayor 1613) committed to prison by order of the Court for 'impertinence' to them, and not liberated till due submission had been made."*

"1562. William Kimpton brought great trouble upon himself for having, contrary to the ordinances, called Stephen Misney, a 'brother of this mystery, *a crafty boy*.' For this misdemeanour he was fined 40*s*., and, not having so much with him, he leaves a gold ring with the master in pawn as security for the amount."†

"1563. William Hector was similarly fined 40*s*. for calling Thomas Wylford '*a prating boy*,' and he, not being prepared to pay, delivers a ring of gold in pledge for the same."‡

The next is taken from the records of the Goldsmiths, from which we learn that they enforced their discipline with Roman severity.

"1529-30, February 14.—This day, John Carsewell, which for working of salts wars (worse) than strlyng som vi. oz., was by Mr. Wardens sent to the Compter, the vth day of this monyth, and this day brought before them to the Goldsmiths' Hall, at viii. of the cloke in the mornyng, and then sette opynly in the stocks, and ther rested tyll after dynner; and then browght into the parlor before Mr. Wardens, the assystents, and all the lyurey, and examyned how many such salts he had made. Whervpon he confessed that he had made a dozen such salts; and it was demandyd of hym what reco'pence he coulde make to the p'rties that had bowght the said sailts.

* Page 190, note. † Ibid. ‡ Ibid.

He answered that he had not wherwth to reco'-pence them. Whervpon Mr. Wardens, by the advise of all the fell'ship, co'mandyd that he shodd be had to Newgate—which was done, there to remayne till his acts were better examyned—*and there he dyed.*" No doubt of shame and a broken heart.

It may appear to some that the fees paid for religious purposes, especially those to the chaplains, were but small in amount. We must not, however, forget that even so distinguished a person as the Archbishop of St. Andrews, when prisoner at Winchester, A.D. 1307, was allowed but a shilling a day for himself and servants, in the following proportions :—

For the Archbishop's own expense	0	0	6
One man-servant to attend him	0	0	3
One boy to attend him likewise	0	0	1½
A chaplain to say daily mass to him . . .	0	0	1½
	0	1	0

When the queen of Robert Bruce was a prisoner in England, in 1314, her allowance was 20*s.* per week for herself and household.*

The crafts or mysteries desired if possible in all things to have the sanction of religion. Their

* The magnificent post of Ambassador to Paris was offered by Queen Elizabeth, on the resignation of Walsingham, to Dr. Dale, the Master of her Court of Requests, with the stipend of 20*s.* a day. Dale pretended to be overwhelmed with gratitude. He could not spend, he said, above 19*s.* daily, and he should be able to send home the remaining shilling for the support of his wife and family! (Duke of Manchester's "Court and Society from Elizabeth to Anne," vol. i. p. 251).

pictures were usually of a scriptural character. Their trade was traced as far back as possible to Old Testament times. Some singularly characteristic pictures were discovered in 1845 accidentally by a workman employed in the restoration of the Carpenters' Hall. Upon the walls in the large hall were found to be a series of four ancient pictures, three feet in height and twenty-three in length, divided into four compartments. To show the antiquity of carpentering, No. I. represents *Noah building the ark*; his three sons are hard at work upon the boat, but Noah is kneeling, hat in hand, receiving instructions from the Almighty. No. II. represents King Josiah ordering the repair of the temple, selected from 2 Kings xxii., on account of the complimentary manner in which "*the carpenters* and builders," are mentioned, for "there was no reckoning made with them of the money that was delivered into their hand, because they dealt faithfully," a circumstance recorded in a black letter inscription above. No. III. represents an incident in the early life of our Saviour. Joseph is engaged at work as a carpenter, the Saviour is engaged in collecting chips in a large basket. The Holy Virgin is seated spinning with the distaff. No. IV. represents the Saviour in his youth teaching in the synagogue. The inscription "*Is not thys that Carpynter's* (son)?" is only partially visible. These remarkable works, which have been much talked of, are supposed to have been by the celebrated John Bossam, and to have been executed in the latter part of the reign of King Henry VIII. The costumes of the figures are of this period, and in the account of the Carpenters' Company, by E. B. Jupp, it is shown that these works of art which have been hidden probably for more than two centuries, were certainly in existence 250 years ago, from letters among the Cottonian MSS. in the British Museum, in which reference is made to them. It is a question of much interest when and for what purpose these able and masterly productions were hidden from the light? Mr. Jupp has no doubt of the reasons which induced the court to secure them. It was done, he says, doubtless to escape notice in times when Puritanical zeal condemned as superstitious, and waged exterminating war against all paintings or other representations of either Person of the Trinity, or of the Virgin. "It will be borne in mind that all the subjects of the paintings are scriptural, and that three of the series contain figures which would have received the condemnation of the ruling party."*

We have thus shown that in modern times religious services, although still, on given occasions, united with the secular, are of not so frequent occurrence as during the early existence of the gild, but we are not aware of any one out of sixty companies still in being, in which all such observances have been abolished. No doubt, in some instances, in days of poverty or reverses, or of national darkness, one or another of the fraternities may have thrown off the avowal of their Christianity, but it has been only for a time, and in better days better thoughts have swayed the brotherhood, and they have returned to

* Page 242.

their due allegiance. A curious instance of this temporary defalcation occurs in the minutes of the Leathersellers' Company, dated 4th August, 1795, thus entered :—

"Present,—

"Resolved and ordered that there be no Church Service performed this day."

That these worthy Leathersellers had a conscience is manifest, for they were ashamed of recording their names, and this is the only minute we have met with in which a blank occurs instead of the names of those present. The next entry, however, displays a charitable feeling, for we read,—

"That on account of the present want and scarcity, five guineas each be paid to the Beadle and the Hall-keeper."

The next year the laudable custom of attendance at church was revived. The clergyman invited to preach the sermon on the occasion being the great and good Romaine, of St. Ann's, Blackfriars, and this now most wealthy and flourishing corporation is amongst the first in London for charity and encouragement of learning, and numbers amongst its Court and Livery some of the greatest and most benevolent of our merchant princes.

From the minutes of this Company we also extract the following entry as an indication of the sacrifice which these traders voluntarily made where their own gratification could only be obtained at the expense of the poor and needy :—

1795, July 23rd. Resolved and ordered—"That, on account of the present scarcity and high price of provisions, the next confirmation dinner be wholly omitted and laid aside for this year, and that the clerk do advertise the same accordingly in the *Times*, *Morning Chronicle*, and *Daily Advertiser*."

The resolution next following, passed at the same court, stands nobly forth, and could not have been placed in a better position to show the generous hearts possessed by these worthy Leathersellers :—

Resolved and ordered—"That the Renter Warden do pay and apply the sum of 50 guineas for the benefit and relief of the poor of the Company and of the ward of Bishopsgate: 20 guineas to the poor of the ward, and 30 guineas to the poor of the company."

A corporation thus conducted was likely to prosper, and such has been the success of this ancient and worshipful company that at the present time they distribute in charity, pensions, gratuities, hospitality, and education, several thousand pounds per annum.

In the commencement of this work we ascribed the continuance of these gilds through so many successive centuries to the religious and social element forming so essential an ingredient in their constitution. In the last four chapters we have considered their religious observances, and the influence which religion has exercised upon their acts. We shall, in future chapters, consider the social element —their banquets and hospitalities.

CHAPTER XIV.

THEIR APPRENTICESHIP.

"All inhabitants within these walls are not properly citizens, but only such as are called freemen."—RALEIGH.

SOME of George Cruikshank's sketches of the Drunkard's Career are very graphic, and no doubt of much value in deterring from the crime of drunkenness; but of all pictorial works of art, Hogarth's inimitable series of scenes in the career of the City Apprentices; the one devoted to the good apprentice who rises to affluence and dignity, the other to the idle one who after wasting his youth and health in riotous living, and squandering "his substance with harlots," sinks into infamy and early death; are undoubtedly the most masterly and valuable productions of any of our moral teachers' pencils. Some years ago, being desirous to witness the process of "binding apprentice," through the kind offices of a mutual friend we obtained an introduction to the then Chamberlain of London, the late Sir James Shaw, in whose province it was to perform all functions in respect to binding or loosing, and admitting to the freedom of the City. Although the age of fourteen is an interesting age, and the act of selecting one's occupation for life an important one, any person of common mind might easily pass through the frequent form of effecting this seven years' compact in a merely perfunctory manner, deeming it a business matter, and passing on the routine to some of the subalterns in the office. Not so thought Sir James Shaw. No youth was ever ushered into the presence of this pious and dignified official, without feeling respect and reverence; and the mode of conducting the ceremony, the fatherly and loving spirit in which he addressed the candidate, the serious tone in which he spoke of the importance, in this life, and the next, of the selection made either of virtue or vice, industry or idleness, in commencing life, left an indelible impression upon the mind, and showed observers the value of such a ceremony when well and religiously conducted.

After a loving address to the lad, the venerable Chamberlain ushered him to the side of the ancient hall, on the walls of which were suspended a noble series of Hogarth's plates, probably having hung there from the day they were first issued from the engraver's hands; and with the most marked simplicity and condescension, and singular talent, explained each scene, and in many instances, we have heard, he has melted the youth into tears. What good intentions and noble aspirations were on these occasions first implanted, culminating in after years and producing good results, only the last day can unfold; but many of the distinguished merchantmen of the present day can testify to the great benefit they in their youth derived from the advice and blessing of this good baronet.

In leaving the hall our friend made the observation—"The emoluments of this office of Chamberlain are under £4000 per annum, but if the City were to offer £40,000 instead of £4000, and to search the world, they could never improve upon the present worthy possessor of the office. His superior does not exist." A life-size and life-like portrait of this officer, taken as he always appeared in his office in his official robes, is to be seen in the Chamberlain's office, one of the ablest works of one of our first and greatest female artists, Mrs. Charles Pearson, whose only child is the wife of Sir Thomas Gabriel, Bart., Lord Mayor 1866-7.

To become on the livery a man must first be free. The present mode of admission to the freedom is threefold, by *servitude*, *patrimony*, or *purchase*. A stranger may become free without any claim beyond the payment of the necessary fees; this is obtaining the freedom by purchase: the son of a freeman, though never apprenticed, may claim his freedom by patrimony upon the payment of a fee much less than that paid by a stranger: and he who has served an apprenticeship becomes free upon a mere nominal fine; this is by servitude. Having thus become free of the City, he may become free of any company he chooses, if he has friends to nominate him, and being free of a company, may then be proposed for the livery, and after a month's delay is balloted for by the court. The fees vary in different companies, from £25 to £100 for the livery fine, which in addition to all other expenses will not exceed from £50 to £200. The highest livery fine we have heard of is that of the Leathersellers, which is 100 guineas. Originally apprenticeship was the only entrance into the gilds.

The origin of the system of apprenticeship is no doubt of a very great antiquity. Sir Francis Palgrave is of opinion that it owes its origin to the customs of the College of Workmen in the Roman empire. After a due term of probation and initiation the admission into the gild was an attestation that the individual had conducted himself with due attention, diligence, and morality. The good resulting from the system must be manifest. Gratitude towards a kind master, who had instructed him in all the mysteries of the craft, emulation, good example, and the unions which the fraternity afforded, "rendered these gilds a continual scene of moral renovation to the commonwealth."*

For a long period subsequent to the Conquest, the City of London, as we have shown, maintained all the peculiarities of the old Saxon system, the same legal polity and usages as belonged to a Saxon county. It was, in fact, a county in itself, being a concentration of leet jurisdictions, each comprising a ward, or, as it was termed, a *gild*, and the whole governed by one chief magistrate. The only difference between it and a county was that it contained no *villeins* or slaves, but all its inhabitants were, as

* Palgrave's "Merchant and Friar."

designated in their charters, free men or "*law-worthy*."

As in the counties, the districts over which the owners possessed a leet jurisdiction were called *sokes* or *socs*, so in the City the various *gilds* over which each alderman (or master) held leet jurisdiction was called his *soke*. The charter of Henry I. provides "that the barons (aldermen or masters) and citizens should have their *sokes* in peace, and that guests tarrying within any of these *sokes* should pay custom to those to whom the *soke* belonged." There can be no doubt that the origin of the city and county *sokes* was the same and that their government was alike. Norton observes that the tenants in *free socage* of the counties, and the burghers or tenants in *free burgage* were of the same quality; for the tenure of *free burgage* was no other than a species of *free socage*. He considers, too, that the proprietary title of the alderman to his *soke* in London (after the title became territorial) was of short duration and never universal throughout the City.

When the Saxon invaders took possession of the soil of Britain, it is probable that they reduced the original inhabitants to a state of dependence or slavery. Prior to the Norman conquest, however, the tenants had, by gradual progress, settled into three distinct classes. The lowest type of individuals remained in their original bondage, oppressed and trodden down, the personal and proprietary *serfs* or slaves of the lord. The next order were somewhat less degraded, the *villeins* (or rustic labourers) who in return for their vassalage and labour had a small portion of land allotted to them. This was, however, a grant only at will, the occupier could not leave the soc, and he was still the personal property of their lord. Occasionally, it is true, by the favour of the proprietor, and from great desert, individuals did arise to a state of freedom and independence, and this gave rise to the third class, viz., the freemen or free tenants, still owing duties for their possessions. They were sometimes termed *Coléberti* and *Radmen*, and were known by the common appellation of *sock-men* or *sokemen*.* Thus we discover how conformably with the imperceptible gradations towards civil freedom in this country the socage tenant advances into the independent freeholder; the villein grows up under the name of copyholder into the true socage tenant; while the miserable bondman or slave disappears altogether from off the land; so that Queen Elizabeth boasted that in her day not one could be found throughout the realm.

We recognize the same principle existing in the City as in the county, except that no bondsmen were admitted within the walls, nor was any one of the order of *villein* eligible for apprenticeship to a craft. The "Liber Albus" states that "from of old no one was made apprentice, unless he was known to be of free condition; and even if, after he had received the freedom, it became known that he was a person of servile condition, through that same fact he lost the freedom of the City; a thing that was the case

* *Vide* Turner's Hist. Ang. Sax. 4th ed., vol. iii. p. 181.

with Thomas le Bedelle and others, who, in the mayoralty of John le Blount (Mayor 1301 to 1307) lost their freedom in consequence of having acknowledged that they held land in villenage of the Bishop of London, and so remained debarred of the freedom of the City."* Great precautions were observed in regard to the admission of strangers within the City; jealousy of their participation in the advantages of their trade, no doubt, had much to do with this exclusiveness, but the system of Frankpledge was the basis of it, and the legal system for the repression and detection of violence, for mutual protection and responsibility, founded under the ancient Saxon polity, prevailed in great force in the City. No stranger was allowed to remain for more than forty days without being enrolled in Frankpledge. No inmates, lodgers, persons under age, or *villeins*, possessed any civic rights. It is true in one sense a residence of a year and a day within the walls conferred an exemption from villenage or slavery, and so high was the privilege of residence within any free city deemed, that by the award of their charter, and by the ancient Saxon custom, whatever slave had fled from his master's soke, and should have remained unreclaimed for a year and day within the walls of a free borough, he thereby effected his effranchisement.† In London inhabitancy constituted full burghership, but as no one was permitted to become a householder unless free of the City and of a craft, and as

* Lib. i., pt. 1, cap. x.

† *Vide* Madox's Firma Burgi, p. 271.

no one could become free of a craft without having first served his seven years of apprenticeship, we thus perceive that in order to full citizenship in the early days this apprenticeship was essential in all cases.

Some writers are of opinion that the system of apprenticeship did not exist prior to the reign of Richard I. (A.D. 1190), because no earlier entry exists among the records of any mercantile distinctions, corporate freeman's oath, nor corporate admission to freedom, prior to that date. It was during the absence of that monarch in the Holy Land that the community of London, as *one body politic*, took its formal origin. It became a member of the national council, and was endued with a political locality and rank. It was necessary that a new form of admission into this fellowship should be adopted, and that the civic freedom should take a new character from that of the ancient Saxon freedom of the leet. As no special mercantile qualification seems at this time to have been recorded, it is supposed therefore that none was required, and as the earliest mention of enrolment amongst the freemen by apprenticeship occurs in the 3rd Edward II. (A.D. 1310), some suggest that at this period we must fix its origin. But as the system of apprenticeship is of great antiquity and the natural one, we think that the absence of positive evidence of its earlier existence is no proof that it was not earlier practised. That it was of a far earlier time, however, is put beyond doubt by an entry in the "Liber Albus," under the date of Edward I., which we have met with since penning the last sentence, and it finally settles the question. In the reign of Edward I. an ordinance of the City declared "that no apprentice after his term fully served shall follow his trade in the City before he shall have been sworn of the freedom, and thereupon enrolled. And that none shall be received for a less term than seven years, *according to the ancient and established usage*."*

Herbert considers that "it is probable that apprenticeship service came into general use during the reign of Henry III., for apprentices both to the trades and law are noticed in records in the reign of Edward I."

All incorporations were anciently termed *universities*, whether of trade, learning, or otherwise. When our great institutions of learning were enrolled, the term of years required to be devoted to study, in order to obtain the degree of Master of Arts, was evidently borrowed from the term of apprenticeship in trades. As to have wrought seven years under a master properly qualified was required in trade before one became a master and able to receive apprentices, so to have studied under a master properly qualified was necessary, in order that he should become master, teacher, or doctor (words anciently synonymous) in the learned arts, and to have scholars or apprentices, also synonymous (from *apprendre* to learn), to study under him. Anciently, benchers in the Inns of Court were called

* "Liber Albus," lib. iii., p. 2, A.D. 1274.

apprentices of the law, "*apprentici juris nobiliores*;" and so the learned Plowden writes himself. Sir Henry Finch styles himself, in his "Nomotechnia," "*apprentice de ley*;" Sir Edward Coke, in his "Institutes," says, "*apprentici legis* are called *homines consiliarii et in lege periti*;" and elsewhere he speaks of apprentices and other counsellors of law. Properly an apprentice at law is a barrister of under sixteen years' standing, and under the degree of serjeant.

CHAPTER XV.

THEIR APPRENTICESHIP, CONTINUED.

THE records of the various gilds afford ample evidence that the regulations of apprenticeships constituted a very important article in the early ordinances of the companies. It was necessary to their standing orders that, for admission to the livery, not only shall the candidate have "served his time," but he must be "of good name." During the period of his pupilage he had the most fatherly care bestowed upon him, and the rules of the gilds were strictly enforced, should occasion require. It may throw some light upon the olden customs, if we extract two or three entries from the books of the companies respecting the treatment of their apprentices. The first is from the Goldsmiths', written in very solemn style; a change of dynasty could hardly have been entered in more emphatic phraseology. We modernize the orthography.

A.D. 1430. "It is to remember how that, in the beginning of April, the third year of King Henry VI., John Hille, citizen and goldsmith of London, had one John Richard to his apprentice; the which apprentice for divers great offences and trespasses that he had done to his master, the same John Hille would have chastised him, as reason and the company's usage is of apprentices to be chastised of their masters; the which apprentice seeing his master would have chastised him, as reason would, of very malice and cursed as an obstinate apprentice to his master, went up forth withon a stair out of the shoppe, bearing with him a short spear, the which he hid in the kitchen 'imagining to kill his maister;' the which spear served to open and to shut the windows of the shop. And when he had so done he came down again, and in the midst of the stairs he reviled his master full despiteously and ungodly, and said to him, 'Come on now, for it is my time, and I have ordained for thee; and as I mote be saved thou shalt never come into my chamber.' And his master considering that time his cursedness, and how he was purposed to kill him, for to eschew all manner of peril of both sides, *fair and soft went out of his house*, and ordained so that the same apprentice was anon wrested and brought unto the Compter, where he was unto the time that the wardens of the craft of Goldsmith appointed to correct the defaults done within the same craft, sent for him to know the matter and rule it to an end, for the said John Hille had complained to them of his apprentice, and told them all the matter above said; and the said apprentice could not say that his master put upon him, but openly acknowledged that he bore the said weapon into the kitchen ready to defend him with against his master as well as he could. Upon which the said wardens said that the same apprentice was found deficient, and asked him how he would make amends; and he said he had no goods. And the next day he made the same reply. And then the said wardens, considering the ungratefulness, rebellion, and cursedness of the said apprentice, the which might turn to the undoing of many others, asked him if he would forswear the craft and the town. And at last by his own will and proper assent he 'chose to forswear the craft and the town.'"

In 1456, William Bowden was charged before the wardens of the same company, for that he had "irreverently, shamefully, and of frowwinesse," beaten his mistress. His punishment was that he shall be "had into y kitchen of the hall," and there stripped naked, and by the hands of his master beaten until such time as he raised blood upon his body, in likewise as he did upon his mistress, and that he should then ask his master and mistress "of grace and mercy nakyd as he was betyn," which he did upon his knees.*

Very stringent rules were enforced against apprentices "wearing weapons within the city," and against "unseemly dress." A curious entry occurs in the Merchant Taylors' books, to the effect that no apprentice of the mystery shall wear any weapon "invasive or defensive within the citie," without reasonable cause, "or els being going forth of the

* Herbert, vol. ii. p. 170.

citie into the countrie with his maister, or with other honest companie." Also a rule was that "every apprentice was to be presented to the master and wardens at the Common Hall," in order that they might be enabled to ascertain whether he was free by birth, not challenged for a bondsman.

Even the length of the hair was a subject not too unimportant to obtain a regulation respecting it. The Ironmongers have the following:—"They were to dress them in soche wise that it be no dishonistye to the companie, but that they be apparalide reysonable and honest, that is to say—For the holy dayes, hose, throwts, shearts, dubblets, cotes, gownes or clokes, with other necessaries, soche as maye be convenyently honest and cleane;" and on the "workyng dayes such as may be honest and profitable to kepe them from cold and wete; and they *shall not suffer their hare to grow to longe.*" The books of the same company have the following curious minute:—

A.D. 1638. "Becausse many young men doe take unto themselves a liberty in their apprentishippe, by their mr. his conivence, to wear their hayre unseemly overlong, more like to ruffians then citizen's apprentizes, and, after their terme of their service ended, come to demand their freedome of the company in that disguised manner; for remedy thereof, it is now ordered that hereafter, if any master shall make free any of his servants before he have orderly cutt and barbed his hayre to the liking of the mr. and wardens of the company for the tyme being, the mr. of the apprentice shall pay to the company for every suche neglect xxs. for a fine."*

We have no doubt that the rulers of the gilds, as well as the masters of the apprentices, had at times great difficulty in directing and governing these young heroes; but, on the other hand, we can easily conceive that the young people were at times sorely tried by the tyranny of laws which detailed such minutiæ as the wearing of the hair and tying a shoe-string. When monarchs could stoop, as Queen Elizabeth and her successor, James I., did, to give laws as to the stockings, caps, and petticoats to be worn by servant girls, and the cloth with which the apprentices were to be clothed, probably the smaller monarchs, the masters of the gilds, amplified and improved upon these laws, and became wearisome to those they governed.

We have already referred to the sumptuary laws of Queen Elizabeth. Those of James were, if possible, still more foolish. "The abuse growing by excesse and strange fashions of apparell, used by many apprentices, and by the inordinate pryde of mayde servaunts and women servaunts in their excesse of apparell and follie in varietie of newe fashions," induced that monarch, in the year 1611, to direct the mayor to issue precepts to the masters of the various gilds, enjoining them to convene and to harangue their fraternities on this grievous sin.

* Nichol's "History of Ironmongers' Company," p. 228.

In the Grocers' Company, "Mr. Warden Burrell," on reading the precept, "made sundrye godlye and charitable exhortacions to each to see reformacion made in his own family according to the meaning of the same," probably hinting that with more finery was less honesty.

> "Hîc ultra vires habitûs nitor: hîc aliquid plus
> Quam satis est; interdum alienâ sumitur arcâ.
> Commune id vitium est."*

Apprentices were to wear no "hats," the facing whereof should exceed three inches in breadth in the head, which with the band and trimming should cost above 5*s.*; the band was to be destitute of lace, made of linen not exceeding 5*s.* the ell, and to have no other work or ornament than a plain hem and one stitch; and if the apprentice should wear a *ruff-band*, it was not to exceed three inches in height before it was gathered and set into the stock, nor more than two inches in depth before the setting into the same stock. The collar of the doublet was to have neither "poynte, whalebone, nor plaits," but to be made close and comely, and, as well as the breeches, was to be made only of "cloth, kersey, sackcloth, canvasse, English leather, or English stuffe," and of not more than 2*s.* 6*d.* the yard; his stockings were to be of woollen yarn or kersey; he was not to wear "Spanish shoes with polonia heels;" or have his hair with any "tufte or lock, but cut short in decent and comely manner" (*à la Jack Sheppard*). The poor servant girl was, if

* Juvenal, Sat. III.

12

possible, even more despitefully treated. She was to wear, alas! "no lawn, kambrick, tiffany, velvet lawns, or white wires on the head or about the kerchief, koyfe, crest cloth, or shadow," but only linen, and that not to exceed 5*s*. the ell. Her ruff was on no account to be of more than four yards in length before the gathering or setting of it in, nor was she to "wear any *fardingal* at all great or little, nor any body or sleeves of wire, whalebone, or other stiffing, saving canvass or buckram only."*

What Chartist apprentice of our own day—after all this—does not repine and mourn over the departed "good old times" of our ancestors?

Nevertheless, a season of trial and restraint is necessary to man. Bishop Butler says that this life is a scene of probation, and Bossuet eloquently remarks that "*Life is an apprenticeship for death.*" St. Paul deemed it a great honour to be a citizen of Rome, having been born in Tarsus, a free city, when he said, "*I am a citizen of no mean city.*" And on another occasion, as if to show that there was even a still higher freedom to be obtained than that of any earthly community, he adds, "our citizenship is in heaven." We doubt not that much of the endurance and courage under difficulties, so characteristic of the English traders in former times, were owing to the seven long years of strict discipline involved under the system of apprenticeship.

The great shrewdness of the early citizens is especially manifested in their strict refusal to allow

* Grocers' Company, p. 88.

apprentices, or even the members of the gilds, "to go to the lawe." The very earliest accounts of these gilds, whether those of Norwich, Chester, or London, afford ample evidence of the great care taken by the founders to prevent litigation amongst their members. All disputes between master and apprentices, or between brethren, as well as claims of debt, were to be arranged by the authority of the master and wardens. "If any debate is between any of the fraternite, or askyng of dette or any other thynges, then anon the party playntiff shall come to the master, and tell his grievaunce, and the master shall make an ende thereof."*

If it proved beyond the power of the master to arrange, as appeared to be the case occasionally in later times, permission from the court had to be obtained, and then the plaintiff might sue at law. Thus, in 1568, the Merchant Taylors' minutes state that "license was granted to one Elston, a member, to arrest Brackshaw;" and in the same year the master granted leave to "Edward Baker to take the lawe of J. Garrett." The Leathersellers have an entry under date January, 1633, granting similar "permission to go to law."

In the reign of George I., a curious point of law was determined by Chief-Justice Sir John Pratt, respecting the suspension of a woman's settlement, owing to her marriage with a City apprentice whose settlement was questioned. The Chief-Justice ruled that a settlement might be absolutely suspended

* Grocers' Ordinances, A.D. 1463.

during marriage; as in this case, in which a woman having a settlement marries a man having no settlement, the principle was, that as the husband could not be sent to the place of the wife's settlement, so neither could the wife, because the husband and wife being, as it were, but one person, could not be parted.

This decision caused much stir at the time, and gave rise to the following

CATCH.

A woman having a settlement
Married a man with none;
The question was, "He being dead,
If that she had was gone?"
Quoth Sir John Pratt, "Her settlement
Suspended did remain
Living the husband; but him dead,
It doth revive again."

Chorus of Puisne Judges.

"Living the husband; but him dead,
It doth revive again."

Sound law as this would appear, it nevertheless was overruled in the 28th George II., in a case in which the parish of St. Botolph, Bishopsgate, were the respondents, and that of St. John's, Wapping, appellants. The court were unanimously of opinion that the woman, whose maiden settlement was in Bishopsgate, although she married a man who had no settlement, did not lose her maiden settlement until she had acquired a new one, but that it was merely suspended during the time she continued under the protection of her husband, and was maintained by him; and that as she was not maintained by him, she should be supported by the parish in which she had gained her maiden settlement.

The Chamberlain of London, as presiding officer in binding apprentices and admitting freemen, should be, if not a lawyer, a man of considerable skill and judgment, as questions of great nicety may occasionally come before him for his decision. He should at least be familiar with the ruling of the judges in cases affecting the question of legitimacy, for when a man is made free by patrimony it is necessary that he should prove that his father was free. But many men find it impossible to discover their father. This, of course, proves an insuperable difficulty to one desirous of being admitted to the freedom by patrimony; but the possibility may occur of a man having more than one father from whom to select, either of whom would secure his legitimacy. He may have two to choose from, and if one be a freeman and the other a non-freeman, he would naturally, in such a case, prefer the former.

The case, as laid down by the authorities, is as follows:—

"*In re*, BASTARDY.

Chiefly a bastard is one born out of lawful matrimony.

The most distinguished cases are—

That a child born of an unmarried woman is illegitimate.

So is a child born so long after the death of the husband, that, by course of nature, it could not be his; but a case may occur in which a child may choose which of two men it will have for its father; as if a widow marry so soon after the death of her first husband, that a child born during the second marriage may be the child of either husband; such child is not only legitimate, but may, on obtaining the age of twenty-one, elect which of its mother's husbands it will have for its father."

While we should ever commiserate those of our fellow-creatures who have had no father, yet, for the credit of society and of the female sex, it is to be hoped that instances of a man possessing two fathers to select from, although possible, are of the most rare occurrence; and that while our present system of apprenticeship continues, no Chamberlain of London shall be called upon to give a decision in any case in which a candidate for the freedom shall be possessed of such affluence of choice as to his paternity as that above indicated.

CHAPTER XVI.

THEIR FEASTS.

"You cannot have a perfect palace, except you have two sides: a side for the banquet, and a side for the household; the one for feasts and triumphs, and the other for dwelling."—BACON.

IN former papers we have laid special emphasis upon the fact that our Saxon ancestors had a high appreciation of the value of sociality and feasting. Was a thing to be done?—then it must be done well! To be done well, it must be accompanied with feasting and good cheer! They were wise men in their day and generation; they knew full well that associations can exist only so long as union of sentiment as well as unity of purpose continue; that man is naturally a self-willed — and, if you please, a quarrelsome animal; that when societies break up it is usually owing to the want of this union—to the existence of unbrotherly feelings amongst the members. To meet this, the invariable expedient of banqueting was hit upon and of "*drynkying togedre.*" They knew that men were never so forgiving and so amiable as when enjoying good cheer, for then the little asperities engendered in their hours of business, which, but for the warmth of the feast, would fester into animosity, melt like the snow before the sun.

That these trade institutions should have continued to exist through so many ages is a matter of great interest, and the inquiry into the "reasons why" must be one of serious importance, especially to philanthropists and statesmen. We think, therefore, that in any historical sketch of these "crafts" or "mysteries," it is time well spent, having discovered and particularized the great cause of their continuity, to examine into their *modus operandi* and to ascertain the details of the system in order that our generation may learn from the example of generations preceding.

Perhaps there are no assemblages less brotherly to be met with in England than Boards of Guardians, and parish vestries, and we know of no deliberative bodies of men, whose meetings, when reported, display more of the qualities of bitterness, anger, and personality. Certain leading orators go of set purpose for a "scene." Some hard words uttered at a former meeting have been allowed to rankle for a week, and revenge must be taken. Had these worthies dined over their former meeting, hard words would have been forgotten. A farthing rate, it is true, has been saved by the ratepayer, but we doubt if it is wise economy. Men who serve the public merit some complimentary return.

In our first paper we showed that, as early as the seventh century, the Frithgilds were essentially a social institution. That even the ecclesiastical gilds of that date were formed for festivity as well as for religion. To this day, not far from York, is retained and maintained a still more ancient system founded by our Saxon ancestors. Before us is lying a notice, placed a few weeks since on the church door in the parish in which we reside, as follows:—

"Manor of ——

"Notice is hereby given that the Court Leet view of Frankpledge and Court Baron of the Worshipful Lords of the said Manor will be holden on Tuesday, 13th day of November instant, at twelve o'clock at noon, and all persons that do owe any suit or service at the said Court are required to attend."

"(Signed) ——

"Steward."

We may add that the ancient accessory of a feast forms not the least important element in this said Court Leet on November 13.

This custom of frankpledge is the most ancient on record in this kingdom. It was known also by the name of *friborg* or *free pledge*, and the assembly was called Court *Leet*, from the Saxon word to *assemble*, and met in each hundred of a county, convened by the reeve by whom the criminal law was administered. In Wilkin's "Saxon Laws" we read that the law was that every freeman of fourteen years should find sureties to keep the peace, certain neighbours being his sureties, and bound to each other to produce him who committed an offence, or to make satisfaction to the injured. To do this the better they formed a common fund, from which all such losses were paid, and by which at stated intervals a common table was provided where they "ate and drank together."

This assembly in the seventh century was called the *Gebeorscipe*, literally *beer-drinking*. From these Frithgilds and their social feastings succeeded the trade gilds and gilds ecclesiastical. That joviality became at times too prominent seems certain, for *Ina* made a law to prevent turbulent proceedings at such meetings.

It is curious that in a rural district in the East Riding this system of frankpledge should have continued, as we know the Normans abolished it where they could, and it was only such powerful cities as London and York, by their charters specially exempted from the Norman code, which were permitted to retain intact the old Saxon institutions under which they had prospered.

Of the intervening centuries between the seventh and the fourteenth, few details remain concerning the festivities of the gilds; but from that period to the present numerous records occur of the sumptuous banquets prepared for the brotherhoods on all occasions of religious ceremonial or business. The earliest entry of the kind is in the books of the "Grossers" *erst* "Pepperers," the most prominent of whose ordinances was, that "on St. Anthony's day, or on any day within the octave thereof, that should be assigned by the wardens, all who were in London should assemble in 'a house' and commune and dine together, and be served according to the ordinances of the wardens." The cost of this feast to those who attended was 5*s*. 6*d*., to those who did not attend 2*s*. 6*d*., which sums went to the joint expense of the dinner and the maintenance of the priest. "Persons not in the livery, and *who kept shops*," were only to pay 12*d.*; and as a *dinner* was supposed to be insufficient after so much business as they usually performed, a supper crowned the day, and "every man being a brother of the felliship, and in the clothyng of the same, that did not come to the dynner or soper that should be made for the elecion of the wardens" yearly, should forfeit 5*s.* "to the use and behoof of the felliship."

From this it will be seen that the custom of possessing magnificent halls had not at this period become general. It was not till the early part of the fifteenth century, the reign of Henry IV., that the Companies acquired a *local habitation* as well as a name. As feasts on a large scale could only be given in commodious rooms, halls in the style of the refectories of the religious houses were soon erected; and should our readers desire to know the style of the room, we can refer them to the halls at Trinity, and St. John's, Cambridge, and other similar halls at Oxford, to the Guildhall, York, and for one on a grand scale we would refer them to the Guildhall of London, capable of feasting from one to two thousand guests.

We can find no records earlier than the fourteenth century of the Companies being possessed of such edifices. At that period such a building became the usual property of the gilds. Many of the Gothic palaces of the nobility still preserved may be mentioned, in addition to those just named, as fair specimens of the City halls, from which, however, the latter differed in certain peculiarities, upon which we may remark.

The chief room was the hall, open-roofed and lofty, with the Companies' banners, standards, and other heraldic devices, used at tournaments, or in war, suspended aloft. Hanging platforms or galleries were also erected for the use of the "*musitioners* and *mynstrylls*." The lofty Gothic windows were richly coloured with the arms of the Company's benefactors, and with incidents in the life of their patron saint. Nor should we omit to specify the elevated *dais* or *haut pas*, for the high table; the *reredos*, which traversed the apartment, and the noble buffets for the plate.

Passages convenient of access led to the wine and ale cellars, the "bachelors'" chamber, the buttery, bakehouse, and brewery; the entrance to the kitchen being guarded by a spiked hatch, while that interesting chamber was replete with "spittes," "rakkes," and implements capable of tossing round the "wild-boar," "whole sheep," and possibly "entire oxen."

About the time of the Reformation many noblemen's houses were purchased by various gilds. The Drapers' obtained Lord Cornwall's, and to this day retain and keep up his beautiful gardens. The Grocers' bought Lord Fitzwilliam's town mansion. The Slaters' secured the residence of the Earl of Oxford.

On the suppression of the religious houses many

of the conventual buildings were purchased by the Companies. The Leathersellers' obtained the ancient priory of St. Helen, and turned the refectory, a very noble and gorgeous specimen of Gothic architecture, into their common hall, A. D. 1537. The Pinners, in like manner, removed to the monastery of the Austin Friars; and the Barber-Surgeons to the hermitage of St. James'-in-the-Wall.

The halls of the larger Companies, then as now, were frequently visited on festive occasions by the monarch of the day, or the royal princes, as well as by the great representative men of the nation. During periods of revolution the party in power not unfrequently made them the great central seat of government; and in Cromwell's time many were seized upon to be used as conventicles. In times prior to the erection of an official residence for the Lord Mayor they were, in many instances, selected as temporary mansion-houses by the successive chief magistrates.

Many of the more ancient halls possessed, in addition to the principal room and those enumerated above, "the great parlour," "the dining parlour," for the Court dinners, "the chekker chamber," "the ladies' chamber," "the King's chamber," "the long gallery" for the portraits of the benefactors, besides the private chapel in which the priest said daily mass. The various smaller apartments were usually hung with tapestry; the Drapers' books of 1494 contain many entries of items paid to "a tapster-man that *amended the hangings of the parlours.*" At that period the "chekker chamber" of this Company was laid with mats, which the other apartments did not boast of. That their hall was spacious is certain, for their livery numbered, at this time 114, the "bachelors" 60, and the invited guests usually 60 or 70 more. They occasionally permitted the ladies to dine alone in the "ladies' chamber." Here none but the married ladies and guests of the highest rank are recorded as being entertained. The "maydens" at these seasons held their festivities in "the chekker chamber." Usually, however, unless a large accession of guests was expected, "the susterne," both wives and maidens, as we shall presently show, joined "the brethren" in the hall.

CHAPTER XVII.

THEIR FEASTS, CONTINUED.

> "The courteous citizen bad me to his feast,
> *   *   *   *   *
> I went: then saw and found the great expense,
> The fare and fashion of our citizens,
> Oh, Cleopatricall! what wanteth there
> For curious cost, and wondrous choice of cheere."
>
> BP. HALL.

THE feast was always welcome to the brethren, and, no doubt, to the sisters also, for they had their seats at the board, whether given in a temporary hostel, or, in later times, in their hall, as described in the last chapter.

Each brother and sister, some days before, had been summoned to appear on a given day and hour, and "*to come in their best liverie.*" The place or meeting was named, from which in due procession, headed by their *bedell*, *minstrels*, and *officiating priests*, the master, wardens, and brethren marched, with all state and dignity, to one of their own churches, to attend a "*solemne masse*," and offer upon the altar each a silver penny. Thus was their feasting preceded with prayer and alms-doing.

The return to the hall was in the same order, and

with the same observance of precedency. The old records of the Companies throw light upon the customs of those ages—even to the minute particular of their "*washing before sitting down to meat.*" That particular attention was paid to all ceremony, etiquette, and the rules of polished life, is evident, from the custom prevailing then as now, of each person occupying a given position at table according to his rank and degree. The Merchant Taylors have the following entry, under date 1578, March 24: "One Jordan, an officer of the King's Artillery, a loving brother, is ordered to have his place in all meetings next to our loving brother, Ralph Hope." No scrambling for the best places—no forward, unknown person, occupying a place above his betters. As the laws of heraldry were strictly observed on occasions of pageantry and ceremonial, and at the obsequies of their members, so at their feasts the strictest attention was given to the observance of the rules of precedency.

The order of arrangement at table was not deemed a matter beneath the most exact definition. The ordinances of the Drapers' Company, 6 Henry IV., contain a distinct article, entitled "A rule ordeyned for the sytting in ye halle."

"That from this day forward, at every general feast or dinner, all those that have been masters and wardens shall 'sitte at the + tabyll,' and none else, unless by the advice and the assignment of the master and wardens, 'to sitte at the hygh tabyll, upon payne of ijs.' No brother of the fraternity to presume to sit at any table in the hall till "the master and the states *have washed* and be sett at the hygh tabyll, on payne of iijs. iiijd."

It was customary to wait personally on distinguished persons to invite them to the feasts. In 1496 the charge is made of iiijd. "for bote hire to desyre my lorde tresorer to our feste." This, it will be found, was William Paulet, first Marquis of Winchester. Great ceremony was used in inviting visitors of rank. Preparatory to a banquet at which King James I. attended, the Merchant Taylors made the following order:—"1607, July 7, Two Earls to invite the King—the Committee to invite the Prince—and the Queen's Lord Chamberlain to invite her Majesty." In those days, however, the favourite and most frequent guests were the mitred abbots, the priors, and masters of the religious houses, names, and titles, which look strange to our eyes as we glance over the ancient records. We meet with the frequent mention of the grand master of St. John of Clerkenwell, the prior of St. Mary, Overy, of Christ Church, of St. Bartholomew's, the master of St. Thomas of Acon, and of St. Lawrence, Poulteney, and a long list of dignified and conventual clergy.

In the year 1519, at the election feast of the Drapers, amongst the guests we find "my Lord Bishop of Carlisle, the master of St. Thomas of Akers, the prior of Crychurch (Holy Trinity, Aldgate), the prior of Seynt Bartholomew's, the prynceyall of freres Austin, the prior of the same place, the prior of St. Mighell's (Michael's), the sheriffs, etc."

The minutes of the same company contain the order observed at the table in 1521, on a like occasion:—

"The prior of Christ Church chief. Sir John Milborn at his left. My lady Fenkyll at his right. My lady Milborn and my lady Bayley chief before." "At the first side table in the hall Mr. Sadler began the bench, and Mr. Bowyer before him on the forme, and so down. Men of the bench, and women before them. Master Dale and Master Praed began the other side table in the hall," etc.

In 1515 the list of guests and order at table, with the particulars of plate, napery, etc., occupy four folio pages. The guests of rank numbered seventy-eight persons, forty-four men and thirty-four women. Among the number are many above-named, with the "lady wardenesses," and the antiquarian author of the "Collectanea"—Mr. Leland.

Having followed the company to their hall and seen them seated at the board "according to degree," before describing their ceremonial observances we must say a few words respecting the "meats" and the "drinks" provided for the occasion.

It may be interesting to know the kind of meats most in request among our ancestors, and the wines in which they most delighted. This fortunately is easily ascertained, for exact copies of the early bills of fare remain on the companies' records to this day. To modern tastes we should think the banquets in the fifteenth century were more substantial than elegant, more gross than choice. That our ancestors had good digestions, or as they termed it "good stomachs," is clear from the amount of "grease" and other coarse ingredients so copiously used in their *cuisine.* "Brawn," "sea-hog," "fat swan," "conger," and even "porpoise," were amongst the delicacies at the "high table," or above *"the salt."* That our readers may not imagine that we are drawing upon our fancy in this list, we subjoin *verbatim et literatim* a bill of fare for a dinner, *temp.* Henry V., A.D. 1419, on the occasion of the election of wardens, in the Brewers' Company.*

"FIRST COURSE.—Brawn with mustard; cabbage to the pottage; swan standard; capons roasted; great custards.

"SECOND COURSE.—Venison in broth, with white mottrews; cony standard; partridges with cocks roasted; leche-Lombard; doucetts with little parneux.

"THIRD COURSE.—Pears in syrop; great birds with little ones together; fritters payn puff, with a cold bake meat."

Standard means *entire* and *erect*, so that a "*swan standard*" must have been a very magnificent dish.

For the particulars of the same dinner we subjoin the following:—

"5 SEP., 1419, 7 HEN. V.

2 necks of mutton, 3 breasts, 12 marrow bones	1 quart of honey with a new pot
	Divers spicery
6 swans	1 pottle of fresh grease
12 conies	4 doz. pigeons
200 eggs	100 pears
2 gals. of frumenty	11 gals. red wine
2 gals. of cream	4 gals. milk
Hire of 2 doz. earthen pots	Half bushel flour
2 doz. white cups	1 kilderkin of good ale."

At a later dinner, given by the Brewers, in the year of grace 1425, we find the following:—

* *Vide* Herbert, vol. i. p. 77.

"FISH.

Porpeys, salmon, 5 pykes, 800 herrings, etc.

POULTRY.

21 swans, at 3*s.* 9*d.*	12 woodcocks, at 4*d.*
2 geese, at 8*d.*	12½ doz. sm. birds, at 6*d.*
40 capons, at 6*d.*	3 doz. plovers, at 3*s.*
40 conies, at 3*d.*	18 larks, at 4*d.*
48 partridges, at 4*d.*	6 doz. little birds, at 1½*d.*

BOCHERY.

2 boars	3½ gal. *fresh grease*, at 16*d.* per gal."*
2 rounds of beef	
40 marrowbones with marrow	

The whole cost of this dinner amounted to £38 4*s.* 2*d.*—a very large sum in that day. Considering that these banquets were usually preceded by a sumptuous breakfast, these worthy liverymen could not be said to be placed on "short commons." Frequently the minutes of the companies afford such entries as the following:—"7 Hen. VI. The expenses at *breakfast* on day of account of the masters, consisting of *two courses*, viz.:—

"FIRST COURSE.—Grewel ferse a la pottage and pestell de porke, ove vertawes.

"SECOND COURSE.—Capons and lambes rosted, and doucettes for the bake meat."

Should it be thought desirable to know the meaning of "leche-Lombard," "mottrews," etc., the explanation is easy. Randle Holme informs us that leche-Lombard was a jelly, made of cream, isinglass, sugar, and almonds, with moreover pork pounded in a mortar with egg, raisins, dates, sugar, salt, pepper, spices, milk, and red wine, the whole boiled in a bladder. Not bad meat, we imagine, and

* Herbert, vol. i. p. 79.

we should think infinitely superior to any species of modern German sausage. We should like to have heard Soyer's opinion upon it! But what is the next mysterious article, mottrews? This, say the learned lexicographers in the "Archæologia," consists "of a rich stew or soup made of pork and poultry powdered in a mortar and strained."

We know not what reward Gunter, or Ring and Brymer, or other great successors of the great cooks of ancient days, may feel inclined to bestow upon us for this most erudite recipe, but for their good, and for the good of mankind, we bring it forth into daylight, and wish all who taste of a viand so choice and rare, the best of digestions.

We give them at the same time the following equally rare recipe:—

"For to make a most choice paste of games to be eaten at the Feast of Chrystemasse."

(17 Richard II., A.D. 1394).

"Take pheasant, hare, chicken, of each one, with two partridges, two pigeons, and two conyngys (rabbits), and smite them in pieces, and pick clean away therefrom all the boonys (bones) that ye may, and therewith do them unto a paste of good pasto, made craftily in the likeness of a bird's body without the livers and hearts, two kidneys of sheep, and seasoning of eggs, made into balls. Cast thereto pouder of pepper, salt, spyce, vinegar, and mushrooms pickled; and then take the bones and let them seeth in a pot to make a good broth for it, and put it into the paste and close 'hit uppe faste,' and bake it well, and so serve it forth; with the head of one of the birds stuck at the one end of the paste and a great tail at the other, and divers of his long feathers 'sette ynne cunnynglye alle about him.'"

The Salters' cook in 1830 made trial of the above recipe, and found it most excellent, as we are informed.

Although, as we have remarked, some of this feeding seems gross to our tastes, it is quite evident that our ancestors were not unacquainted with many luxuries indicating a certain amount of refinement. They used costly aromatic woods and spices at their banquets to perfume with sweet scents their apartments, and the Ironmongers, in 1541, have the heavy charge of 3*d.* for "*roses*, *lavender*, and *sweet holy-water*;" the Salters, in 1506, enter "*perfume* 2*d.*;" and in 1559, the Carpenters are so profuse as to expend on "a quart of rosewater xiid."

"This was a present at the time worthy of a king," as says Mr. Jupp, for in the Privy Purse expenses of Henry VIII., 1530, we read:—

"Item paid to a man in reward for bringing a glass of rosewater from Guildford to Windsor, 5*s.*"

The Carpenters' Company would seem to have taken the lead in luxury, for as early as the reign of Elizabeth we meet with the following entry:—

"1560, paid for a table cloth for the 'hy-tabyll' of dyaper, and for iij. dozen of '*napkyns of dyaper*' £4 3*s.* 6*d.*"

When we bear in mind that the use of forks did not become general till long after this period, it will be evident that table napkins must have been a necessary article at all feasts; and it is singular that we have not met with their mention in any of the inventories of linen in the other companies, unless where the Ironmongers specify "one doz. diaper cloths." Finger-glasses being unknown, washing after dinner, as well as before, was usual, in imitation of the Romans, who in their later and luxurious days had water handed to them by servants as they reclined at table.

> ——" Stratoque super discumbitur ostro;
> Dant manibus famuli lymphas."—*Virg. Æn.* 1, 705.

With such provision and the best of cheer, happiness reigned supreme. Care was driven from the scene. Thus our gay ancestors surrounded the festive board! How they fared—how the "*minstrels*" sang—how the "*London clerks*" performed the *holy play*—how the master and wardens were "*crowned with garlands*"—how the hall re-echoed with the sound of mirth and good fellowship—how the fragments of these mighty feasts were distributed to the needy, who ever found a welcome under these hospitable roofs,—cannot now be told. We must defer that pleasant duty to a future page.

CHAPTER XVIII.

THEIR FEASTS, CONTINUED.

THE CROWNING WITH GARLANDS.

"This day (September 21, 1671) I din'd in the city, at the Fraternity Feast, in Yronmongers' Hall, where the four stewards chose their successors for the next year, with a solemn procession, garlands about their heads, and music playing before them; so coming up to the upper tables they drank to the new stewards."—EVELYN'S *Diary*.

AFTER the grand feast of the year, that on election day, the most interesting incident to all the brethren was, immediately upon the removal of the cloth, the crowning with garlands the new master and wardens.

In the Drapers' books, under date 1522, we read that dinner being finished, the old master rose and went into the parlour, having a garland on his head and his cup-bearer before him, and so he went straight to the upper end of the high board, without any minstrels, and "then chewsed Mr. Rudston, being then sheriff, for our new master, and sat down again." Then the master and wardens went into the parlour and took their four cup-bearers before them, without minstrels, and then crossed the great parlour, entering the hall, and so they went about till they came to the upper end of the *high board*, and there the chief warden delivered his garland to Sir Laurence Aylmer, as the eldest alderman, because Mr. Brewer was absent.

In Malcolm's "History of the Ironmongers' Company" is a detailed account of the election ceremonies in 1565 (more than a century earlier than that at which good John Evelyn attended), when it is agreed that the two wardens at the dinner shall rise to go out, and then shall come in with garlands for the master only in the chief warden's hands, with the minstrels before them and the bedell, and, making their obeisance to the master, shall deliver him the same garland; and there shall remain and attend the master till the master hath assayed the garland upon the heads of such of the most worshipful as he shall think meet. And then the master to receive it again and set it on his own head. And the wardens to depart, the garland remaining still on the old master's head. And immediately the wardens to come in again, with the bedell and minstrels before them, either of them having his garland upon his head, and one to bear a cup before the chief warden, and to go once about the house, and after obeisance made, the chief warden to take the cup and to deliver it to the old master. And then the old master to take the garland off his own head and put it on the new master's head. And then the old master to take the cup and drink to the new master; and after that the wardens, after due reverence, to depart to assay their garlands; and then to go out, and to come in again, with the minstrels and bedell before them, with their garlands on their heads, and in like manner place their garlands on the heads of the new wardens, as if saying, "Let merit crowns, and justice laurels give."

Malcolm informs us that the garlands are like the heraldic wreath, except that they are made of red velvet, and have pieces of silver fastened on them engraved with the company's arms. This is precisely the description of garlands still preserved, although not used at elections, by the Leathersellers' Company, except that the silver ornamentations, consisting of their arms, crest, and supporters, are more elaborate and pretentious than those described by Malcolm.

Caps of maintenance (or, perhaps, more correctly, *caps of honour*) are to this day used by the Skinners, instead of garlands, with just the same ceremonies as those above described, but which caps mysteriously happen to fit only those who have been selected as new master and wardens, and when they are found to fit, loud and prolonged acclamations ring through the hall, the drinking-cups are brought in by a procession of certain blue-coat boys, the almsmen, livery, and trumpeters, all of whom must "be clothed in their best."

The earliest description of this ceremony is that of the Grocers, whose "wardens were to come with garlondes on their hedes;" after the feast or "mangerie" was finished, and they were to be chosen wardens for the year, "upon whom the forseid garlondes shullen be sette." The Carpenters' Company have an entry under the date August 11, 1657, to the effect that "after dinner the said election was openly published in the hall, and their election caps and garlands particularly presented to them that were present according to ancient custom. But forasmuch as Mr. Hawkins, the youngest warden elect, was now absent, his garland was presented at the upper end of the table where his usual place hath been, and he was drunk to and openly published."*

The custom of crowning prevails to this day also in this ancient company, the same caps of honour being used which were in use three hundred years ago. The master's is described as being of velvet, embroidered with gold and silver, bearing date 1561, and those of the three wardens very similar.

Should any corporate body, *proprio motu*, introduce or institute such a ceremony in our day, we should look upon the whole proceeding with contempt; and persons not acquainted with the origin of this custom and its vast antiquity, may approve of the taste displayed by such of the city gilds as have permitted it to fall into abeyance. For ourselves we think more highly of the rulers of those gilds which continue to observe these and similar usages of their ancestors, as the discontinuance of any of them indicates rather an ignorance of their meaning and deep significance. Just as unwise and imprudent would it be to abolish the ceremony observed at the universities in conferring upon the doctors their degree; or, at Westminster, upon the

* Jupp, p. 210.

sovereign assuming his crown, for the nation to cease the practices usual at coronations.

From the earliest historic period, crowns or wreaths have been held in high estimation. What would the Greeks have cared for their Pythian, Isthmian, Nemean, and Olympic games, with all their exciting pageantry, attracting people to witness them, not only from all Greece but from the whole civilized world, if it were not for the highest ceremony of the whole, the crowning of the victors? The intrinsic value of these garlands was nothing; it was the honourable significance of the rite which made it beyond all price.

At Delphi, a garland of *apple* rewarded the victor; at Corinth, a wreath of *pine;* and at Olympia, a *laurel wreath.* Such, then, was the crown awarded to the successful competitors at these celebrated games, and yet Cicero says that a victory at the Olympic games was not much less honourable than a triumph at Rome. Though a mere contest of skill, strength, or prowess, success indicated not only great natural gifts, but the possession of undaunted spirit and resolution, and the victor was deserving of honour.

> "Qui studet optatam cursu contingere metam
> Multa tulit fecitque puer; sudavit, et alsit,
> Abstinuit Venere et Baccho."—*De Arte Poet.*

Although the Romans, equally with the Greeks, made use of the corona in cases of success and eminence, their rite was usually reserved for the encouragement and honouring of valour and industry.

The soldier who saved the life of a Roman citizen in an engagement, received with all honour and pomp the *corona civica*, the most valued of all their wreaths, composed of oaken boughs. Virgil designates it "*civilis quercus*." However humble in rank otherwise the possessor of this wreath might be, yet, if he visited any public show, the whole assembly, senators as well as people, rose *en masse* to receive him, and, escorting him to the seats of honour, placed him with the senators.* He who first scaled the walls of a city in a general assault received a *corona muralis;* he who first forced the enemy's entrenchments had as reward the *corona castrensis;* and the successful sea captain was crowned with the *corona navalis.*

> "Cui belli insigne superbum
> Tempora navali fulgent rostrata corona."
> *Virg. Æn.* viii., 684.

Besides these was the *corona obsidionalis*, given by the soldiers to their general after a victorious siege; the *corona triumphalis*, made of laurel wreaths, but afterwards changed to gold, as was also the castrensis, the mural, and the naval. The ceremony of crowning these heroes was very imposing, and termed a Triumph; but another similar rite was called an Ovation (not from shouting *Evion!* as some say, but from *ovis*, a sheep, which was usually offered in the procession). Plutarch considers that the Triumph was for conquerors; the Ovation for those who, without force, by benevolence and civil behaviour, had secured peace.†

* Plin., lib. 16, cap. 4.

† Plut. in Marcell.

Thus, then, the masters of the trade gilds were received not with a conqueror's triumph, but an ovation was awarded them, for cultivating by civil behaviour and benevolence the arts of peace, and endeavouring to maintain peaceable relations with their fellow-men. But, it may be argued, why should the ancient English traders imitate such customs of the Greek and Romans? Such a borrowing is as unmeaning as if themselves had first instituted them! No doubt of it, if unsanctioned by authority of their sovereign; and we hesitate not to venture the opinion that no item of pageantry, no device or symbol of heraldry, no civic ceremonial similar in character to those observed by sovereigns in the investiture of the orders of nobility, has ever been adopted or used by these gilds unless in every instance, and to the most minute detail, the King of Arms and the sovereign prince had first in due form conferred upon them the right.

The early occupants of England, both the Anglo-Saxons and Normans, with all their love of pomp and ceremonial in matters religious, military, and civil, had no vain, unmeaning customs. Some deep significance was in every symbol and in every rite. This is especially observable in more recent times, when the symbols of heraldry became a science. So in the forms observed on the creation of a peer of the realm. The crowning of the wardens of the gilds with garlands or caps is exceedingly significant. Patrouillet says that the giving of the cap to the students in the Universities was to denote that they had acquired full liberty, and were no longer subject to the rod of their superiors, in imitation of the ancient Romans, who gave the *pileus*, or cap, to their slaves in the ceremony of making them free; whence the proverb *vocare servos ad pileum*. Hence also on medals the cap is the symbol of liberty, whom they represent holding a cap in her right hand by the point.

In the year 1362, when King Edward III. created his son John of Gaunt Duke of Lancaster, he invested him with a sword, and also himself put upon him a *cap of fur* under a coronet of gold set with precious stones. The first introduction of this order of the peerage into this country was in the eleventh of this reign (A.D. 1337), when the eldest son of the King, commonly called the Black Prince, was created Duke of Cornwall. Heralds assure us that the only ceremony at his investiture was girding him with a sword. The cap was used, however, in 1362, and continued in use on all investitures of dukes until the custom obtained of creation by patent, when these forms ceased. The cap of the marquis, earl, viscount, and baron is of crimson velvet, lined with ermine, having a gold tassel at the top. The crest of the city of London is a *cap of fur* similar to that of the duke, and also to that for many centuries worn by the city swordbearer.

In former chapters we have shown that the City gilds were most careful to observe the strict rules of heraldry and of precedency; that their arms and other honourable grants, such as supporters, earls' helmets, etc., were amongst the first conferred in this country; that their gorgeous palls, adorned with heraldic devices, were manufactured under the supervision of the Lancaster herald; and that even to the details of the cut and colour of their livery, they deemed it incumbent upon them to obtain the royal sanction. We think, therefore, that although we can find no commencement of the custom at their feasts of crowning with garlands or caps of honour, nor have we been enabled at present to meet with any records of authority for the usage, still, from our knowledge of the spirit which actuated these ancient traders, from their minute correctness in all details of courtesy and ritualism, from the intimate relations which they have held in all ages with the various monarchs and royal princes, many of whom themselves, be it noted, have witnessed this crowning, and some themselves submitted to the rite, we hesitate not to say that this, like all their other usages, is not only suggestive and valuable, but honourable, as having been one of the most ancient of all their royal grants and privileges.

Since writing the above lines, by the favour of the learned author we have been enabled to peruse a most valuable pamphlet printed in York for private circulation the 9th of November, 1865, on "the York Cap of Maintenance;" and although some of the points just named in this chapter do not come under consideration in that able essay, the tendency of the whole is most fully to corroborate the views here enunciated; and other matters are there referred to which indicate great research, and in a manner contributing much to enhance the value of that addition to our antiquarian literature.

A reference to the other proceedings of these splendid ancient feasts—the "songs of the minstrels"—the acting of the "holy play" by the London clerks"—the pledging of each other in the "loving cup," and the like, must be deferred to future chapters.

CHAPTER XIX.

THEIR FEASTS, CONTINUED.

THE MINSTRELS.

"Hark how the minstrels 'gin to shrill aloud
Their merry musick that resounds from far;
The pipe, the tabor, and the trembling *croud* (fiddle),
That well agree withouten breach or jar."
SPENSER, *Epith.*

As the master of the company was in all cavalcades preceded by his bedell in his scarlet suit, and by his minstrels in their golden chains and gay attire, all on horseback, so was he also attended by the same at all the most sumptuous feasts. During the time of dinner the minstrels were bountifully provided for with "meats and wines of the best," probably in an adjoining chamber. At the election feasts, as we have just seen, their services were required in the hall, to attend the master with the garlands. After the ancient ceremony of crowning, and the passing of the "loving cup," followed the time-honoured custom of "toasting" and of "wine drinking," the latter accompanied by the varied performances of the minstrels.

Little is now known of this singular class of men, and less of the songs they sang at these festive meetings. In ancient days we know they tuned their voices to their harps, and perhaps they continued so to do to the end. Mean as our present estimate of these men may be, they once held an honourable rank; they were, undoubtedly, most able singers, players, and composers, in their most prosperous days. In times of universal ignorance, these gifted men were held in the highest estimation by all classes; they were the companions of kings, and received the highest honours and rewards. In the days of King Alfred, each prince or monarch had a minstrel as one of his most eminent officers, and kings themselves deemed the occupation of minstrelsy not beneath them.

When the Saxons first invaded Britain, Colgrin, son of Ella, who succeeded Hengist, was closely besieged at York by Arthur and the British. Baldulph, his brother, we read, desiring to tell him of a reinforcement, dressed himself as a minstrel, took his harp in his hand, and thus obtained an entrance into the very citadel of Old York. All chroniclers inform us that the genius of the great King Alfred was first aroused by listening to the stirring strains of the bards, whose poetry fired his soul to effort and endurance, and resulted in his being enabled to read their productions, and himself to equal and excel his teachers. The knowledge of this art saved his kingdom, for when outnumbered by the Danes, and compelled to dismiss his followers, he, disguised as a harper, entered the camp of his enemy, Guthrum; was there entertained for many days, learned their tactics, saw their negligence, returned,—re-assembled his nobles, expelled the invaders, and peace, and security, and sovereignty resulted from the chanting of this minstrel-king.

King Richard I. was equally successful as a bard. After a whole year's imprisonment he obtained his liberty and kingdom owing to his skill in song, for Blondell, his faithful minstrel, from outside the castle in which he was detained, began to sing a song which King Richard and Blondell had learned together, so that when the King heard the song he knew that it was Blondell that sung it, and when he paused at half the song, the King began the other half and completed it. "Thus Blondell won knowledge of the King, and returning into England made the barons of the country acquainted where the King was." This happened, adds the chronicler, about the year 1193. This monarch had several minstrels in his pay, one of whom, the celebrated Fouquette, upon the death of Richard, became a monk, and at length rose to be Archbishop of Toulouse.

In the palmy days of minstrelsy, no doubt, the great and royal feasts of the companies would be graced by the presence of such poets as the royal bards, the noble flights of whose genius, and melting strains of whose melodies, would add greatly to the dignity and happiness of the festival. How far superior must have been the soul-stirring rhapsodies of these ancient bards, such as "Chevy Chase" or "Cœur de Leon," to the mediocre, unmeaning, sentimental ballads usually forming the staple commodity of our after-dinner singers in this year of grace one thousand eight hundred and sixty-nine!

From the mention made of this ancient order of men in the books of the companies, it would appear that as a class they did not always take the highest rank; and at one time that they had forsaken London altogether, notwithstanding that that mighty city must have been the very centre of their engagements. In the year 1401, when Joan, queen of Henry IV., made her entrance into London, the Grocers, with the other crafts, "met her and brought her into London, where for her were ordeyned sumptuous and costly pageants, and resemblance of divers old histories, to the great comfort of her and of such as came with her," says Stow. On this occasion the Grocers enter a charge of 6*s*. 8*d*. paid to Robert Sterns, their bedell, to ride into Suffolk to furnish minstrels. He was so fortunate as to procure six of them, to whom was paid £4 for riding with the company to Blackheath, and 2*s*. for their dinner and wine. That their appearance should not disgrace so wealthy a company, 10*s*. 2*d*. was expended on "new caps and hoods." The next day 13*s*. 4*d*. is charged for the minstrels' attendance when the Queen passed through Cheapside; for wine while there, 18*d*.; and for a horse for the bedell, 12*d*.

The dress of the minstrels at this period was very showy, and they were adorned with chains of gold and silver; their horses also were richly caparisoned. At an earlier period they assumed the clerical garb, and ever retained the tonsure.

In 1401, the same company expend 40*s.* for six minstrels, 8*d.* for their "chaprons," * 21*d.* for their dinner and wine by the way, and 4*d.* for a horse for the bedell. (We learn from this and the former entry that the minstrels found their own horses.) Again, the same year is a charge of 46*s.* 8*d.* for seven minstrels to ride with their sheriffs, 8*s.* 10*d.* for cloth for their "chaperons," 16*d.* for their dinner and wine, and 13*d.* for the "bedell's horse."

In 1481, it would appear that the Drapers found horses, for only 1*s.* iij*d.* is charged for "the mynstrellis for the Mayre Sir Wm. Heriot," and even then the pay is small. In 1486, we read, "Paid to nine mynstrels and their marshall, 66*s.* 8*d.*; twelve crimson hats for the mynstrels, 6*s.* 8*d.*"

In the reigns of Edward II. and Edward III., the minstrels' profession reached its zenith of popularity in England; they were encouraged by the wealthy and applauded by all, but in the succeeding reigns they declined in public favour; probably they became dissipated and licentious, and unwilling to make advances in education and refinement. A change was gradually taking place throughout the kingdom; the great were beginning to sanction education; the Latin classics were becoming their study and delight, and at length the minstrel's song sounded coarse and rude after the flowing periods of Virgil and the Roman poets. Soon they were no longer to be seen in the ancient halls of the kingly and the noble, but were glad henceforth to amuse

* Little escutcheons on the horses' foreheads.

the vulgar at the tournament, the pageant, or the fair.

> "A wandering harper, scorned and poor,
> He begged his bread from door to door,
> And tuned to please a peasant's ear
> The harp a king had loved to hear."

The noble bearing and manly dignity, for which they were once so famed, gave place to a low and ignoble address; their songs were now, like themselves, licentious and depraved, and they at length became outcasts from all virtuous communities. To such a depth had they fallen, that in Sandys's paraphrases they are thus mentioned—

> "I to the vulgar am become a jest,
> Esteemed as a minstrel at a feast."

And Dryden is still more severe in his strictures upon them—

> "These fellows
> Were once the minstrels of a country show;
> Followed the prizes through each paltry town,
> By trumpet cheeks and bloated faces known."

Even as early as the reign of Richard II., many of the profession were engaged in duties very unfitting the poet or musician. In the "Liber Albus," we read that punishments were inflicted upon malefactors, by their being openly brought from prison with minstrels unto the thew (pillory for women), where "their hair was to be cut about their heads." If any woman be a brawler or a scold, let such be taken unto the thew with a distaff dressed with flax in her hand, with minstrels, and be set thereon for a certain time, at the Mayor's discretion.*

At an early period a powerful set of rivals began to grow up in London, doomed eventually to abolish the whole race of minstrels. This was the parish clerks, a very numerous and respectable class of men, who, as early as the reign of Henry III., had become sufficiently powerful to obtain from that monarch a charter of incorporation, under the title of the Fraternity of Clerks. These were the "London Clerks" so often spoken of by modern writers as the actors of the "holy plays" at the civic feasts. Within a few months an able writer in one of the magazines, in reference to this, remarks: "It requires a not-easily-made stretch of modern imagination to picture to ourselves a set of 'London Clerks'—say, for instance, the members of Sion College, with their President for prompter—*playing some holy play* as an adjunct to the festivities of a London Livery dinner, or a Lord Mayor's feast."†

Had this well-informed writer searched diligently, he would have found continually in the Companies' records this expression—"*The priests, and London clerks.*" We do not dispute that in very early times the monks have themselves acted certain holy plays or mysteries—"Isaac's Wedding," or the "Storie of Sampsone," or "Noah's Flood," but we maintain that whenever we meet in the Companies' records mention of the "London clerks," since the year of our Lord 1220, nothing else is meant than

* Lib. iii., pt. iv., fol. 239.

† *The Argosy*, Dec. 1866, p. 55.

the "Society of Parish Clerks," as at that time incorporated by royal charter, under the name of the fraternity of "clerks." Herbert, in his "History of the Twelve Great Companies," falls into this same mistake, when speaking of the holy plays by the London clerks at the great City feasts. He says, "the payment of London clerks for their 'play,' confirms other accounts as to the ecclesiastics being the first actors of the middle ages" (vol. i., p. 85), at which remark our readers will be equally surprised with ourselves if they will read the following extracts from the books of the various companies, quoted by Herbert himself:—

"A. D. 1444.—Obit founded in the Goldsmiths' Company by Thomas Polle.

To pay the Rector - - - - - - - -	8*d*.
„ Chaplain of the Chantry - - - - -	6*d*.
„ every other Chaplain - - - - - -	6*d*.
„ and every Clerk - - - - - - -	4*d*."

The same year, the next item is for the obit of John Carter, when precisely the same charges occur (p. 207, v. 2).

"A. D. 1496.—Drinking money for the Clerk of Seynt Myguills, and for the ryngyng - - -	2*s*. 8*d*.
1426.—Agnes Palmer directs the Fishmongers, by Will, to pay to the three priests of the Company to pray for her soule - - - -	4*d*. each.
To every of the three clerks of the Company for warning the fellowship - - -	4*d*. each.
To the Person - - - - - - -	4*d*.
	(P. 45, v. 2).
1513.—At the Funeral of Sir Roger Achilley (p. 445, v. 1.)	
Paid for the greatest bell, six hours - -	3*s*. 4*d*.
The Clerk for ringing, tolling, and peals - -	2*s*. 0*d*.

To the Priests and Clerks for dirge and masse	0*s.* 8*d.*
To 2 childn. that bore 2 branches of wt. wax, and the Sexton, *in surplices*, helping at the dirge - - - - - - - - -	20*d.*

1524.—At the Funeral of Sir Thomas Lovell, "the dirge was solemnly sung by all the Clerks of London" (p. 75, v. 1).

1426.—The Skinners had in procession "200 clerks and priests in surplices and copes" (p. 68, v. 1).

7 Hen. VIII., 1516.—Sir John Percival's obit.

To two chantry priests - - - -	£43 6*s.* 8*d.*
To the person (parson) - - - -	0*s.* 12*d.*
To his deputy, in his absence - -	0*s.* 13*d.*
To three other chantry priests - -	2*s.* 0*d.*
To two 'clarks for ringing of belles' -	2*s.* 0*d.*

(P. 453, v. 2)."

In the various records innumerable instances occur of the engagement, by the companies, of priests and chaplains, at a yearly salary, but no such mention is ever made of a "clerk," nor is the name ever used as synonymous with that of priest or parson. Every mention of clerks above extracted has evident reference to parish clerks, the class of men upon whom the upper clergy depended in those days for all the music they were able to introduce into their services at a period anterior to the introduction of organs. The crest granted to the Company and used by them to this day is a *music score*, and their heraldic devices, various small instruments of music then in use. In Stow's "Survey," underneath the head "Parish Clerks' Company," we read "Some certain days in the year they had their publick feasts, which they celebrated with singing and music, and they received into their society such persons as delighted in singing or were studious of it. Thus the 27th of

September, 1560, or the eve thereof, they had *even song* and on the *morrow* there was a *communion.* And after they retired to Carpenters' Hall to dinner.''*

Before dismissing this curious question we would briefly refer to the Carpenters' records *in re.* Entries are made of the following items :—

"1462.—To the persons of Allhallows for the tryntall	3s. 4d.
(A trentall is a service of 30 masses celebrated on as many different days for the dead).	
1454.—For two hoods for the priests - - -	Xs.
1491.—To the priests and clerk for dirige after feast	15d.
1555.—To the pryst for hy masse - - - -	12d.
To the clerke of the prysche for ryngyng of the belles - - - - - - -	
1560.—To the prcher for sermon - - - -	3s. 4d.
,, ye curate of the prych - - - -	16d.
,, ye clarke of powlls - - - - -	2s. 6d.
,, ye mynstrels - - - - - -	8s. 4d."

(Jupp, *in loc.*)

In the Ironmongers' books a word not previously used occurs, A.D. 1541 :—

"To the curate of the church - - - - -	1s. 0d.
,, two deacons - - - - - - - -	1s. 2d.
,, the clerk for ringing of the bells - - -	2s. 0d."

We might multiply indefinitely these extracts from the various minutes of the crafts, but enough has been said to satisfy any careful reader that whenever the trading companies speak of their upper clergy they use the terms "priest," "person," "chaplain," "rector," "deacon," "curate," or "preacher," and never that of "clerk."

* Quoted by Jupp, p. 244.

The London clerks then, and not the priests, were the men engaged by the gilds to play some holy play at their great feasts. As music was the chief and almost only study of this company of clerks, we doubt not that these plays were rather operatic, and as Shakespeare had not then arisen to enlighten and delight mankind, the good citizens being prepared to expect but little from their musical players, no doubt were not disappointed. The truth is, it was the feast and the feast alone, with its forms and ceremonies, its fair guests and nobles, its good things both of wines and meats, that were to them the chief attractions; and the London clergy—whether priests or clerks—and the jovial minstrels with their harps and rhapsodies were but secondary and accessory, and not by any means essential to their day's enjoyment.

The last historical record of the unhappy minstrels with which we meet is in the reign of Queen Elizabeth, when a law is passed refusing permission to "beggars, mountebanks, thieves, and minstrels, to congregate at the country fairs to excite the ignorant to wickedness and dissipation." Men who, a century or two before, were the idols of the people, and the favourites of kings—the associates of nobles and of the learned; who could rouse the slothful, cheer the sorrowful; could sing of the battle, the tournament, and the love scene; could tell of the "fairies" and "magacians," themselves "magacians," able to conduct us where

> "As imagination bodies forth
> The forms of things unknown,
> The poet's pen turns them to shapes,
> And gives to airy nothing
> A local habitation and a name,"—

such were the men who, through vice and licentiousness, fell from their high estate, were driven from the festive hall, and were classed among "thieves, vagabonds, and beggars."

The waits, for a long time, shared with the clerks the patronage which the gilds had formerly bestowed upon the minstrels, and henceforth for a time their feasts were attended by *waits*, *clerks*, *musitioners*, and *singers*. Shakespeare says there is "*good in everything*." No doubt there was and is much good in their feasts, ancient and modern, yet the wise man says "it is better to go to the house of mourning than to the house of feasting." So our citizens attended more often at the obsequies and obits of their departed brethren than at the house of feasting. They knew that there is "a time to mourn, and a time to dance," that all things are good in their season, that "He hath made every thing good in his time." Neither were they ignorant of the injunction of the man of wisdom nor loath to yield a ready obedience, when he directs "*that every man shall eat and drink, and enjoy the good of all his labour; it is the gift of God.*"

CHAPTER XX.

THEIR FEASTS, CONTINUED.

THE LOVING-CUP AND THE PLAYERS.

"Quando propinat
Virro tibi, sumitque tuis contacta labellis
Pocula? quis vestrum temerarius usque adeo, quis
Perditus, ut dicat regi, bibe?"—JUVENAL.

THAT the custom of drinking to one another is very ancient there can be no doubt. Our ancestors received it, with many others, from the Romans. The satirist in the lines above quoted clearly shows that it was a prevalent fashion at old Rome eighteen centuries ago. But he complains that the poorer guests at their banquets were unhonoured by the great man of the feast, who drank wine only with the nobles, and left the commoner visitors unpledged. "Does Virro ever drink your health, or take the cup touched by your lips?" We perceive also from these lines that it was not usual for the inferior to challenge the superior—a rule continued in English society to the present time.

The loving-cup is certainly an improvement upon the ancient plan of pledging each other. There is no true hospitality in slighting one set of guests by omitting paying to them an honour which the more wealthy and distinguished enjoy, and therefore it was that our ancestors introduced the custom which we shall now explain.

The loving-cup, either of gold or silver-gilt, is a massive bowl with two handles and an elegantly-embroidered cover, and is capable of receiving some three or four quarts of wine. In the mediæval times, as soon as the ceremony of crowning with garlands was completed, the cup filled with savoury hippocras was carried to the chair of state by the usher, who in a loud voice warned the company that the right worshipful the master welcomed them to the board, and pledged them one and all in the loving-cup. He then handed the cup to the master, who, removing the lid, took it by the two handles, and turning to the senior warden at his right hand drank to him, "lowly bowing," and then having handed the cup into his hands, he wiped the edge of the bowl which his lips had touched with a napkin used for that purpose. The senior warden then in turn, bowing lowly, pledged in like manner his right-hand man, passed to him the cup, and having wiped it with the damask resumed his seat. A second cup, in a similar manner, at the same time was passed from right to left by the two renter wardens, who sit on the master's left, and thus the two cups passed from guest to guest, and met at the bottom of the table.

The learned in vinology inform us that hippocras is a medicated wine, the chief distinction of which is the excellent manner in which it is spiced. King and other poets have written in its praise, and its properties must have been good in order to have commanded a place at the board for several centuries. It was a very costly wine, as we find from the Goldsmiths' books, where, under the date 1449 (27 Henry VI.), the entry occurs of "one gallon of ypocras, 10*s.* 6*d.*," where at the same feast the whole of the "flesh" consumed cost only 11*s.* Should our readers care to know the ingredients, they are specified, in 1518, at the St. Dunstan's feast of the same company:—"For Ipocras. Cynamon, 4lb., 21*s.* 4*d.*; gynger, 2lb., 4*s.* 4*d.*; cloves, 1oz., 5*d.*; sugar, 11lb., 22*s.* 8*d.*; small raysons, 11lb., 6*d.*; dates, 1lb., 4*d.*; total, £2 9*s.* 7*d.*" When on the same occasion the butcher's meat cost only 16*s.* 10*d.*, and a hogshead of red wine and a hogshead of claret only 52*s.*

> "Sack and the well-spiced hippocras, the wine,
> Wassail the bowl, with ancient ribbands fine."

At the present day, the grateful and cooling beverage called claret-cup usually takes the place of hippocras in the loving-cup.

In some of the less distinguished of the livery companies this ancient custom of pledging in the loving-cup has disappeared. Of the discontinuance of that and other significant and ancient forms and ceremonies we would say, as we did of the crowning with garlands, that the abolition of any time-honoured and suggestive right sanctioned by authority (in which no religious doctrine is symbolized opposed to the articles of our reformed religion as by law established), indicates a deficiency of taste on the part of the rulers of the gilds, or a want of acquaintance with its origin and history.

This ceremony performed, next followed the usual loyal and gallant toasts, thus described by King:—

> "The cheerful master, 'midst his joyous friends,
> His glass to their best wishes recommends;
> Then 'midst their gravest furs shall mirth arise,
> And all the gild pursue with joyous cries."

Drinking toasts at banquets was much in vogue in the middle ages, especially in the religious houses, where, Fosbroke informs us, it was usual when any benefactors were entertained to drink to their health in very laudatory terms, and when dead to drink to their blessed memory. It was between these loyal, patriotic, and grateful toasts that the City companies were refreshed by the minstrels' strains, and the whole was succeeded by the performance of some "holy play" by the London clerks.

Where the players played, whether in the "gallery," or whether the whole company of liverymen adjourned while the tables were removed, that the dais might be appropriated to the performers, historians tell us not. There was not, we believe, much variety in the subjects of the plays; the brethren and sisters must have made up their minds frequently to listen to an oft-told tale. But they were simple times, and little satisfied those who expected little.

We have already, in our last chapter, mentioned

15

the names of two or three of the most frequently acted of these "holy plays," nor can we find any others specified in the records of the various companies. It is just possible, however, that they might occasionally have borrowed a favourite play from the provinces, for in the fourteenth century very many subjects from Holy Scripture, we know, had been dramatized. In the year 1327, some very celebrated plays came to light in the ancient city of Chester, on the occasion of the religious festival of the trade gilds, when the monks not only composed the plays, but, jointly with the minstrels, assisted the trades in their performances.

As it is not at all unlikely that some of these may have been re-acted in the City halls, we subjoin the titles of a few of these holy plays, and the companies by whom supported:—"The Fall of Lucifer" was played by the Tanners; "The Creation," by the Drapers; "The Deluge," by the Dyers; "Abraham, Melchisedec, and Lot," by the Barbers; "Moses, Balak, and Balaam," by the Horseboilers; "The Shepherds feeding their flocks by night," by the Painters and Glaziers; "The Killing of the Innocents," by the Mercers; besides other plays with the following titles:—"The Temptation," "The Last Supper," "The Descent into Hell," "The Resurrection," "The Ascension," "The Day of Judgment." The titles alone of these plays will suffice to show the great depravity of taste at that period, and it speaks well for London citizens that no trace can be found of the same disregard by them of the sacredness and reverence due to the narratives and doctrines of the sacred book.

Certain writers have endeavoured to shield the monks from censure in regard to their composing these blasphemous works, and it is but fair to them that their apologists should be heard. In the dark period of our history, say they, the merchants and traders throughout England resorted for commerce to the central towns. To secure the presence of large numbers of people, they patronized buffoons and mountebanks, and brought them to the fairs to amuse the crowd. By degree players became organized, companies formed, and dramatic representations of the most debasing and infamous character were introduced. The priests, to save their flock, suppressed these plays, and fearing rebellion against their authority, themselves undertook the task of playing, that they might introduce scriptural stories for their plays. In a word, say these apologists, they hoped to give the people a relish for the Scriptures and a knowledge of their contents. We are free to confess that these arguments are not to our mind quite satisfactory, and no doubt they had more weight when enunciated before the Reformation than they are likely to have in the nineteenth century. Anything more revolting and debasing we cannot conceive. A surer way of training men to become scoffers and infidels we know not, than rendering ridiculous the word of God, and exposing to the gaze of the licentious the most solemn and sacred of the truths of sacred writ.

"To instruct a people you must please them; but unless you instruct them, you cannot please them long."

But to return to our banquet. Whatever the play might be, it had to be performed after the other matters already referred to had been duly executed; and seeing that these venerable citizens were religious men, the play must be a "holy play." From the cost of this entertainment we should not imagine that the scenic representation could have been on a particularly grand scale; nor were the parish clerks, the actors, though usually only four in number, paid exorbitantly. In the Carpenters' books, in the year 1490, the modest charge of 4*s.* 4*d.* only is entered.

"Payd for a play........iiijs. iiij*d.*" *

In order to show relatively the value of that sum, we quote the next entry:—

"A hole schepe save the scholderys, ijs." †

As, therefore, 4*s.* 4*d.* is to 2*s.*, so is a holy play with four players to a whole sheep save the shoulders.

In 1454, the same worthy craft postponed the play till the day after the feast, and we think wisely, for after early mass, then a heavy breakfast with swan and conger, then church and perhaps a sermon, followed by the "processions," "music," "washing," "garlanding," "minstrelling," and "toasting," we do think that a full day's work had been done in

* Jupp, p. 198. † *Ibid.*

the day, and that a limit might fairly be put to "working overtime" by even the most conscientious of carpenters. The item is as follows :—

"1454, 33rd Henry 6.—"Payd for ye play on ye morowe after ye feste day iij*s*. iiij*d*." *

We think even Joseph Hume himself could never have complained of the largeness of this sum for a whole play. If the audience did not exceed a hundred, which is a moderate number to calculate upon being present at a "holy play," surely an entertainment furnished at a cost of less than a halfpenny each must have been cheap for the money.

Many of the companies were occupied three days with their election ceremonies. Herbert extracts from the Drapers' book the account of their proceeding in 1522, which informs us that on Saturday, the feast of the "Assumption of our Lady," after even song was the nomination of the new wardens, with potation in the parlour afterwards. On Sunday, after the solemn mass of our Lady, here dined in the parlour the master and his lady, the four wardens and their wives, our two chaplains, and Richardson and his wife. The fare for the Sunday dinner, besides a cold sirloin of beef that had served for breakfast, consisted of four pair of capons, half a buck (baked), five conies, two swans, five pasties, eighteen pigeons, two geese, two pike, and for a reward two tarts, and afterwards pears and filberts.

* Jupp, p. 213.

The guests "*washed* after dinner standing." For fourteen people the above is not a bad bill of fare.

On Monday, after mass of requiem, "all our aldermen in skarlet" and all the livery came to the hall; all that had served wardens sat at the *high table*, below the aldermen, and all the rest of the livery at the side table on the north side; and at the other side table in the hall "sat our *two chaplains*, and no more at that table." Then followed the crowning with garlands already described, and the "wafers and hippocras." The proceedings at supper are thus specified. At supper the old wardens, their wives, the officers and the wardens' servants, sat at the side table in the hall, and had "swanneys pudding," one neck of mutton in pike broth, two shoulders of mutton roast, four conies, eight chickens, six pigeons, and cold meat plenty, and so departed.

On Tuesday dined again in the parlour the old master and lady, Sir John Brugg, the parson of Michael's, and six others named, with their wives, but this day no supper! (alas!) but fragments among the servants.*

If such a succession of feasting obtained in the Carpenters' Company, we cannot be at all surprised to learn that on one occasion they felt constrained to postpone the "holy play" from the election feast to the morrow.

We have thus very hastily sketched in outline the great mediæval livery feasts, with their numerous

* Vol. i. pp. 442, 444.

forms and ceremonies. We have refrained from reflections upon these usages, nor have we made comparisons between the customs of our ancestors and those of modern times. Our readers will make their own inferences and draw their own comparisons. We think, however, that they will agree, that amidst all the pomps and vanities of the City feasts, there was much of excellence and significance, and that, notwithstanding the many improvements of our time, we may still learn many things from a study of the customs and ceremonies of the decorous and dignified, charitable and jovial, citizens of olden time.

CHAPTER XXI.

THEIR MAIDENS.

> "Nor was there one, of all the nymphs that rov'd
> Amid the maiden throng, more favour'd once."
>
> ADDISON'S *Ovid.*

MENTION is made, in one of our former chapters on the ancient feasts, of a portion of the festive hall called the Maidens' Chamber. In that chamber it was usual, on the great day of the feast, for the damsels to dine with great splendour by themselves. It may be interesting to inquire somewhat respecting these most honoured guests. That the rulers of the gilds paid them great respect is clear from the provision made for their reception and their cheer. It is a very curious fact that no records are extant which make mention of dancing as forming part of the entertainments at these civic feasts. All kinds of amusements seem to have been provided but this. There were singers, players, minstrels, fools, poets, but no dancers. We are at a loss to understand this. Dancing throughout the period referred to we know was a favourite pastime. It was indulged in even to daybreak. Froissart tells us of grand doings in the reign of Richard II., and says, "On the morrow, Tuesday, the tournament was continued. The supper was magnificent as before at the palace of the Bishop of London, near St. Paul's, where the King and Queen lodged, and the *dancing lasted until daybreak*."* "On Wednesday, the tournament again, and the supper and *dancing* as the preceding days." In all the old chronicles we find mention of dancing as closing the day's amusements, but never is any mention to be found among the ancient records of the gilds of the exercise of this accomplishment.

It cannot be that the daughters of the citizens were educated in a degree inferior to those about the Court; we know, indeed, that this was not the case; the citizens were great encouragers of education, and, as the daughters of these rich liverymen frequently became allied to members of the peerage, and were accustomed to meet on public occasions persons of the highest eminence, we doubt not that they were in all respects fitted by education for their position and their wealth.

There appears to be evidence that the maidens, after the feast, adjourned to the hall to witness, with the liverymen and their ladies, the performance of the minstrels and of the holy play, and no doubt their presence was hailed by very many of the brethren as a welcome accession to their ranks. Some of these maidens, we are told, had rather extravagant ideas of what was needed in a household,

* Vol. iv. p. 233.

and we subjoin, for the edification of those who are interested in domestic economy, a letter written by one of the most accomplished of these visitors at the City banquets, the only daughter and heiress of Sir John Spencer, Lord Mayor of London, A.D. 1594, better known by the name of "rich Spencer," as furnishing a curious specimen of the state in which a rich City heiress of the sixteenth century expected to be maintained after her marriage with a branch of the nobility. This fair Eliza Spencer married a descendant of Sir William Compton, a distinguished courtier in the reign of Henry VIII., and became the mother of the future Earls of Northampton, so celebrated during the civil wars, "a worthy mother of a noble race."

"My Sweete Life,—

"Now I have declared to you my mind for the settling of your state, I supposed that it were best for me to bethink, or consider with myself, what allowance were meetest for me. For, considering what care I ever had of your estate, and how respectfully I dealt with those, which, by the laws of God, of nature, and civil polity, wit, religion, government, and honesty, you, my dear, are bound to, I pray and beseech you to grant to me, your most kind and loving wife, the sum of £1600 per annum, quarterly to be paid.

"Also, I would (besides the allowance for my apparel) have £600 added yearly (quarterly to be paid) for the performance of charitable works, and those I would not, neither will be accountable for.

"Also, I will have three horses for my own saddle, that none shall dare to lend or borrow; none lend but I; none borrow but you.

"Also, I would have two gentlewomen, lest one should be sick, or have some other lett. Also, I believe that it is an indecent thing for a gentlewoman to stand mumping alone, when God hath blessed their lord and lady with a great estate.

"Also, when I ride a hunting, or hawking, or travel from one house to another, I will have them attending; so, for either of these said women, I must and will have for either of them a horse.

"Also, I will have six or eight gentlemen; and I will have my two coaches—one lined with velvet to myself, with four very fair horses, and a coach for my women, lined with cloth; one laced with gold, the other with scarlet, and laced with watch-lace and silver, with four good horses.

"Also, I will have two coachmen; one for my own coach, the other for my women's.

Also, at any time when I travel, I will be allowed, not only carriages and spare horses for me and my women, but I will have such carriages as shall be fitting for all, or duly; not pestering my things with my women's, nor theirs with chambermaids', or theirs with washmaids'.

"Also, for laundresses, when I travel, I will have them sent away with the carriages, to see all safe; and the chambermaids I will have go before with the grooms, that the chambers may be ready, sweet, and clean.

"Also, for that it is indecent to crowd up myself with my gentleman usher in my coach, I will have him to have a convenient horse to attend me either in city or country; and I must have two footmen; and my desire is, that you defray all the charges for me.

"And, for myself (besides my yearly allowance), I would have twenty gowns of apparel; six of them excellent good ones, eight of them for the country, and six others of them very excellent good ones.

"Also, I would have put into my purse £2000 and £200, and so you to pay my debts.

"Also, I would have £6000 to buy me jewels, and £4000 to buy me a pearl chain.

"Now, seeing I have been and am so reasonable unto you, I pray you do find my children apparel, and their schooling; and all my servants, men and women, their wages.

"Also, I will have all my houses furnished, and all my lodging-chambers to be suited with all such furniture as is fit; as beds, stools, chairs, suitable cushions, carpets, silver warming-pans, cupboards of plate, fair hangings, and such like. So, for my drawing chamber, in all houses, I will have them delicately furnished, both with hangings, couch, canopy, glass, chairs, cushions, and all things thereunto belonging.

"Also, my desire is, that you would pay your debts, build Ashby House, and purchase lands, and lend no money (as you love God) to the lord chamberlain, which would have all, perhaps your life, from you. Remember his son, my Lord Waldon, what entertainment he gave me when you were at Tilt Yard. If you were dead, he said he would marry me. I protest, I grieve to see the poor man have so little wit and honesty to use his friends so vilely. Also, he fed me with untruths concerning the Charter House; but that is the least: he wished me much harm; you know him. God keep you and me from him, and such as he is.

"So, now that I have declared to you what I would have, and what that is I would not have, I pray, when you be an earl, to allow me £1000 more than now desired, and double attendance.

"Your loving wife,

"ELIZA COMPTON."

This letter, for the period at which it was written, displays great literary excellence, and considerable ability on the part of the fair writer. Considering her vast wealth, her requirements are but reasonable, and evidence taste and refinement in their selection. We know little of the history of this accomplished dame, but we think, from what we learn from this epistle to her lord and master, that she was one worthy to be the bride of a prince; and from it we gain a little insight into the kind of education and the tone of mind prevailing in the sixteenth century amongst the damsels of the higher class of City merchants, or, as we would now term them, the "girls of the period."

The father of this lady was interred, A.D. 1609, in St. Helen's Church, Bishopsgate, by the side of Sir John Crosby, Sir Thomas Gresham, and other civic worthies, whose descendants to this day pay reverence to the ashes of their ancestors, as may be seen from the following announcement recently made in the London papers:—

"The most noble the Marquis of Northampton has forwarded a donation of £50 on behalf of the St. Helen's Church Restoration Fund, and has also announced his intention of restoring, by the aid of an old drawing in his possession, the noble monument of his ancestor, Sir John Spencer, situated in the chapel of the B. V. Mary, and which, during the last century, was reduced to a uniform white by the injudicious treatment, known as 'beautifying.' Mr. G. L. Gower, M.P., the lineal descendant of Sir T. Gresham, has also promised the sum of £25. Some few weeks back, the Gresham Committee assembled in the church to inspect the new window erected at their cost, when Mr. Gower exhibited the nuptial ring of Sir Thomas Gresham."

Peace be to their ashes!

We may add that the father of the fair Eliza, Sir John Spencer, was possessed of a country mansion at Canonbury, from which place the second Lord Compton, Lord President of Wales in the year 1594, carried her away,—it is said hidden in a basket which usually contained the family's bread. Sir John was greatly enraged at her elopement, and renounced her. Queen Elizabeth, however, upon the birth of the heir to the Compton estates, desiring that so vast a fortune should not be diverted from its proper channel, offered to stand sponsor to the child, and requested Sir John to unite with her in the duties, informing him that the parents were very happy in each other's love, but that the lady's father had discarded her for marrying without his consent. Sir John was pleased to act, and told the Queen that, having renounced his own daughter, he would adopt this his god-child for his heir. At the ceremony, the Queen, to his surprise, presented to him his own daughter as the happy mother, and effected thus a reconciliation. The child had the name of Spencer given as his Christian name, and lived to inherit the Compton and Spencer estates, his father, August 2, 1618, having been created Earl of Northampton. The letter from the daughter of Sir John Spencer to Lord Compton, her husband, was first printed in the "European Magazine" for June, 1782. The Lord Chamberlain she names was Thomas, Earl of Suffolk, appointed treasurer, July 10th, 1613. His son, who had so greatly offended her, was Theophilus, Lord Howard of Walden, who succeeded his father as Earl of Suffolk, May 28th, 1626.*

As recently as the reign of George I., a lady of the Princess's bed-chamber thus writes, under date October, 1715:—"I was now at Kensington, where I intended to stay as long as the camp was in Hyde Park, the roads being so secure that one might come from London any time of the night without danger."† We wish we could say that our roads in and about London were equally safe, and free from footpads and garotters, in our own times. They might be worse, however, as may be seen from the following extraordinary passage, showing the wildness of the times, which occurs in a rare little work, entitled "The Vanity of the Lives and Passions of Men," by D. Papillon, Gent.:—"In Queen Elizabeth's time, a pirate of Dunkerk laid a plot, with twelve of his mates, to carry away Sir John Spencer, which, if he had done, £50,000 had not redeemed him. They came over the sea, left their bark in the river, six of

* Nichol's "History of Canonbury."

† "Diary of Countess Cowper," p. 49. London, 1864.

them went to Canonbury to lie in wait for the rich citizen as he returns home at night, but, by the providence of God, he stayed the night in the city at his town mansion, Crosby Place (formerly the residence of the Duke of Gloucester, afterwards Richard III.), or assuredly he would have been carried away prisoner." This wealthy merchant was Sheriff of London A.D. 1583. In the records of the parish of St. Helen's, Bishopsgate, it appears that the family vault in which Sir John was interred became forfeited to the parish, "the Earl of Northampton refusing to repair it." The family, it would seem, afterwards satisfied the parish, and in 1727 the marriage register bears the inscription :—"Married Aug. 13th, the Honourable Charles Compton to Mrs. Mary Lucy."

In Strype's "Stow" is an epitaph on Baptist Hickes, Viscount Campden (referred to at page 6), said to be from the pen of one of his daughters, and although much admired in its day, modern readers will, perhaps, not hesitate to give the palm for literary merit to the prose composition of the fair Eliza Compton :—

"IN MEMORY OF BAPTIST LORD HICKES, VISCOUNT CAMPDEN.

"Reader, know,
Whoe'er ye be,
Here lies faith, hope,
And charitie.

"Faith true, hope firm,
Charity free,
Baptist Lord Campden
Was these three.

"Faith in God,
Charity as a brother,
Hope for himself,
What ought he other?

"Faith is no more,
Charity is crowned,
'Tis only hope
Is underground."

When Scotland's ablest poets, in paraphrasing the Book of Psalms for use in their churches, could indite such lines as the following—

"The finny monsters of the deep
Their Maker's praises shout,
And codlings of the sandbank leap,
And wag their tails about,"—

it cannot be considered surprising that verses so musical and pious as those we quote from the pen of the City heiress, although not quite up to the modern standard of excellence, should have found admirers two centuries and a half ago.

We do not instance the two ladies just referred to as specimens of the average literary ability of the City ladies; but considering how many of England's nobles selected their wives from amongst their number, we can entertain no doubt that the City maidens were then, as now, not undistinguished by all feminine excellences and graces. That their presence at the assemblages of the gilds formed a great attraction to the other sex there can be no doubt, nor that much of the success of their banquets was due to the same cause.

Not only were they admitted to the feasts, but, as we have shown, the privilege of membership was granted them, some of the queens, and even a queen regnant (Elizabeth), having taken upon themselves "the liverie of companie." It is much to be regretted that in some few of the gilds the female element has been displaced, and at the festive board the ladies are conspicuous by their absence. We are informed that an attempt has been recently made in the Court of the Worshipful the Leathersellers' Company to restore to the livery the privilege granted to them by royal charter—but abrogated during the civil wars—of bringing a lady to the election banquet; which attempt, however, was not successful. We are pleased to learn that a truly antiquarian spirit has long displayed itself amongst many of the gilds, and we doubt not that this praiseworthy effort, although for the present unsuccessful, will very shortly be triumphant, and that whoever may have to describe their future banquets will find the brightest pages those descriptive of the fair maidens which shall grace even the Leathersellers' festivals.

It is a noteworthy fact that, although we frequently meet with mention in the records of charges made against the "members of the clothing" of "unhandsome, unseemly, and naughty words," used by one against another; sometimes of quarrels; and even of a brother knocking down the beadle through "hytting hym on the hedde with a pewter potte;" yet, and it speaks much for the civilizing influence of the presence of the ladies, in no one instance can we discover any such ill conduct to have been committed in their presence; nor does a most diligent scrutiny of the companies' minutes afford even a shadow of a charge of impropriety or misbehaviour on the part of any one of the fair "maydens of the lyverie." Women, no doubt, had in the early days their detractors, as now; but that the large majority of the members of the crafts felt it to be a great privilege to bring a lady to the banquets, and that many happy marriages were thus brought about, there can be little room for doubt. Cynics then, as now, were to be found who spoke bitterly of marriage, as Sir John, the father of Sir Thomas More, who likened marriage to one "taking a dip into a bag containing twenty snakes and one eel, the chances were twenty to one he caught not the eel." Notwithstanding the odds, the worthy knight himself ventured to take three dips; so in the Ashmole library is a manuscript containing the following stanza:—

> "Marriage, saith one, hath oft compared bin
> Unto a feast, where meet a public rout,
> Where those that are without would fain get in,
> And those that are within would fain get out."

After a careful consideration of this matter, we unhesitatingly give our vote and interest in favour of the presence at certain of the banquets, as in the olden time, of the "maidens of the livery."

We think it greatly to the credit of those of the City gilds which have maintained, from ancient times, the laudable custom of inviting the ladies to their banquets, and we rejoice to learn that efforts are being made in some others of them to revive this excellent custom. No public dinner of our day is so popular and agreeable as that of the Dramatic Sick Fund Association, and entirely on account of this humanizing custom of introducing ladies, not as spectators, but as guests at the table. Surely no man is such a fool as seriously to hold with the poet who could not bear to see a woman eat. The good things of life are as welcome to them as to us, nor would we wish them to look upon such things as if they lived in a nunnery, and as if eating and drinking were a sin. The ladies of the present day are as qualified as the men to judge of the qualities of the ingredients of the feast, and if good-fellowship be the main consideration, they add to it tone and life. Some years ago, no doubt, many men objected to the presence of the ladies, fearing to exhibit themselves before them "in their cups." But times are now so thoroughly changed, that such an exhibition is not probable. Others, who loved a coarse jest or vulgar oath, would rather the ladies were absent. A gentleman now uses neither the one nor the other in good society, so this can be no longer a reason for the exclusion of women. Of course, women are very properly more exclusive than men in their acquaintanceship, and some of them might hesitate to meet at dinner with neighbours whom they did not wish to know. This hesitancy need not exist, for without a special introduction, which must be by mutual consent, no acquaintanceship can be claimed by any one, either man or woman, merely upon the plea of sitting at the same public dinner, any more than at the same *table d'hôte.* Many ladies, no doubt, would regard the revival of this privilege as a very questionable advantage, and by no means worth the trouble of dressing for; but, as it has been well replied, they should at least have the choice, and if one will not accept the invitation another will.

CHAPTER XXII.

THEIR HOLIDAYS.

"All work and no play
Makes Jack a dull boy."—Old Proverb.

In few things did our ancestors, and especially the ancient citizens, display their good sense more than in the provision they made for the recreation of all classes. There was something fatherly in the treatment which the poor received at the hands of the rich in respect to their amusements which were most liberally and considerately provided for them. The present day presents a sad contrast to the past in the matter of public holidays, and frequent periodical games and pastimes. In our time the rural districts are utterly unprovided with healthful amusements under the sanction of authority. In the early ages the tilts, and tournaments, and jousts were open to all spectators, and afforded intense excitement to those classes whose avocations are of so thoroughly monotonous a character, that in the absence of some such pastime they are now driven to seek for stimulants either at the alehouse, or the camp meeting, or revival.

We do not say that we would advocate a return

exactly to the dangerous and cruel pastimes of our ancestors, either the tournament, or cock-fighting, or bull-baiting. But the grand distinguishing feature of their holiday festivals we would call back, namely, the presence of the great proprietors, and the nobility, and even of the monarchs, to unite with the common people in their festivities, and thus add a charm to that which all should be anxious to make as jubilant and national as possible. One almost sickens at the recollections of the only recreation which we in the East Riding provide for our labouring population in this nineteenth century; the series of daily and nightly orgies; the youth of both sexes brought together without restraint, without oversight, to spend the Martinmas week in revelling and licentiousness. Had society entered into a conspiracy to debase and brutalize the labouring people, no scheme could by possibility have been devised by which so thoroughly and entirely they could have succeeded in training the youth to immorality, and in depriving woman of every vestige of shame or of virtue. The Martinmas hirings are the hot-beds, the forcing-houses, of vice and debauchery.

All classes require occasional cessation from toil. But this is not sufficient: they require stimulating recreations as well as rest. Some of the religious sects in our country appear to be the only people who understand how necessary excitement is to working people, and, as they cannot provide for them healthy games or sports, they have invented expedients of a most curious character—some original inventions, others borrowed from the customs and rites of heathenism. Next to the hirings we would class camp-meetings and revival prayer-meetings in the list of unwholesome and vicious recreations of our day, which have taken the place of those less unwholesome pastimes which our forefathers so liberally and judiciously instituted. We owe it to the mistaken Puritans that many exercises were displaced and national sports abolished. We think the change is for the worse. Not many weeks ago, at Derby, immense placards announced that a sermon was to be preached by the *infant Samuel and his father and mother!* How all three could preach one sermon we cannot imagine; probably the infant Samuel—who, if we remember rightly, was only six years old—would take the leading part, while his father and mother would be satisfied with "expounding." The idea of this triune preacher is not original. It is borrowed from the old American tale of the deacon who was so great a saint that when he died it took two men and a boy to preach his funeral sermon. The Derby people, we heard, flocked in multitudes to listen to this wonderful sermon; and, if society provides no wholesome recreation for the working classes, who can be surprised if infant Samuels arise to amuse a people who must be amused well or ill?

The late exhibition at York afforded a practical illustration of the value of intellectual occupations in drawing people away from less harmless employments. The manager of one of the principal dramshops in York complained bitterly to the writer that, although many strangers who visited the exhibition came to his shop in the daytime, he had lost all his regular evening customers, who now gave to the works of art and music the time which formerly they spent in his parlour.

We all need seasons of vacation and of recreation. The Mosaic dispensation sanctioned these seasons and made them religious institutions. The Pagan festivals were, no doubt, borrowed from the Mosaic. The Romish system observes many festivals, and enforces many days of cessation from toil. When the reformers removed numerous Popish corruptions, they accomplished a great work, but it is a question whether they might not have retained and enforced the observance of many days for holiday and worship, and thus have given a religious sanction to the recreation of the people from which we are at present debarred.

The ancient citizens were great patrons of public games. The May games which they celebrated with so much pomp, acquired an European celebrity. People from other lands visited London in the days of Bluff King Hal to attend him and his good Queen Catherine of Arragon as far as Shooter's Hill, where the great Lord Mayor and his grave brethren of the livery were accustomed to make a pilgrimage to gather May for the due observance of the festivities. It was the union of classes in those rollicking days which gave the charm to the holiday. How happily did the day pass off—how merry was the dance, when the squire and his lady joined in the sport, and even the monarch deigned to dance on the village green.

In the early days our great Christian festivals were observed as national holidays, and the gilds were the foremost in their religious and festival celebrations. Christmas was an universal holiday; Easter equally joyous; and Whitsuntide not less jubilant than either. The dauphin in Shakespeare's "Henry V.," refers to this gay season in which all England was engrossed with these games:—

> "No, with no more than if we heard that England
> Were busied with a Whitsun morris dance."

The London pageants of Easter were peculiarly grand and costly; they, with the excesses and vulgarities of Greenwich fair, have now passed away, but Easter Monday is still celebrated by the Lord Mayor with one of his most splendid banquets, and the "Spital" sermon is still annually preached to his lordship and the Court of Aldermen.

The Norman and Plantagenet kings kept Whitsuntide with special pomp in tourneys and tilts and games of prowess; like King Arthur who "would not go to meat in the time of Pentecost until he had heard or seen some great adventure or marvel." It was on the first four days of Whitsun week that the Chester miracle plays were acted by the gilds, to which reference was made in a former chapter.

The Londoners appear to have been ever the foremost in providing costly holidays and recreations for the people, and eagerly took advantage of all royal entries into their city for this purpose. The entry of Richard I. after his captivity was observed with unusual splendour. When Edward returned from the Holy Land, the very walls of the houses were hung with silks and tapestries; the conduits, we are told by Holinshed, ran with rich wines, and the members of the liveries threw gold and silver among the people. Still more magnificent were the preparations made after the battle of Poictiers, when John, King of France, with his chivalric conqueror Edward, the Black Prince, were marshalled through the City in a procession so numerous as to last from three in the morning till noon. When Richard II. twice entered the City, the citizens vied with each other in the costliness and splendour of their costumes, and thus gorgeously attired lined the streets through which he passed, observing the occasions as universal holidays. The conduits ran with wine, pageants were provided, castles curiously wrought were erected, a boy to imitate an angel presented the king with a gorgeous crown set in jewels, and the like to the queen, while four fair virgins scattered gold leaves upon the king's head. Similar displays took place in the reign of Henry V., upon a scale of equal magnificence, very splendid tapestry work, upon which had been embroidered the exploits of the king in France, being suspended from the houses. Each succeeding reign vied in these costly spectacles; but in that of Henry VIII. the profusion of expense rose to such a height as to be almost beyond belief, did we not know the immense wealth of individual citizens, and the pretentious spirit of that age of display.

One of the most pompous displays of this reign occurred on the occasion of mustering the Midsummer watch when the king and queen (Catherine of Arragon) "came roially riding to the signe of the 'King's Head,' in Cheape, and there beheld the watch of the Citie, which watch was set out with divers goodly shewes, as had been accustomed." We are told that not less than two thousand men, on foot and on stately chargers, all equipped in costly fashion, with minstrels, pages, dancers, musicians, and wonderful pageants, formed the procession. On a noble charger richly caparisoned and attended by a numerous cavalcade of servants, knights, and esquires, together with the sheriffs, rode the great Lord Mayor. Stow is quite eloquent in descanting upon this watch. He says, in 1510, on St. John's Eve, Henry VIII. came into the City to witness and increase the pomp of the City March, to set the watch, repeated on St. Peter's Eve, when he was again present. The march commenced with music; then came the City officers, in particoloured liveries. The sword-bearer, in armour, mounted, went before the Lord Mayor, on a noble charger, attended by a giant and two pages, three pageants, and a company of morris-dancers. The sheriffs, too, had their giants, morris-men; then followed a body of demi-lancers, in bright armour, on stately horses, a company of carabineers, in white fustian, the City arms embroidered on their tabards, back and front. Then a division of archers, with bows and arrows at their sides, pikemen with corslets and helmets, and halberdiers, also in armour, the whole march being closed by a troop of billmen, helmed, and wearing aprons of steel. This nocturnal display was illuminated by fiery cressets carried on men's shoulders. The procession passed through Cheapside, Cornhill, and Leadenhall Street, to Aldgate, and thence by Fenchurch Street and Grasschurch, back to the conduit at Cornhill. Every house in the line of march was adorned with greens and flowers, wrought into garlands, and intermixed with innumerable lamps.

That the preparations made for the setting of the watch were somewhat elaborate may be judged from an entry in the Drapers' books, where in 1520 is the following entry of an agreement made with William Whyting, "payn tour steynowe," to make substantially and well 12 new banneretts of double blue sarsynet in oyle, every bannerett to contain in length besides the fringe 3½ yards and 1¼ nail, and in breadth three-quarters of a yard, besides the buckram and fringe, and he to make them in fine gold for £4 16*s*. In 1521, they resolved to have no Midsummer pageant, but to send 30 men in harness instead. But, notwithstanding, the items occur of "yellow cotton towards the dresses of the archers and minstrels; 5*s*. to John Wakelyn for playing the King of the Moors (the company finding him his apparel, his stage, and his wild fire), and sums for the said king's girdle, his garland or turban of white feathers and black satin, and sylver paper for his shoes," etc. In 1523, the amount is somewhat enlarged by the additional entry of "the hire of the Giant of Barking." Who this giant was, history informs us not. Probably he was not an historic character, but a figure of pasteboard, of which we know many have existed.

In Strutt's "Sports and Pastimes" are many particulars respecting the setting out of the Midsummer watch at Chester in 1564—borrowed, no doubt, from the London programme—in which we are informed that "the pageant, according to ancient custom, should consist of four giants, one unicorn, one dromedary, one lucern,* one camel, one ass? (query, only one?) one dragon, six hobby-horses, and sixteen naked boys." On the revival of the custom at the restoration of Charles II., he mentions a calculation of costs for getting up the same, all things being required new ("by reason the ould modells were all broken"). The giants, he computes, if well made and comely, could not be produced under *five pounds a giant!* and four men to carry them would add to the expense, two shillings and sixpence each!

So costly, at length, became these spectacles that Henry VIII. prohibited their continuance; but the citizens found other means of displaying their prodigious wealth and their love of recreation; especially when a monarch visited their City was the occasion

* Probably, a bear from Lucerne.

seized upon as an excuse for an universal holiday. The pageants of the great Midsummer-night watch, however, held on the Eve of St. John, or Midsummer's Eve, so great a favourite with the citizens, though put down by Henry VIII., was soon again revived, and was not finally abolished until 1569. We think that the great prosperity of these City merchants is evidence sufficient to show that success in business does not necessarily imply a state of slavery to its pursuits, but that a fair share of pleasure and relaxation from toil is a surer way to wealth and happiness than uninterrupted application and toil which must tend to make life a weariness and to shorten its duration. In this age of industry and labour let us take a lesson from the past and make some better provision for this great want of the labouring people.

CHAPTER XXIII.

THEIR HOLIDAYS, CONTINUED.

THEIR MAYINGS.

"You must wake and call me early, call me early, mother dear,
To-morrow 'll be the happiest time of all the glad new year;
Of all the glad new year, mother, the maddest, merriest day;
For I'm to be Queen o' the May, mother, I'm to be Queen o' the
May."
TENNYSON.

MANY of the public holidays of the ancient Romans originated in their religious ceremonies. In this respect the religion of the ancient Britons and the pagan Romans was very similar. Indeed, there can be little doubt that from the latter the Druids borrowed much of their ceremonial. Both worshipped the same gods under different denominations, and very nearly accorded in the manner of their sacrifices.

Belin, the British name for Apollo, was a favourite deity with the Britons, and the ancient temple once standing in his honour near London Bridge gave rise to the present name of Billingsgate, or, as it was formerly called, Belinsgate. The very learned John Bagford informs us that a custom existed till of late years for the porters who plied at Belinsgate, to entreat civilly every man that passed that way to salute a post that stood there in a vacant place. If he refused, they compelled him by force, but if he quietly submitted to kiss the same, and paid 6*d.*, then they gave him a name, and chose some one of the gang for his godfather. "I believe this was done," he adds, "in memory of some old image that formerly stood there, perhaps of Belin."* This author very ably demonstrates that the religion of the ancient Britons and the pagan Romans was in many respects alike; that Luna (another name for Diana, and from which he thinks the word London is derived), and her brother Apollo, under the name of Belin, were two chief deities amongst the Britons as well as amongst the Romans. Fosbroke, an equally high authority in matters antiquarian, is of the same opinion. He shows how much we owe to the Romans in respect also of our national sports and holidays. In descanting upon the May games, so popular in this country until the seventeenth century, he suggests, that as Claudius instituted the Maiuma, celebrated with such splendour at Ostia, and grafted them upon the Floralia, and which games were suppressed by Constantine for their licentiousness, but were afterwards re-established by Acadius and Honorius; so our nation adopted the Maiuma under the familiar title of May games, and in imitation of the goddess of Ovid, they selected the most beautiful maiden as the Queen of the May, whom, after the olden model, they decorated with ribbons and crowned with chaplets of a thousand flowers. "*Mille venit variis florum Dea nexa coronis.*" Tennyson has many pretty allusions

* Leland's "Collectanea," A.D. 1714.

to the rustic ceremony of gathering the may, and the flowers, and he even makes the May Queen herself to join in this preliminary pastime.

> "I sleep so sound all night, mother, that I shall never wake,
> If you do not call me loud when the day begins to break;
> But I must gather knots of flowers, and buds and garlands gay,
> For I'm to be Queen o' the May, mother, I'm to be Queen o' the May."

The same poet, in his "King Arthur," describes the King, Queen, and the Knights of the Round Table, with the ladies of the court, all going forth a-maying:—

> "For thus it chanced one morn when all the Court,
> Green-suited, but with plumes that mock'd the may,
> Had been, their wont, a-maying, and returned."

In the reign of Henry VIII., as we have shown, vast cost was expended upon these national games, in which the king and queen and court joined the citizens of London in celebrating them with great pomp. On May-day all the citizens went forth to the woods and meadows to divert themselves. Edward Hall, the quaint old chronicler, tells how King Henry, in the seventh year of his reign, on May-day morning, with Queen Catherine, and many lords and ladies, rode a-maying from Greenwich to Shooter's Hill, where, as they passed, they saw a company of tall yeomen all in green, with green hoods, bows, and arrows; their chieftain was called Robin Hood, who desired the king to stay and see his merry men shoot. The king consented, and Robin Hood whistling, all his two hundred archers shot off. The shafts were so contrived in the heads that they whistled when discharged, so that the strange loud noise greatly delighted the royal company. Moreover, Robin bade the king and queen to enter the woods, where in arbours of boughs, decked with flowers, they were served plentifully with venison and wine to their great content. But probably the reign of Queen Elizabeth witnessed the May games at their highest point of extravagance and profusion. The various City companies record the large expenses incurred by them in furthering the preparations of these spectacles. The Ironmongers' books, A.D. 1559, inform us, that by the queen's order they "sent men in armour to the May game that went before the queen's majesty to Greenwich;" and in April of the year following, it was ordered by the court that, in obedience to the Lord Mayor's precept, "twenty-eight hansome men, well and hansomely arrayed, and ten whifflers (fifers) should go with them to feaching the queen's majesty," to be furnished with two new streamers of silk, a great flag, and twelve small banners.

In 1571, the Merchant Taylors furnished no fewer than 187 men in military costume as their share towards providing another spectacle at the May games. In the following year a precept was received, demanding "a company of 188 men of the mystery, 94 of whom were to be supplied with corslets and pikes, 36 with corslets and halberds, and 58 with kalivers and morryens for a shew." The books of the several companies bear similar entries, and show that these "mayings" were celebrated annually, and with royal profusion of expense.

Several sites in London were set apart for the erection of the May-pole, and Pennant, in writing as recently as A.D. 1790, observes, that "in the beginning of the present century, somewhat east of the site of the Cross,* was the rural appearance of a May-pole." In 1717 it fell to decay, and the remainder was begged by Sir Isaac Newton, who conveyed it to Wanstead, in Essex, where it was erected in the park, and, says Pennant, had the honour of raising the greatest telescope then known. By its place rose the first of the fifty new churches, which is known by the name of the *New Church in the Strand.* The first stone was laid in 1714, the architect being Gibbs, of some repute in his day. Malcolm, in his account of the games and pastimes of the English in the olden time, mentions the universal popularity of the mayings, and states that the grand and wealthy resort to Hyde Park, while the next in order throng to Gray's Inn.

Another celebrated spot was in the City, in which a very notable May-pole stood in Leadenhall Street, near Aldgate, by the church of *St. Andrew Undershaft.* The church has ever borne this name to the present day, and to the fact of the May-pole or shaft being erected near to it is owing this curious addition of *undershaft.* The glory of this shaft ceased at the period of what is termed the "*evil*

* Opposite *Chester Inn* in the Strand. Pennant, p. 155.

May-day," the occasion of a great riot, chiefly originating with the City apprentices. It appears from Stow and other chroniclers, that, in 1517, a quarrel arose between the London workmen and the foreigners, between whom great jealousy existed, and the May-day was chosen for the trial of strength. The apprentices as usual mustered in great numbers, and it required considerable force to put an end to the riot. No fewer than three hundred of them were sent to the Tower, many of whom were lads of thirteen and fourteen years of age. Sentence of death was passed upon many of them, and on the 4th of May eleven pairs of gallows were set up in divers places where the offences were done, set on wheels, to be removed from street to street, and from door to door, whereat the prisoners were to be executed. After all these preparations, it was rather disappointing to the sightseers that only one culprit was put to death. All the rest, on the 13th of May, were brought to Westminster before the King, "every one with a halter about his neck," but at the intercession of three queens, Catherine of Arragon, Mary Queen of France, and Margaret Queen of Scots, the King's sisters, who were in London, they were all pardoned.

Pennant ascribes this insurrection to the May-pole at St. Andrew Undershaft. He means probably that it was near to it that the riot occurred. He informs us, moreover, that from that day the May-pole was hung on a range of hooks over the doors of a long row of neighbouring houses. In a word, we suppose that inasmuch as the authorities, deeming a large crowd of youths in so densely populated a street dangerous to the peace, abolished the games in that locality; but so popular was the pastime that the shaft was preserved almost as a sacred relic, and the day henceforth, which deprived the people of their holiday, was called the "Evil May-day." The poor harmless log remained in peace for many years in its safe abode, until, in the third year of Edward VI., a fanatic, Sir Stephen, curate of the adjoining parish, preached against it as an idol, and so inflamed his audience that the owners of the several houses over which the shaft hung, with the assistance of others, sawed off as much of it as hung over their own premises; "each took his share and committed to the flames the tremendous idol."*

In 1522, the Goldsmiths' records have the following entry:—"That no man of the felishipp shall go forth on May-day, or suffer their servants to go a maying." This, be it noted, was five years after the "Evil May-day," showing that, although the particular mayings in the neighbourhood of Aldgate had been discontinued, the custom still prevailed in other parts of the City. There can be no doubt that sometimes great danger has arisen to the State in troublous times from vast aggregations of people at these games. It is true they have sometimes been made use of as an excuse for the assemblage of large multitudes for political purposes, and the

* Pennant, p. 431.

rulers of the nation have had to be well on their guard when treasonable measures were suspected. Bacon, in narrating Perkin Warbeck's insurrection, A.D. 1493, records an instance of the shrewdness of the King (Henry VII.), who, "though he seemed to account of the designs of Perkin but as a May-game, yet had given orders for the watching of beacons upon the coasts."

The May-games, though in process of time abolished, gave place to other holidays not less boisterous, and the May-fair which took their place, kept about the spot now occupied by the May-fair chapel and neighbourhood, was attended with such disorders, riots, thefts, and even murders, that in 1708 it was prevented by the magistrates; and although again revived for a time, had to yield at length to the inroads of bricks and mortar which now possess the whole locality.

We must not forget that our ancestors were a simple and childlike race in respect of their amusements. Even as late as the reign of Charles II., Pepys tells us that going through the royal chambers at Whitehall one day, he found the Duke of York, afterwards King James II., with his first Duchess (Anne Hyde) and the great ladies of the Court, sitting on the floor playing at honey-pots. The decorous and dignified serjeants-at-law even could romp and sport at their grand entertainments like so many children. In a curious and amusing work, entitled "Origines juridiciales," giving a description of the hospitable manner in which

Christmas was kept in the sixteenth century, especially minute is the account of a great feast given by the serjeants in the hall of the Inner Temple, in 1555, when the notable sport of hunting the fox and the cat round the old hall with ten couples of hounds, and all the other merry disports of those joyous days, occupied the evening.

With such examples, then, before them, we cannot be surprised if, in process of time, irregularities occurred at the mayings, the favourite pastimes of the whole nation. No doubt the advantages conferred were not unalloyed, and when at length the squire and the landlord, with their families, absented themselves, the chief charm had vanished, and the games were given up to misrule and boisterous conviviality. If instead of abolishing them, however, they could have been reformed, it would have been better for us all; for out-of-door amusements for the people, when well and wisely directed, are the most efficacious instruments in fostering health, happiness, and contentment, and become the finest preventives and antidotes in the world to those unhealthy and much to be deprecated political gatherings, called together by selfish and unprincipled demagogues, those pests and curses of the present day, who, for their own wicked ends, hesitate not to delude their poor ignorant followers, and instil into their minds the venom of discontentment with their lot in life, and disloyalty to the country of their birth.

CHAPTER XXIV.

THEIR HOLIDAYS, CONTINUED.

THE ROYAL PROCESSIONS.

"A prentis whilom dwelt in our citie,
And of a craft of vitaillers was he;
At every bridale would he sing and hoppe;
He loved bet the taverne than the shoppe.
For whan ther any riding was in chepe,
Out of the shoppe thider wold he lepe,
And til that he had all the sight ysein,
And danced wel, he wold not come agein;
And gadred him a meinie of his sort,
To hoppe and sing, and maken swiche disport."

CHAUCER—*The Coke's Tale.*

THE intention of the London citizens in making such costly preparations for all royal processions which passed near their limits, and which were designated "ridings," as those concerned were chiefly mounted on horseback, was undoubtedly to secure an universal holiday. Chaucer therefore is unduly severe upon the race of apprentices, who loved to be present at these "ridings," and who refused to return to their shops "til that they had all the sight ysein." This was the intention of their masters, all the principal of whom themselves were engaged in taking part in the pageant, and the entire trade and labour of the metropolis being suspended for the day. In the present chapter we purpose briefly describing these "ridings against (or in company of) the king," occupying as they did so prominent a place amongst the great holidays of the London gilds.

In the reign of Henry III., on the occasion of the marriage of that monarch, A.D. 1236, and again on the marriage of his daughter, 1252, the citizens were called upon to furnish a large proportion of the royal pageantry; but we cannot learn that the liveries, as such, took part in the display.

The return of Edward I. from his victory over the Scots, A.D., 1298, was the occasion of the first royal triumph we can find on record in which the City gilds took part. Stow mentions that on this occasion "every citizen, according to their several trades, made their several show, but especially the Fishmongers, which in a solemn procession passed through the citie, and having amongst other pageants and shows foure sturgeons gilt carried on foure horses; then foure salmons of silver on foure horses; and after them sixe and fortie armed knightes riding on horses, made like sluces of the sea; and then one representing St. Magnus, because it was on St. Magnus' Day, with a thousand horsemen to complete the triumph." These ancient worthies evidently did not trouble themselves respecting the *unities*, nor can we discover the meaning of all their symbols; and indeed, to be consistent, if the fishes must ride on horseback, we cannot at all conceive why the "sixe and fortie armed knights" should not have been represented as swimming in the sea.

In 1384, 6 Richard II., the Goldsmiths' Company record the particulars of dresses worn by their craft in the procession to meet the new queen, Anne of Bohemia, from which it is evident they must have made a very magnificent appearance, for they "did wear on the red of their dress bars of silver work and powders of trefoils of silver; and each man of the same mystery, to the number of seven score, had upon the black part five knots of gold and silk; and upon their heads hats covered with red and powdered with the said trefoils." The cost of seven minstrels in attendance upon them, and their splendid dresses, is entered at £4 16*s*. 1*d*. They were served with a pageant with three female characters, the whole cost of which, the three minstrels included, amounted to £35 0*s*. 9½*d*.

Froissart describes the coronation procession of Henry IV., in 1399, as very imposing, on account of the splendid appearance of the City companies, led by their wardens, all clothed in their proper liveries, bearing banners of their trades.

Fabian's "Chronicles" narrate the entry of Queen Margaret into London A.D. 1446, who was received on the 28th of May in most goodly wise with all the citizens on horseback in blue gowns and red hoods. The Mayor, Aldermen, and Sheriffs of the City, and the crafts of the same, every mystery or craft with their conysance of their mystery embroidered on their sleeves, and red hoods upon either of their heads, and so she was brought into London, where for her were ordained sumptuous and costly pageants, resembling of divers old histories, to the great comfort of her and such as came with her. This, however, was far surpassed in grandeur by the preparations made upon the return of Henry V. from France in 1415, when, according to Hall, "the Mayre of London and the Senate, apparelled in orient grayned skarlet and three hundred Commoners clad in beautiful murrey,* well mounted and gorgeously horsed, with rich collars and greete chaynes, met the King at Blackeheathe, rejoicing at his victorious returne."

Stow describes the entry of King Henry VI. at Dover on his return from being crowned King of France in 1432, and his reception by the London gilds, as affording a fine opportunity of pageantry and display. On this occasion occurs the first mention of a pageant with an attempt at scenic illustrations with which we have met. The Mayor, John Wells,† a grocer, had prepared a representation of a grove with the foreign fruits in which the grocers traded; and seeing that his name was *Wells*, three wells were placed in the midst, the waters of which, at the King's presence, seemed miraculously changed into wine, like the water at Cana of Galilee. Lydgate has recorded in a long poem the marvels of the whole representation, and describes this grove as an island in which were found

---

* Murrey, crimson.

† Herbert, vol. i. p. 93—4.

"Oranges, almondys, and the pomegranade,
Lymons, dates, there colours fresh and glade
Pypyns, quynces, chandrells to disport,
And the pom cedre, corageous to recomfort;
Quenygges, peches, costardes, and wardens,
And othere manye full faire and freshe to se.
Damasyns, which with there tast delight,
Ful gret plente bothe of blak and white."

No ordinary mortals were allowed to serve at the wells; but the cardinal virtues, Faith, Hope, and Charity, or as they are termed, Mercy, Grace, and Pity, handed forth the wine. These superhuman servitors were well overlooked by the patriarchs Enoch! and Elias! We cannot suppose that the cardinal virtues needed any one from the ghostly world to keep them to their duty; the patriarch and the prophet were brought hither therefore, no doubt, for the purpose of paying a compliment to the King and to present him with some of the delicious fruit, and to pray for his welfare—

"That God conferme his state ay to be stable,
Thus old Ennock, the processe gan well telle,
And praid for the Kyng as he rood by the welle;
After Elias, with his lokkes hore,
Well devoutly seyde, lokyng on the Kyng,
'God conserve the, and kepe the evermore,
And make hym blessyd in erthe here levyng,
And preserve hym in al manere of thyng,
And special among kynges alle,
In enamyes handes that he nevere falle.'"

The prayer certainly is excellent, better than the poetry. But the Muse was young in those early days, and our plain, simple ancestors looked more at the thoughts than at the language; they cared more for the jewel than for the casket.

In 1501 (17 Henry VII.), a gay ceremony took place in London, on the occasion of the entry of the Princess Katharine, of Spain (as she was then designated), when the several City companies, as usual, took the most prominent part. We subjoin a short summary from Stow of her subsequent marriage with Prince Arthur:—Nov. 12, 1501, Lady Princess Catherine of Spain, with many lords and ladies, riding from the "Archbishop's Inne" at Lambeth, came to London Bridge, where was a costly pageant of St. Catherine and St. Ursula, with divers virgins. At Grace Street was a second pageant; and by the Conduit, Cornhill, a third. The great conduite at Chepe ran with Gascoyne wine, and was furnished with musicians. At the Standard and Paul's Gate were two other pageants; and at Soper Lane end a sixth. Now, within the Church of Paul was ordered a standing like unto a mountain, with steps on all sides, covered with red worsted, nigh which was a standing for the King; and on the south stood the Maior and his brethren. Also upon the 14th, upon the said mountain, was Prince Arthur, aged fifteen, and Lady Catherine, about eighteen, both clad in white satin, married by the Archbishop of Canterbury, assisted by nineteen bishops and abbots, all mitred. The King (Henry VII.) beheld the solemnity. Then the spouses, king, and bishops passed from the mountain by a passage, under foote, covered with blue ray cloth, unto the choir. Then followed 100 ladies and gentlemen, in rich apparell; the Maior in crimson, and his brethren in scarlet velvet, and sate in the choir, for mass. Wonderful were the riches worn that day. The poisant chains of gold. Sir T. Brandon's chain was valued at £1400, and William de Rivers, Esq., "Master of the King's Hawkes," had one worth £1000. Some were noted not for the length, but for the size of the links. Also, the Duke of Buckingham wore a gown of wrought needlework, furred with sables, valued at £1500. Sir Nicholas Vane's robe of purple velvet, bright with pieces of gold, cost of the fanciers £1000. Henry, Duke of Yorke, led the bride, with a train of 160 gentlemen. Then Sir Richard Crofts, the Prince's steward, brought the Maior and Aldermen to a great table, set for dinner, where they were served, each with 12 dishes for the first course, 15 at the second, and 18 at the third. In the dining-hall was a cupboard of five stages, triangled and set with plate, valued at £1200, and where the Princess dined was a cupboard of gold plate, garnished with pearles, valued at £2000. The King and Queen abode at Barnard's Castell, and when Sir Nicholas Vane waited upon them, he wore a collar of SS. which weyed, as the goldsmiths affirmed, 800 pound of nobles.

Two years after this gorgeous marriage, A.D. 1503, died at the Tower, universally beloved, Elizabeth of York, consort of Henry VII. Her obsequies were conducted with all the pomp usual in those times, and we refer to the event for the purpose of mentioning one particular circumstance, the effect of which must have been very beautiful. The Lord Mayor and the citizens headed the procession from the Tower to Westminster, and within the City, at every door by which the cavalcade passed, stood a person bearing a lighted torch, the sight of which, in the darkness of night, we are informed, "surpassed description." In Fenchurch Street and Cheapside stood thirty-seven virgins, the number of years of the queen's age, each elegantly apparelled in garments of white, with chaplets of white and green, and bearing lighted tapers. All the parish churches were illuminated, and from Mark Lane to Temple Bar were no less than five thousand torches burning, in addition to a vast number borne by innumerable processions of religious persons from every fraternity, who met the royal corpse, each bearing a cross, and all singing some holy chant.

Dazzling and splendid as all these spectacles must have appeared, there was one individual subject of the king who, in his progresses, far exceeded in magnificence any of the royal processions and pageants. A dignitary of the Church, the ruler of the nation, the great Archbishop of York, Cardinal Wolsey, outvied and surpassed in his equipage and retinue all monarchs before or since. A description is extant of several of his cavalcades, from which we select that on the occasion of his appointment (A.D. 1527) as ambassador to France, when he rode through the City in great pomp, with a numerous train of the prime nobility, gentry, and prelates, forming a company of one thousand horsemen. The cavalcade was led by sixty sumpter horses and mules, eighty baggage-carriages, followed by a great number of gentlemen, three abreast, dressed in velvet, with heavy gold chains round their necks. Then two attendants, each bearing a massive silver cross; two others, each with a tall silver column; two great officers, one carrying the great seal of England, the other the lord cardinal's hat; then rode a gentleman alone, bearing the cardinal's portmanteau of scarlet, richly embroidered. Next the cardinal, gorgeously apparelled, riding on a stately mule, attended by a led horse, and a mule richly trapped with crimson velvet. Then a following of nobility and clergy, all clothed in dark orange-coloured coats, with T.C.—that is, "Thomas, Cardinal," embroidered on each. His own servants that attended were about four hundred in number. His domestic arrangements were on an equally grand scale. He had in his hall, constantly, three tables with three chief officers, a steward, a treasurer, and a comptroller, also a cofferer, being a doctor, three marshals, three yeomen ushers, besides grooms and almoners; also two clerks of the kitchen, a surveyor of the dresser, a clerk of the spicery, in addition to which were two master cooks, and twelve assistants in the kitchen, four yeomen of the scullery, two yeomen of the pastry, with divers other pastelers under the yeomen. In the privy kitchen his chief cook wore velvet and satin, and a chain of gold. He also retained above a hundred other servants constantly, besides sixty clergy in orders, governed by a dean and sub-dean, for his chapel. The chapel furniture was rich, with rich ornaments and inestimable jewels. The attendants at chapel, including the Earl of Derby, numbered over two hundred. His physicians, chaplains, clerks in Chancery, running footmen, heralds, etc., amounted to several hundred persons, all wearing his livery. The great dining-hall at each of his mansions—for he had many, though York House was the most magnificent of them all—was constantly furnished with numerous tables, liberally supplied with every variety of food and abundance of wine, and open to all comers.

We may here pause to consider whether all this love of display was the result of the weakness of a great mind—for no one can doubt the greatness of that proud man—or whether really some deeper motive than the mere love of it led to so much ostentation. We find the same peculiarity in the life of another of the mighty men of England, some centuries earlier, the Archbishop of Canterbury, Thomas à Becket. Before he rose to the primacy, when holding the office of Chancellor of England, and Constable of the Tower, and tutor of the Prince Royal, his household surpassed in feudal splendour that of all the Norman nobility. Seven hundred cavaliers in splendid harness attended him. Their trappings glittered with gold and silver. Nothing could surpass the gorgeousness of his retinue, and he kept open table for all comers. But that he loved not this display is certain, for upon reaching the summit of his ambition, and becoming primate of all England, A.D. 1160, he broke up his vast establishment, dismissed his splendid retinue, no longer appeared in the gorgeous vestments which so well became him, but assumed henceforth the coarse frock of the monk, and selected his companions from among the poor and despised.

It is remarkable that two of England's greatest statesmen were churchmen. Both of humble origin, but possessed of vast mental power, quick to read the characters of those around them, and ready to appease prejudices by a careful study of the public tastes. Becket was a man of loftier character than Wolsey, and devoid of that personal ambition which so marred his character; but to suppose that either of them indulged in all these pomps and vanities for the love of them is to mistake their genius. These were used as means to an end—in an age in which the love of display, and of outward adornings, and of gorgeous cavalcades gay and glittering, was the rage. They, like Queen Elizabeth in later times, yielded to the popular fancy in this respect, and in the display of all this millinery and finery, were merely paying a sort of homage to the public taste, and adopting the only means to secure the end they proposed.

In later times we have seen a stern, inflexible hero rise to greatness by the mere power of the sword and the force of a mighty will; but even he, upon reaching eminence, had to yield his natural inclination to Puritan plainness in costume and equipage, and gratify the public by a display of almost regal magnificence. Who can for a moment imagine that Cromwell felt any satisfaction in the trappings and surroundings of a royal court? If the nation would have borne it, he would gladly have maintained no more state than that observed by an American president; and his great fitness for the office of a ruler of a nation was manifested alike in his foreign relations and in his domestic political rule, especially in his power of thus reading the national mind.

Wolsey was well suited to the office of responsible minister of such a monarch as Harry. Unprincipled and unscrupulous, but bold as a lion. His treatment of the City gilds could hardly be termed mild or courteous, yet he always found the citizens submissive. In 1521, the Drapers' Company rather demurred to a command of the King that they should provide a ship for some foreign enterprise under Sebastian Cabot, and they used many ingenious arguments to show that the scheme was not feasible; but the answer from the Cardinal soon brought them to their senses. Word came "fro' my Lord Cardynall the King would have the premises performed, and would have no nay therein." The ship was soon ready. Nevertheless, they seem to have entertained no ill-will to the great man, for the same year two entries occur in which the names of my Lord Cardinal's grace "and the King's highness" occur on very familiar terms of equality. One is the entry of £22 15*s.* "for 32 yards of crimson satten for my lord Cardinall," and in the second 20 marks are paid him "as a pleasure," so they denominate it, "for his services with the King."

We close this chapter with the entry of Queen Mary, September, 1553, for the purpose of recording the exploits of Peter the Dutchman (who, it would seem, surpassed even Blondin in his audacity), and of showing that the same love of sensational exhibitions, which so greatly disgrace the present age, existed three centuries ago even in a surpassing degree. Great as was his risk, the City was not niggardly in paying the Dutchman for "his costs and paines and all his stuffe." The chronicler narrates that this year (1553), Mary Tudor, the Queen, rode through London to Westminster (to her coronation), sitting in a chariot of tissue, with six horses, all trapped in tissue. She wore a gowne of purple velvet, furred with powdered ermine; on her head was a caul of tussell, rich with pearls and stones, and above a circlet of gold, sown thick with precious gems, in value inestimable, and so heavy that she was fain to support her head with her hand. A canopy was borne over her chariot. Then followed the nobles of the realm, and the Lord Mayor, in a gown of crimson velvet, bearing the sceptre of gold. Sir Edward Hastings led the Queen's horse; after came a chariot, trapped with silver tissue, drawn by six horses, trapped in like manner, wherein sat the Lady Elizabeth and the Lady Anne of Cleves, with many ladies in red velvet on horseback. Forty-six gentlemen rode in this fashion. There were various pageants, and the conduits ran wine. When Mary came to the Little Conduit in Chepe, the Chamberlaine for the City gave a purse containing 1000 marks of gold. Then did one Peter, a Dutchman, stand on the weather-cock of Paule's steeple, waving a long streamer, sometimes standing on one foote, and then kneeling on his knees, to the great "marvel of all people." He also sate on a scaffolde lighted with torches above the crosse. "The said Peter had 16 pounds 13 shillings and 4 pence paide him by the City for his costs and paines and all his stuffe." On the morrow the Queen was solemnly crowned, when the citizens kept the day with all kinds of festivities and rejoicings.

A general notion prevails that, previously to the invention of wheeled carriages, the ladies, as well as the men, always appeared in these grand processions on horseback; but very elegant carriages were sometimes made use of, called "litters," of very costly workmanship, as appears from Leland's description. He informs us that at the coronation of Elizabeth of York "she rode in a litter, the tymbre* work thereof coverde with cloth of golde of damaske, and large pelowes of doune coverde with lik cloth of golde, laide about her moost roiall person to susteyne the same."†

* Not *timber*, but *strong leather*. † "Collectanea," iv. 220.

To be present at these "processions," or "ridings," was not optional with the brethren. The ordinances of nearly all the gilds made it compulsory that all who "were not lawfully let" should answer to the bedell's summons. From "An Act of Mercyment," that is, of amercing or fining, we extract the following:—"It is ordained that whoever shall omit to come in due time, when called by the bedell to the court quarter-day, to ryding against the king, queene, or other lords, with the maire, sheriff, or going on p'cession with the maire, as common course is, at Christmasse and other tymes, congregacion, or any other thynges, that they be warned, to pay the penalty or amercement to the bedell." The fine being "for the kyng, queene, or maire's ryding iijs. iijd., and on other occasions is. or ijs."*

The picturesque appearance of so large a multitude was greatly heightened by the presence of "the merchant strangers," established in London, consisting of the "Geneweuse, Florentines" (Genoese and Venetians), "and Easterlings," † who, dressed in the peculiar costume of their countries, or, as it is stated, "*clad in their manere*," and attended by sergeants and other officers, "statly horsyd," joined in the processions riding after the mayor.

What, then, with kings and queens, lord mayors, sheriffs, men of the livery, all clad in their best "*in their own manere*," the minstrels and marshals,

* Grocers' Ordinances.

† Merchants of the Hanse Towns in Germany.

the sergeants and bedells, all "statly horsyd," who can wonder that the city apprentices loved to be present, and refused to return to their shops

> "Until that they had all the sight ysein"?

*** "Running footmen" (mentioned in this chapter, p. 273, and elsewhere), according to Fosbroke's Berkeley MSS. extracts (p. 204), were no mean race of men, for we read of one (*temp.* James the First), who performed a "run" well worthy of notice:—"Langham, an Irish footman of this lord (Henry, Lord Berkeley), upon the sickness of the Lady Catherine, this Lord's wife, carryd a letter from Collowden to old Doctor Fryer, a physician, dwelling in *Little Britaine*, in London; and returned with a glass bottle in his hand, compounded by the doctor for the recovery of her health, a journey of 148 miles, performed by him in less than *forty-two hours;* notwithstanding his stay of one night at the physician's and apothecary's houses; which no one horse could have soe well and safely performed: for which the lady shall after give him a newe suite of cloaths." (MS. Veel, p. 919.)

CHAPTER XXV.

THEIR HOLIDAYS, CONTINUED.

LORD MAYOR'S DAY.

"Thus unlamented pass the proud away,
The gaze of fools, and pageant of a day."
POPE.

THE chief holiday in the year in old London was certainly the Lord Mayor's day. Although at the present time it has become shorn of much of its splendour, it is still the sight of the year to all London apprentices. Modern improvements have suggested that the knights in armour and all such antique personages should be dispensed with, and the good and excellent aldermen of our day being neither antiquarians nor warriors, have yielded to the foolish penny-a-liners of the newspapers who have recommended to them that, inasmuch as this race of beings is now extinct, there should be no representation of them in the procession. But the first Lord Mayor who dispensed with these knights in armour, whoever he was, was unworthy of his proud position. A ceremony which for four, five, or even six centuries, has been observed and honoured, ought not lightly to be thrown aside; and had that

Lord Mayor only known the history of his City, and the debt which the nation owed that City, for the prowess and bravery of its magistrates and citizens in the olden time, he would not, at the suggestion of a mere ignoramus, have deprived the Londoners of a pageant so ancient and so suggestive. We should indeed rejoice to see some learned liveryman like Gough Nichols installed in the prætorian chair, in order that all the ancient, historic, and suggestive symbolism of the old Lord Mayor's show might be restored in its original state and magnificence.*

In the Bodleian Library is a copy of the order of the day on the occasion of the inauguration of Sir Charles Duncombe, Knight, Lord Mayor 1708-9, on which day the literary part of the pageant was committed to the celebrated Elkanah Settle. The title runs thus: "The Triumphs of London: for the inauguration of the Right Honourable Sir Charles Duncombe, Knight, Lord Mayor of the City of London: containing the description (and also the sculptures) of the Pageants, and the whole solemnity of the day. Performed on Friday, the 29th of October, anno 1708. All set forth at the proper cost and charge of the honourable Company of Goldsmiths. Published by authority. London: printed for and to

* The earliest Lord Mayor's Show which we have found on record, was in 1401, when the Grocers' books have the following:—

"At the chevauche of John Walcote, Grocer and Mayor—
Paid 40*s*. for six minstrels (and their horses).
,, 8*d*. for their chaprons and fessures.
,, 21*d*. for their dinner and wine by the way, and
,, 4*d*. for a horse for the bedell."

be sold by A. Baldwin, at the Oxford Arms, in Warwick Lane." This Sir Charles Duncombe (so severely treated by Lord Macaulay) left his estates to his sister, Mrs. Brown, who, taking her brother's name, became the founder of the present family of Earl Feversham.

For a more minute description of these pageants we may turn to the programme, where we find—

"First Pageant.—A large triumphant chariot of gold, richly set with divers inestimable and various-coloured jewels of dazzling splendour, adorned with sundry curious figures, fictitious stories, and delightful landskips; an ascent of steps up to a throne, whereon a person of majestic aspect sitteth. The representer of justice, hieroglyphically attired, in a long red robe, and on it a golden mantle fringed with silver: on her head a long dishevel'd hair of flaxen colour, curiously curled, on which is a coronet of silver; in her left hand she advanceth a touchstone (the tryer of truth and the discoverer of falsehood); in her right hand she holdeth up a golden balance with silver scales, equi-ponderant, to weigh justly and impartially; her arms dependent on the heads of two leopards, which emblematically indicate courage and constancy. The chariot is drawn by two golden unicorns in excellent carving work, with equal magnitude to the life; on whose backs are mounted two beautiful raven black negroes attired according to the dress of India; on their heads wreaths of divers coloured feathers; in their right hands they hold golden cups; in their left hands two displayed banners, the one of the King's, the other of the Company's arms. All which represent the crest and the supporters of the ancient, famous, and worshipful Company of Goldsmiths.

"Second Pageant, on a very large pageant, is a very rich seat of state, containing the representer of the patron of the Goldsmiths' Company, Saint Dunstan, attired in a dress properly expressing his prelatical dignity in a robe of fine white lawn, over which he weareth a cope or vest of costly bright cloth of gold down to the ground; on his reverend grey head, a golden mitre set with topaz, ruby, emerald, amethyst, and saphyr; in his left hand he holdeth a golden crozier, and in his right hand he useth a pair of goldsmith's tongs. Beneath these steps of ascension to his chair, in opposition to St. Dunstan, is properly painted a goldsmith's forge and furnace, with fire and gold in it, and a workman blowing with a bellows. On his right and left hand there is a large press of gold and silver plate, representing a shop of trade, and further in front are several artificers at work on anvils with hammers, beating out plate for the formation of several vessels in gold and silver. A step below St. Dunstan sitteth an assay-master, with his class frame and balance for trial of gold and silver, according to the standard. In a march are divers miners in canvas breeches, red waistcoats, and red caps, bearing spades, pickaxes, twibills, and crows. The devil also appearing to St. Dunstan, is catched by the nose at a proper qu, which is given in his speech."

When we read of "one," "two," or "three

pageants," we understand large painted scenes, before which the actors stood and delivered their speeches. Some of these paintings must have been of considerable extent, as large platforms and scaffolds had to be erected on which to affix them. In describing the ancient hall of the Fishmongers, it is specially mentioned that "so lofty was the roof of the dining-hall, that it was high enough to suspend the largest pageant from, which was used at Sir John Lemon's inauguration as Lord Mayor (A.D. 1616)." This painting, we believe, is still preserved by the company, and is explanatory of the procession of Sir William Walworth, in 1380. Strype says, in reference to this pageant, "There rode several men in armour, one whereof had the head of Wat Tyler upon his spear erected." There was then also a pageant representing Walworth lying dead on his monument; and an angel, the genius of London, making him arise; who forthwith sat up, and standing, made a speech to the mayor passing by (ii. p. 269).

We cannot lay our hands at the present moment upon a programme of any of the very earliest Lord Mayors' shows, but we know that the military display was very imposing, illustrating the warlike character and habits of the people, all of whom, before the existence of a standing army, were trained to arms. Besides the long cavalcade of armed warriors and knights in mail, the pennons, banners, bannerets, trumpets, war-horses, and all the illustrations of "war's magnificently stern array," were the minstrels, with their sergeant, and the splendidly-arrayed bedells of all the companies, in scarlet gowns, and, like the minstrels, mounted on horseback. Then came the various liveries, headed by their masters and wardens, the aldermen, sheriffs, and lord mayor, all suitably attended.

Taubman's "London Yearly Jubilee" at the inauguration of Sir John Peake, mercer, 1686, gives the order of their "morning procession," which usually set out from Mercers' Hall about eight o'clock, and as showing the manner of the thing in the seventeenth century, we extract a portion, reminding our readers that this is only the list of one company out of sixty or more which would take part in the "jubilee." 1. The master and wardens, and assistants, in their gowns faced with foins, and hoods. 2. The livery, in their gowns faced with satin, and in their hoods. 3. Three score poor men (almsmen), in gowns and caps, each bearing a banner. 4. Fifty gentlemen ushers, in velvet coats, each having a chain of gold about the shoulders, and in his right hand a white staff. 5. A splendid train of bachelors, in gowns, and scarlet satin hoods. 6. The rest of the bachelors. 7. Twelve more gentlemen, bearing banners and colours, with scarfs of the company's colours. 8. Thirty-six trumpeters. 9. Fourteen drummers. 10. Drums and fifes, with scarfs. 11. The two city marshals on horseback, and six scarfs to attend them. 12. The six foot marshals. 13. The Master of Defence, with six persons of the same noble service to attend him.

14. Pensioners in red gowns, with white staves and flat white caps, each carrying a javelin in one hand and a target in the other, with the arms painted. 15. A body of the gentlemen of the Honourable Artillery Company as Grenadiers, with crimson velvet caps lined with rich furs, led that day by Sir John Moore. At St. Paul's Churchyard they were met by the pageants. The first of these, allusive to the company in their character of *merchants*, was a rock of coral with seaweeds, and Neptune mounted on a dolphin at the summit on a throne of mother-of-pearl, accompanied by tritons, mermaids, etc. Then followed the *maiden's chariot*, to which we must refer hereafter, merely here quoting from Strype these few lines:—"When any of this company is chosen Mayor, the day wherein he goes to Westminster to be sworn, a most beautiful maiden is carried through the streets in a chariot, with all the glory and majesty possible, with her hair all dishevelled about her shoulders. This lady is plentifully gratified for her pains, besides the gift of all the rich attire she wears."

Sometimes unseemly quarrels took place in very early times respecting the question of precedence. At the mayoralty procession of John Gedney, A.D. 1417, the butchers, it seems, wished to take rank above the goldsmiths, and we think without the slightest claim to such honour. The Goldsmiths' books thus record:—

"1417. 6 Henry VI. Remembrance, the 3 Nov. in this year, that how of holde custome of the worshipful citie of London the craftes of the saide citie have used to ride withe the maire of the same citie to the Palyes of Westminster, atte eche makyng of the maire, and fro' thens to the citie ridyn ayen, and the craftes ridyng afore the maire. And when they come in *chepe*, every craft, eche be other holdyng, a horsbak, abod tille the maire rode thurgh hem. And of olde tyme the Goldsmythes of the same citie, whan of her craft is no maire, they have used to have and stonde above the *Cross of chepe* afore the *Goldsmythe-Rowe*, withoute long forstallyng afore eny of the craftes: tille nowe late it felle that in the monoth of the Apostles Symond and Jude last past, John Gedney, draper, then beyng mayer, as the said Goldsmythes rode afore hym, comyng into Chepe for to stonde in the place afore seide, as they have of old tyme out of a mynde, cam the Bochers of the same citie and hoved into place there as the said Goldsmythes were wontyd to stonde; and for no prayer of the wardens of the said Goldsmythes, the said Bocheres wolde not voide; where thurgh hit happyd that there fell grete variance and strife amonge hem. For the whiche stryfe the said Bocheres compleyned hem to the said John Gedney, mayer, and submityd hem to stonde to his award; and axed the Goldsmythes if they wolde do the same: and the wardeins of the Goldsmythes answered the mayer and seyd they wolde be rewled hight and lowe at hys award, knowing well hys disposicon substantiall, wyse, and rightfull. Whereon the saide mayer, the day of the commemoracion of all sowls, sitting in his parisshe churche of Seynt Christofers, by the Stokkys and as well the wardeins of the Goldsmythes as the wardeins of the Bochers, being present afore hym—the matter of every partie herde and consideryd—the same mayer awarded that the crafte of Goldsmythes, as they have used of olde tyme, fro hensfoward, shulde ayen have their stondying in the same place; and charged the wardeins of both craftes aforesaide to take eche other be the handys, in sign of love and pees,—and so they dede—and chargyd hem that alle things afore doo shulde be no more spoke of, but every crafte to love and cherisse other, as they owyd (ought) to doo."

In curious contrast to Lord Mayor's Days of former times, we subjoin a summary lately published of certain particulars of a recent Lord Mayor's Day, and the expenses thereof, from which it will be seen that a large proportion is for the banquet, and a very small share allotted to the "show."

"EXPENDITURE FOR THE BANQUET AND PROCESSION ON LORD MAYOR'S DAY, 1866.

"The banquet and procession on Lord Mayor's Day last cost £3,325 19*s.*; of that sum £1,665 19*s.* 4*d.* was paid to Messrs. Staples for the dinner and wine. The cost of the general decorations, including armour, flags, looking-glasses, flowering plants, shrubs, awning, gas, gas-fitting, upholstery, plumbing, painting, carpentry, removal of statuary, pictures, etc., £878 16*s.* 7*d.* There was paid for the services of the seven bands, who took part in the procession, £101 1*s.*; banners and bearers, £32 11*s.*; rosettes, scarfs, etc., £25 9*s.* 6*d.*; refreshments to troops, police, etc., £63 5*s.* 3*d.*; gravelling the streets, £14. The bands, the trumpeters, and the vocalists in the Guildhall, and the Guildhall Yard, were engaged at a cost of £104 7*s.* The accounts for printing and stationery amounted to £147 9*s.* The general expenses included, decorations for committee, £47 10*s.*; wands for committee, £30 17*s.* 6*d.*; cutlery, £10 16*s.*; gold pens and pencil-cases for chairman and secretary, and engraving the same, £12 16*s.*; seal for chairman of committee, and engraving ditto, £7 12*s.*; toilet articles, £13 10*s.*; gloves, £12 8*s.* 6*d.*; perfumery, £36 3*s.* 6*d.* Among other items we find the customary four men on the roof, at 10*s.* 6*d.* each, £2 2*s.*; bell-ringers at seven churches, £14 14*s.*; refreshments for committee and guard of honour, £17 18*s.*; assistant-secretary, £15; remembrancer's clerks, issuing tickets, and disbursements, £17 17*s.* 11*d.*"

One-half of the whole amount, viz., £1,663, was paid by the Lord Mayor, Sir Thomas Gabriel, Bart., and the other moiety by the sheriffs—viz., Sheriff Sir Sydney Waterlow, £831 10*s.*, and Sheriff Sir Francis Lycett, £831 10*s.*,—rather a handsome amount to be expended in hospitality by three individuals, especially when we consider that this was only for one banquet out of many. Had this entertainment been given in the reign of Henry VIII., instead of Queen Victoria, we might have expected some regulations from headquarters respecting the expense. A writer on the former reign remarks that the extravagant mode of living of the City magistrates had risen to such a height in this age, that many merchants left London to avoid the expense of office, whereon an act of Common Council passed, enacting—That the Mayor should have but one course on a flesh day, either at dinner or supper, to consist of only seven dishes, hot or cold, and on fish days, eight dishes, on common days seven dishes, exclusive of brawn, collops, with eggs, sallads, pottage, butter, cheese, herrings, sprats, shrimps, with all sorts of shell fish and fruits. Aldermen and sheriffs to have one dish less, the same number of dishes allowed for City companies, but neither swan, crane, or bustard, under a penalty of 40*s.* When foreign ministers or privy counsellors were invited, additions might be made at the discretion of the Lord Mayor, but no entertainment could be given after dinner, except hippocras and wafers. No Lord Mayor or sheriff was to keep a lord of misrule.

In these days of liberty the above restrictions appear rather hard and tyrannical, but we cannot be surprised that the Common Council should pass such strict regulations, for they had precedents in abundance for these severe rules enacted by the sovereign. Even the powerful benchers of Lincoln's Inn were denied the privilege of engaging at their revels the *Lord of Misrule*, and instead thereof had their *King of the Cockneys*. They had also a *Jack Straw*, but, in the reign of Elizabeth, he and his adherents utterly vanished. In the same reign sumptuary laws were made to regulate the members of the House, who were forbidden to wear long hair, or great ruffs, cloaks, boots, or spurs. In the reign of Henry VIII. beards were prohibited at the great table, under pain of paying double commons. His daughter Elizabeth, in the first year of her reign, confined them to a fortnight's growth, under penalty of 3*s.* 4*d.*, but the fashion prevailed so strongly that the prohibition was repealed, and no manner of size limited to that venerable excrescence.* We believe that in these times of universal beards amongst all professions, the members of the bar (having revived Elizabeth's statutes) are the only men in England who are cleanly shaved.

With what astonishment should we receive intimation of an Act of Parliament to compel all mechanics and workmen during harvest to leave their occupations to work in the fields; but notwithstanding the power of the London gilds, and the loss to trade by such a measure, King Richard II., by an Act (2 Richard II., c. 11), ordained that "as well artificers as people of mystery (men of the crafts or mysteries), and of which craft or mystery a man hath no great need in harvest time, shall be compelled to serve in harvest, to cut, gather, and bring in the corn."

The records of the various companies afford occasional curious and interesting pictures of the tyrannical customs of former times. The King was despotic with the Mayor, the Mayor with the masters;

* Pennant, p. 171.

the masters with their livery, and so on.* The books of the Leathersellers' Company, the most perfect of any of the companies' records, forming as they do an uninterrupted diary of their proceedings from the year A.D. 1470, bring to light the prevalence of a custom of which we had not been aware previously to discovering it in these minutes, viz., of the City fining a citizen for not serving as alderman, after his election to such office, and of a company electing a master out of his rotation, with the evident expectation that as he had fined for alderman, he would also fine for master. Under the date June 28, 1650, we read, "Stephen Beale, who had lately fined for alderman of this City, was elected master or uppermost warden." At the next court his son-in-law, Captain Forbes, attends to excuse Mr. Beale from the office, "his habitation being altogether forth of London," and submitting to pay any fine inflicted by the court. £30 was the sum fixed, which the captain immediately paid, with many and hearty thanks for the Company's courtesy in releasing him from the honourable duty. It is only fair to this distinguished Company to admit that this mode of proceeding on their part is quite exceptional. The tyranny of the Parliament had been exercised towards them, and most of the other great companies, and after seizing their plate and money, in many in-

* Dean Swift had this in his eye when he wrote the following:—

"Big fleas have small fleas
Upon their backs to bite 'em;
And these fleas have other fleas,
And so on 'ad infinitum.'"

stances they had forced them to borrow large sums on their common seal. About this period continual entries occur of the difficulties of this Company, in language similar to the following:—"Sept. 27, 1649, In consideration of the great debt due to our Company by Parliament, no quarterly dinner be given, and a livery be taken in;" also, "no court dinners—but the master and wardens to pay the usual fines for providing the same to accumulate." The members taken in or compelled to become liverymen, consisted of twenty-six persons, amongst whom was John Ironside; and just before (October, 1634), we read "this day Praisegod Barebone was admitted to the clothing (made a liveryman), and paid the fine according." In August, 1635, four brothers, no doubt of the same school with Praisegod, were introduced, viz., Joshua, Caleb, Obadiah, and Zephaniah Bromley. Indeed, this loyal and honourable Company appear just at this period of their history to be given up almost entirely to the Cromwell party, if we may judge from the names so frequent amongst them, one of their most active spirits being no less a personage than Mr. Jumper. In 1649 we meet with the first instance for two centuries of the livery dining without their wives, and to these same Puritan gentlemen the ladies owe their disfranchisement, for they had hitherto dined with the livery by right of Royal Charter. "July, 1649:—Agreed that the master and wardens shall give their feast on election day (first Tuesday in August next) to all the livery (without their wives), to which shall be allowed £28.

£4 shall be allowed towards venison, and £20, the gift of Mr. Jumper, for a dynner for the lyvery, and the remainder out of the gift of Mr. Humble for a repast not yet expended."

We do not say that all these worthy Leather-sellers were anti-monarchical. The Mr. Humble just mentioned—the son of a great benefactor of the Company, ancestor of the Lords Dudley and Ward—was a staunch loyal alderman, and was created a baronet by Charles II. at the Restoration.* He must have had hard times of it during the interregnum amidst these "Jumpers," and "Barebones," and "Zephaniahs." We may mention just one instance in which fanaticism seems to peep out, wherein these worthies deface and destroy their ancient common seal, it being evidently too Papistical for their tastes, notwithstanding it had stood the severe ordeal of the onslaught upon all such emblems at the Reformation. In the minutes of the same court as that upon which Praisegod Barebone was admitted, October, 1634:—"It is agreed that a new common seal be designed and executed to bear the arms of the Company with its supporters, and the old seal, bearing the assumption of St. Mary, the blessed Virgin, being very ancient, to be broken and defaced." In the minutes for January, 1634-5 (the following January), we read that "the new seal was

* Mr. Humble's sister Honor married Sir Thomas Vyner, who was Lord Mayor 1653, and created a Baronet, with Sir William Humble, at the Restoration, 1660. Sir Robert Vyner, King Charles's great friend, has been mentioned at p. 82.

used," and the old one is ordered "to be locked in the chest till all the leases signed with it shall have expired."

Whatever their shortcomings may have been, however, in no period of their history have these worthy sellers of leather been untrue to their trusts, nor wanting in their duty to the Mayor, especially on the great day of his inauguration—"The Lord Mayor's Day."

CHAPTER XXVI.

THEIR HOLIDAYS, CONTINUED.

THE WATER PAGEANTS.

"The barge she sat in, like a burnish'd throne,
Burnt on the water."

ANTHONY AND CLEOPATRA.

PERSONS familiar with London at the present day can hardly believe that, three centuries ago, the roads leading from the City to Westminster were almost impassable. This, however, was the case, and accounts for the fact that almost all the traffic between the West-end of London and the City was by water. Each nobleman and gentleman possessed a pleasure boat, many of them highly ornamental, and, like Venetian gondolas, glittering with gold and gay colours. A state barge was certainly a picturesque object, and in the olden time a procession by water was worth beholding. Each of the City gilds of any note of course possessed a state barge, and on all occasions of royal progresses they were required, one and all, to take part in the spectacle.

For the information of those of our readers who may not have seen one of these very handsome little vessels, we may state that the larger barges were usually fitted up with two decks, the upper deck capable of affording accommodation for forty couples of dancers, and between-decks was a spacious saloon, in which as large a number might be entertained at dinner, should the company choose to dine on the water. As the cost of purchasing and maintaining in ornamental repair one of these splendid vessels was considerable, the wealthier companies only, as we have said, possessed one; those less favoured had to be satisfied with the hire of one on all occasions of aquatic holiday.

The barge of the Drapers' Company seems to have been decayed in 1533, for in October of that year they agreed with Mr. Edward Wade, the bargeman of the Archbishop of Canterbury, "for his grate barge, at such tymes as we shall have need to occupy it, either with the mayor or shreves, or for any other business, he to have xxviii. oars furnished and cysshons for the said barge, at every voyage wher we shall have need thereof with our compaignie in the lyvery for the sum of xxxs."

On the occasion of the marriage of Anne of Cleves, the company appear to have had sufficient influence with the royal bargeman to hire one of the king's barges, for we read in their minutes as follows: "Agreed with Carter, master of the king's barge 'Greyhound,' to serve the feliship at the comyn in of the Lady of Cleveland for the sum of 54*s.* 3*d.*" It was usual for these barges to be covered, on occasions of civic triumphs, with blue cloth or *plunket*, and on royal ones with red cloth or *murrey*. This cloth measured twenty-four yards. They were accompanied by minstrels or trumpets with crimson hats, and headed by their marshal; the barge was decorated with costly banners, pennons, and streamers fringed with silk and "beaten with gold." In 1488 the charge is made for xi. yards of tartern for a new banner; for painting and beting the said banners and streamers and silk fringe xls., besides iij. yards of red buckram for the sockets.

Stow states "that John Norman (Lord Mayor 1450) was the first that rowed by water to Westminster to take the oath, for before that time they rode on horseback." But the books of the Grocers' Company show that water processions were known before that period, for under the date 1436, is an entry of the payment for the hire of a barge to attend the sheriffs' show by water. Also for minstrels and their hoods, for amending of banners, etc., £4 6*s*. 4*d*. The Carpenters' Company seemed to have hired their barge on very economical terms, from the following entries which occur in their books:—"1460 (39 Hen. VI.), hire of barge to Westminster with the shireves, iiijs. 1470 (10 Ed. IV.), hire of one barge to meet the kyng, vs. ijd. 1485 (1 Hen. VII.), barge at metyng of the kyng on the water, vijs. vijd.; barge hyre to reseyve the kyng on the water, viijs. ivd. 1490 (6 Hen. VII.), hyre of barge when the prince was created, xijs. viijd."

From the minutes of the various companies it is evident that, although the voyage from the City to

Westminster could not have been expected to be a long one, especially when the boat was "furnished with twenty-eight oars;" yet our ancient citizens, feeling impressed with the uncertainty of all human plans, made every provision for a lengthened sojourn on the way, and every care was taken to secure a good supply of creature comforts in case of any accident which might produce delay. The Drapers deemed this a matter of so grave importance that their minutes bear the following entry, A.D. 1485:—"1 Hen. VII. Paid £2 for boat hire to Westmynstre to put up our bill for the reformacion of cloth making. For pippyns put into the barge, 11d.; ij. rybbes of beefe, xijs.; and for a bottell of wyne, viid." This boat would be a small shallop, it being for business purposes to wait upon Parliament then sitting. Mr. Jupp quotes the following from the Carpenters' minutes, dated 1616:—"Chardge laid out the 31st Oct., when the companye went to meete the prince, before the companye tooke bardge and in the bardge. Paid for bread, ijs.; carryeing the wine sellers to and fro, xijd.; for sugar and cakes, ijs.; beare at our masters (!) ixd.; claret wyne, one gallon, ijs.; sack, j. pottle and halfe pynt, xviijd.; canarye, one quart, xijd.; which is in all xs. iijd." This merely for a voyage to Chelsea to meet Prince Charles. A curious item occurs in the Drapers' books, throwing much light upon the customs of that period, A.D. 1496:—"For a barge two times to Shene to speak with the King for reformacion of our act to be made for woollen cloth, which cost us and the taylors in vytels, supplicacion, and learned counsell, 3li. xiijs. iiijd." At a later period the books of another company have the solemn entry, that on state occasions "pipes and tobacco shall not be taken on board, as is usual on Lord Mayor's Day." Probably the smell of tobacco was objectionable to the king and court—or, possibly, some rising spirits in the gild had taught the doctrine that such an indulgence was beneath the dignity of ancient and grave brethren.

Some curious particulars respecting the coronation of Elizabeth, queen of Henry VII., A.D. 1487, from the Cottonian Library, are given in Leland's "Collectanea" (b. iv. pp. 218—220), containing a description of this water pageant. The Lord Mayor, sheriffs, and aldermen of the City, and divers and many worshipful commoners, chosen out of every craft, in their liveries, in barges, freshly furnished with banners and streamers of silk, richly besene with the arms and "bagges of their crafts;" and, in especial, a *barge*, called *Bachelor's Barge*, garnished and apparelled, passing all others, wherein was ordained a great red dragon, spouting flames of fire into the Thames; also many other gentlemanly pageants, well and curiously devised, to do her highness sport and pleasure with. On her passage, the next day, from the Tower to Westminster, all the streets which she should pass by were cleanly dressed, and besene with cloths of tapestry and arras; and some streets, as Cheap, hanged with rich cloth of gold, velvet, and silks. Along the streets, from the

Tower to St. Paul's, stood in order all the crafts of London, in their liveries; and in divers parts of the City were ordained well-singing children: some arrayed like angels, and others like virgins, to sing sweet songs as her grace passed by.

The great honour paid by Henry VII. to the Livery of London is never more marked than on the occasion of the marriage of Prince Arthur to Katherine, when, as we have before stated, on the authority of Stow, in "the Banketts and Disguy-syngs, the chiefs of the Companies, together with the Lord Mayor, were seated next to the King and Queen." Again, on the Court removing to Richmond, there was assembled "a great and goodly number of barges, for the most partie of evry lord in England," either moored "or roweing and skymmyng in the riv' Thamys," but "first, for the cittie of London, was the mayer's barge, the sherevys barge, and aldermen dyv'rs bargs; and then the crafts of the cytie having their standards and stremers, wt. ther conizances right weel dekkyd, and replenyshid wt. wrshipful company of the citizens."

At Easter, 1533, Anne Boleyne was publicly acknowledged as Queen, and Henry sent missives to the Lord Mayor, requiring him to convey her Grace in State from Greenwich to the Tower on Whit-Sunday. Here is the authentic chronicle*:—The Mayor, etc., all in scarlet, the knights, with collars of SS, and the rest with gold chains, went from St. Mary's Hill to the City barge, which was gar-

* Nichols's "Progresses;" also Taylor's "Glory of Regality."

nished with banners, etc., and had in it shalmes, shagebushes, and other instruments of musicke plaing continually. The other City barges, fifty in number, with their accustomed banners, their sides decked with targets, and such seemly banners and bannerets as they had in their halls, or could get to furnish the said barges; and every barge provided with a minstrel joined in the procession. First went a foiste,* for a wafter, full of ordnance, with a great red dragon, incessantly moving, and casting aboute wildefire; and thereby stoode terrible, monstrous wilde men casting fire, and making hideous noises. The batchelor's barge came nigh unto the Mayor's, in which were trumpets, etc., the decks and yards were hung with cloth of gold, and two great banners with the arms of their Majesties; also divers other flags, etc., hung with little bels at the ends. On the left of the Mayor was another foiste, where, on a mount, stood a white faulcon crowned upon a roote of gold, adorned with white and red roses, the Queen's device, and round about sate fair women, singing melodiously. At Greenwich they anchored, making great melodie. At three o'clock (May 29), the Queene, apparelled in rich cloth of gold, entered her barge, with many ladies and gentlemen. Then all the barges set forward, her Majesty having great pleasure in beholding the batchelor's barge. A train of noblemen accompanied her, and she moved towards the Tower, and

* A "*foyst*" was a small vessel or galley to convey fireworks. "*Foist*," a barge or pinnace, from *fuste*. Dutch or French.

being come, there was a marvellous shot out of the Tower, never was heard the like. The Lord Chamberlaine brought her to the King, who received her with loving countenance, and kissed her. Then she turned and thanked the citizens with many goodlie words. "To speak of the people that stood on every shoare to behold this sight, he that saw it not will not believe it." On the second day was a procession from the Tower to Westminster. The Queen was borne on a "litter of white cloth of gold, led by palfreys, clad in white damask." She wore a kirtle of white tumic, and a mantle furred of the same. Her hair hung loose, but she wore a coif, with a circlet of rich stones, and over her was carried a canopy of cloth of gold. Her guards had on coats of goldsmith's worke. In Fenchurch Street, a pageant of children, dressed as merchants, welcomed her; thence came she to Grace Church, where was a cunning pageant, made by the Stilyard merchants, whereon was Parnassus and Helicon, of white marble, and four streams, "without pipe," rose on high, meeting in a cuppe over the fountain, which ran freely with rich Rhenish wine till night. Around sat Apollo and Calliope, and the Muses playing on sweet instruments, poesies being written at their feete, each Muse praysing the Queene. There were other pageants in Cornhill and Chepe, also at Temple Bar; the standard and crosse were newly painted and gilt, and near the little Conduit, where the Aldermen stood, Mr. Recorder came to the Queen "with a low reverence, and presented her, in the name of the City, with 1000 marks in a gold purse, which she thankfully accepted, with many good words," and so rode on, meeting another rich pageant, full of melody, the actors being Pallas, Juno, and Venus, with whom was Mercury, who gave her Majesty a gold ball, divided into three, signifying three gifts—Wisdom, Riches, and Felicity. At last she came to Westminster, and in the middle of the hall, which was richly hung with "cloth of arras, and newly glazed," the Queen was taken out of her litter, and after "a solemn service" of "wines, spices, subtleties, etc.," she gave hearty thanks to the lords and ladies, the Lord Mayor, and others that had attended on her," and withdrew to her chamber. Next day was the coronation in the Abbey. At dinner twelve chief citizens assisted Lord Arundel as Chief Butler, and after the feast, the Queen, according to old custom, gave the Lord Mayor, with her own hands, the gold cup, which devolved upon him as chief cup-bearer at the coronation.

How sad is the contrast which the next public ceremony connected with this unhappy woman affords to the one just recorded. In less than three years the citizens who had taken so distinguished a part in her coronation pageants, attended at the Tower-green to witness the beheading of that fair and beauteous Queen, whose bereaved husband consoled himself for her loss by marrying, on the following day, her successor, Jane Seymour. Much of the property left by Alderman Boleyne (the Queen's grandfather) was situated in Kent, in the neighbourhood of which estates, a worthy innkeeper, indignant at the treatment of his old master's relative, altered his sign from "The Boleyne Arms," to "The Boleyne Butchered." Queen Elizabeth, they say, who took every means to hush up her mother's sorrows and end, induced the host to amend it into "The Bull and Butcher," which henceforth became a popular sign throughout all England.

The minutes of the several gilds throw much light upon many points of history, though otherwise too unimportant to be recorded. The Carpenters' Company have many entries of this kind, curious and valuable in their way, brought to light by Mr. Jupp in his most able history of that ancient company. They record that, in 1610, the company attended to bring Prince Henry from Richmond, and "paid 5*s.* for barge hyer, by consent, in regard it was ex-ordinarye." For the supper (which, we suppose, was not extraordinary), "when the company came home from the water, when they attended in their barge to bring the Prince from Richmond to Whitehall to be created Prince of Wales, iiijli. vs. vid."

Thus we learn that in the reign of the first James, the eldest son was not born Prince of Wales. Three years after this ceremony this young Prince died, and, in 1616, Prince Charles (afterwards King Charles I.) was created Prince of Wales in his stead, and with the same magnificence, when the Carpenters expend the large sum of £3 "upon Master Watt for barge hyre when the company went to meet the Prince." But this sum is largely exceeded in 1662, shortly after the marriage of Charles II. with Catherine of Braganza, when, for boat hire and other charges to attend the King and Queen from Hampton Court, the large sum is entered of £18 11*s*. 6*d*.

The water pageants on Lord Mayor's day were sometimes very curious. At the inauguration of Sir John Frederick, Lord Mayor, 1661, in the Grocers' pageant, was a large ship rigged and manned; at the head was Galatea, a sea-nymph drawn in a sea-chariot by dolphins, and accompanied by syrens, tritons, and sea-lions. These, upon the Mayor's taking the water, saluted him on the river near the Temple.

In 1768, on the occasion of a visit to London of the King of Denmark, the Lord Mayor issued a precept to all the companies to attend his Majesty in their state barges, with the usual accompaniments. The minutes of the Merchant Taylors' Company record this fact, and contain the order respecting pipes and tobacco just quoted, and direct that there should be no breakfast at the hall, and the cook attending with a bill of fare, the same, with some few alterations, was approved of.

How quaint these minutes sound after the lapse of a century! One cannot read these musty records of the past, without a feeling of regret that the primitive and child-like customs of our fathers have passed away, to yield to others, more intellectual truly, but certainly not so joyous or so exhilarating.

CHAPTER XXVII.

THEIR HOLIDAYS, CONTINUED.

THEIR OUT-DOOR GAMES.

"Dull and monotonous would the circle of existence have been had not the Divinity decreed moments when the mind, fatigued with thought, seeks for relaxation in frivolity. No matter of what kind, so that immorality be absent."—MALCOLM.

LONDON, at the present day, is remarkably unlike the great city, as it stood three or four centuries ago. Improvements, no doubt, are manifest in many respects, prosperity abounds, and money-making seems as easy now as it ever was. But in many respects the change is for the worse; the bright picturesqueness of the old city has gone, and masonry and smoke have completely destroyed or hidden her many shady walks and romantic nooks. London was once the city of green trees and fields, with many bright gardens and lovely retreats—many open spots, inviting men to exercise and recreation—greens, where

"Young and old came forth to play,
On some pleasant holiday."

All this has gone now. Clerkenwell "Green" still

remains, it is true; but—who could keep holiday there? Instead of from sixty to eighty thousand inhabitants to house, there are now some three millions to domicile.

The change in the manners and customs of the citizens is as great as that which has been effected in the fabric of the city. Our ancestors delighted in out-door games and spectacles. We have shown how the early citizens spared no cost in gratifying their dependents by a lavish display of all kinds of finery and costly apparel on the occasion of processions and public shows; how king and cardinal vied with each other in the display of gorgeous equipments to please the public eye. But this is all now a thing of the past. Even the Lord Mayor's Show, that sight of all City sights, has been shorn of much of its trappings; and utilitarians tell us, alas! that "it must go," that the "show," and "Temple Bar," with Gog and Magog, and other "relics of a barbarous age," are doomed—that they must depart to the tomb of all the Capulets, with the merry swan-hopping, and the Easter Epping hunt, and all that true citizens held most dear.

Some moderns may prefer fewer of the manly games, even, than at present prevail amongst us. They may think more of the dangers attending rude sport than they do of the importance of a manly training. We must, of course, allow that even cricket has its dangers. Many a leg or arm has been broken by a blow; and in wrestling, how many a one has come away with a broken head. This is but the fortune of war, and the dangers and perils are by no means so numerous as in the pastimes of the early citizens. They were indeed rather desperate men, and by no means nice as to weapons or place. Even apprentices carried arms, and were well skilled in their use. It may be curious to quote a proclamation to the citizens, *temp.* Edward II., 1308, 14th February :—

"1st. That on Coronation Day, no one be so bold as to carry sword or knife, with point or misericorde,* mace, club, or any other, on pain of imprisonment for a year and a day. 2nd. That all persons shall receive and pay honour to the French and other foreigners, who have come, or shall come to the said coronation; and that none do them wrong, in word and deed, on pain of one year's imprisonment, and for forfeiture of all they have to the king. 3rd. That no person shall strike another, or lay hand on another in evil manners, on pain of losing the hand; and if any person shall brandish sword or any other arm, with such arm as he shall have so brandished let him be pierced through the hand." †

It does not follow that severity of punishment has been followed by a decrease in crime, nor that the dangers of any pastime have deterred men from its exercise. The Mayor, in the fourteenth century, had power to enforce penalties, however severe; and even capital punishment, in a most

* A dagger, so called from its being used to put the wounded in battle out of their pain.

† Riley's "Memorials of London."

summary manner, was sometimes inflicted by his authority, as may be seen from the following commendatory letter from King Edward III. to Andrew Aubrey, Mayor:—

"1340. *6th December.*

"Whereas because you would prevent unseemly riots in the City and conflicts between the pelterers and fishmongers, in the course of your duty you were assaulted by Thomas, son of John Hannsard fishmonger, who seized you by the throat, and John le Brewere, a porter, who wounded a City sergeant so that his life was despaired. When you caused Thomas and John to be brought to the Guildhall, where, being arraigned, they confessed their violence, and by you were condemned to death, and beheaded in Chepe. Wherefore we say you did well in thus punishing the guilty and comforting the good, for we hold such contempts committed against our servants as committed against ourselves, and if you had not done so we should have taken it very grievously." *

"Thomas" and "John," no doubt, behaved very badly on the occasion referred to by the King, but the Mayor might have been less severe in the penalty inflicted, and probably lost two of his bravest wrestlers by his heat. It is possible, however, to relax too greatly in the infliction of punishment for heinous offences; and while we would not advocate a vindictive or cruel system, still we should be sorry to witness in this country the existence of a sickly sentimentality, as may be seen in America, in the use of *chloroform on the scaffold*, and the like. This is nothing better than a weak and apologetic attempt to neutralize the death itself, so to speak; either capital punishment should be abolished, or, if enforced, it should be carried out in the usual way. A New York journal informs us "that nar-

* Riley's "Memorials of London."

cosis on the scaffold is apparently novel, unless we except *the occasional execution of somebody in a state of intoxication;*" but the writer confesses that "there is a ghastly sarcasm about the whole proceeding that trenches on the ludicrous."*

Many of the rising politicians of the present day, "highfliers," as a great statesmen lately termed them, some of whom have spent considerable time in America, and consequently may be supposed to be well acquainted with the manners and customs of that great and interesting nation, sneer at all our old-fashioned modes of amusing our people, ridicule the pastimes and country sports of the past as childish and foolish, and in their place would grant enlarged political rights as the only panacea for a people's wants. In fact, democracy, say they, with its attendant liberty, is *the one thing needful.* They tell us of the advantages of the theory, such as they are, but keep in the background all its dark features. Thoughtful men should not, however, be ready to yield them support, without first satisfying themselves of the working of those theories, and before giving up all our old English principles and old English practices, and substituting for the out-door games the political club-room, and monster meetings for agitation and clamour, should fully realize the ultimate workings of their doctrines. We quote a

* The same writer says: "On the second Friday of the new year 1869), a man named Carswell was hung, while under anæsthetic influence, at Utica, for the violation and subsequent murder of a mere child. He suffered justly, if we once admit that vindictive retaliation is just."—*New York Round Table.*

passage recently appearing in one of the influential democratic journals of New York to illustrate our meaning:—

"Take, again, a New York voter of a certain class. To say that he is illiterate, is inadequately to express the density of his ignorance; to say that he is unscrupulous, is to do injustice to his audacity; to say that he is for sale at every recurring election, is to state a fact as notorious as sunrise; to say that he is ready to commit any crime which may be pleasing to his leaders, is simply to acknowledge his bad loyalty; to say that he is dirty and brutal, drunken and degraded, a bully, a sluggard, and a sneak, is merely to record his natural history. There is not a good citizen who would not prevent this creature from voting, if it were possible to do so; but it is impossible, and we submit; thankful, alas! if we can keep the iniquity from being multiplied, and the excellent citizen from voting the democratic ticket twenty times upon the same day. Yet the citizens of New York, honest, intelligent, wealthy, and refined, go on, year after year, permitting voters of this kidney to rule them, and, above all, to spend their money; and there is not one word said of depriving repeaters and perjurers of the ballot which they have abused. We shrink from class distinctions. We would fain be true to the democratic idea, although, in the concrete, it may devour us. And we are right. Until we are ready to give up democracy altogether, we must be content, for its sake, to run all risks, great and small. The adage of 'Nothing venture, nothing have,' applies to the case exactly." *

We do not see the necessity of "venturing" anything. We have, we maintain, all we want. "Let well alone," is our motto; and instead of going-in for all sorts of new-fangled notions, and teaching the labouring people that they are of all men the most miserable, we would rather remind them of their many privileges and advantages, and add to the amount of their happiness by every means in our power. For this reason we dwell so much, and so emphatically, on the importance of holidays, recreations, and amusements, especially those which can be enjoyed out-of-doors; this is why we desire, in so marked a manner, to call attention at the present day to the sound discretion and wisdom of our ancestors, that we may imitate their example, and walk in their footsteps. Let us maintain all our open spaces, our commons, with their rights, and our forests. To have our "games," we require suitable localities. Cruel is that proprietor who robs his poorer neighbours of their rights in this respect.

> "'Tis surely wrong in man or woman
> To steal a goose from off a common;
> But who shall plead that man's excuse
> Who steals the common from the goose?"

We are thankful to say that to modern times we owe the appropriation of some noble breathing grounds in our metropolis, such as Victoria and Battersea

* *New York Tribune*, Feb. 25, 1869.

Parks; and at one time we heard of a similar open space to be made in Islington. The latter scheme, we fear, has fallen through. Every quarter of London should possess recreation grounds, according to its circumstances, and then future historians need have no occasion to mourn over the physical and moral deterioration of the labouring classes.

Fitz-Stephen (secretary to Thomas à Becket), who wrote in the reign of King Henry II., informs us that the citizens of London were devotedly attached to all manly games, and excelled in running, wrestling, and riding. They held periodical wrestling matches, shooting with the bow and arrow, and casting the stone, at Islington Fields. He adds that youths with their teachers came to the fields to play at ball; while the ancient and wealthy citizens came on horseback "to see these youngsters contending at their sport." They exercised also on horseback to qualify for military pursuits, in which all citizens were experts. On every Sunday during Lent great numbers of the sons of the citizens assembled after early mass to ride and leap their horses for severe discipline. At other times great interest was taken in sparrowhawks, goshawks, and all the manly sports of the field!*

Stow fully corroborates the above, and describes at length some games held in the year 1222 (6 Hen. III.), "on St. James's Day, when the citizens of London kept games of defence and wrestling near to the Hospital of St. Giles, where they got the mas-

* *Vide* "Descriptio Nob. Civit. Lond."

tery of the men of the suburbs."* The same author adds that it was customary for the officers, the sheriffs, and others of the City, to be challengers of all men in the suburbs to wrestle, shoot the standard, broad arrow, and other games at Clerkenwell and Finsbury Fields. But the long-bow was the favourite weapon, and in 1365 Edward III. ordered the sheriffs to encourage its use, and it became henceforth a practice accompanied with much ceremony, and to which was attached much importance. In this exercise Henry VIII. took great delight. At a special shooting match at Windsor before the king, when the shooting for the day was nearly over, his majesty observing one of his guard named Barlo preparing his bow for the mark, and being himself greatly excited with the excellence of the previous competitors, shouted to him, "Beat them all, Barlo, and thou shalt be Duke of Archers." The thousands of spectators present stood in breathless silence to mark the result, for Barlo was known to be greatly skilled as an archer. He drew his bow, executed the king's command, and received the promised reward, being created Duke of Shoreditch, that then being the place of his abode.† But the king's patronage of archery did not terminate here. At future contests he offered other similar rewards, and distinguished the several heroes by the titles of Earl of Islington, Earl of Pancridge (Pancras), and the like, from the villages in which they respectively lived. These titles, though not hereditary by blood, de-

* Survey, 710. † Strype's Stow, i. 302.

scended for several generations to the winners of the great prizes at the archery contests. For several succeeding reigns we meet with the name of the Duke of Shoreditch, Captain of the London Archers, as taking a conspicuous part in all royal pageants and processions. Barlo, the first duke, held for many years periodical shooting matches at Smithfield, at which he challenged the world, and also at Mile End; both King Henry VIII. and his son Arthur are recorded to have witnessed these and similar spectacles.

It is gratifying that in the present day we as a nation are in a measure imitating our ancestors in this regard for athletic and military exercises. Boating, rifle shooting, military discipline, games of prowess and strength, are much encouraged amongst us, and the result of the volunteer movement has already become manifest in the improvement evident in the bearing of the young men of this generation. But we fail still in one respect: the benefits of this movement are confined almost entirely to the middle and upper classes; and the masses of the people, the artisans, and the poor, reap but little advantage from all these commendable efforts to make soldiers of the male population. We should look to this, and take care to provide funds not only to meet all expenses of the working men who enlist, but also to pay them for the time lost to their avocations while under training, and during all musters for duty.

To the clergy we owe a debt of obligation for the

encouragement given by so many of them to cricket clubs and all manly exercises. But great improvement is needed. Every parish in England should have its cricket club and its quoits, and the parson should be the leader and fosterer of the movement. How much better for the young man to spend his leisure in running, leaping, throwing the hammer, etc., under the eye and sanction of the squire and clergyman and their families, than frequenting the public-house for drinking purposes and gambling.

Let us learn from the old citizens and imitate their example, encouraging not only military and athletic exercises, but even the mere pastimes for recreation and enjoyment. To noblemen like Lord Londesborough we owe much. The patronage of that noble lord of all the ancient country games annually witnessed in the park at Londesborough is most praiseworthy. We should gladly see his example widely followed by our large landed proprietors.

It may be objected that such pastimes are but trifling, and the inventors of them all great triflers. Let this be granted. Still the sum of human happiness is made up of trifles, and it may happen that a great trifler may really be a great benefactor to his species. Our only fear should be lest, by immoderate pleasure and fun, we abuse that which should be only a relaxation, by devoting to gaiety more of our precious time than is required for our benefit. But it is not wise to make no provision for man's enjoyment. The present age, we fancy, expends more upon building and maintaining prisons and jails than our forefathers spent upon their pageants and holiday-makings. The result is also a diminution in the reverence paid by youth to old age. In the olden time the young reverenced the aged; now, the merest boy will prate familiarly with his grandfather. Then discipline was maintained—the rod was never spared when deserved—recreation never withheld at proper intervals without a reason why. Now, we fear to punish, and hesitate to reward. If our people obtain a holiday, we neither know nor care in what way they spend it.

By our present system, which neglects providing recreation, not only do we separate class from class and destroy that feeling of affection and regard which in the past existed between the employed and the employer, but what is of far greater moment, we fear that the tendency of the present arrangements tends materially to shorten the lives of the working people. In a Parliamentary report, prepared some years since by the sanitary commissioners, the startling fact was manifested that the labourers and mechanics lived upon an average not half so long as the gentry, who are enabled to obtain recreation and repose. For instance, the average duration of life in the borough of Leeds is reported to be—

Of gentry	44 years.
Labourers, mechanics, etc.	19 „
In the Whitechapel Union—	
Of gentry	45 years.
Labourers, etc.	22 „

In the Kensington Union—	
Of gentry	44 years.
Labourers, etc.	26 „
In Bethnal Green—	
Of gentry	45 years.
Labourers, etc.	16 „

We have seen these statistics quoted in proof of the effects of dirt and filth upon a population; and it cannot be denied that in Whitechapel, Bethnal Green, and Leeds a larger proportion of uncleanliness exists than at Kensington; but although the effects of filth are manifest in engendering all kinds of fevers, cholera, and consumption, yet no one can deny that pure air, relaxation, and the flow of spirits resulting from a quickened circulation, are all-powerful in resisting disease, if not in preventing it. By all means let us get rid of filth—but debasing a people will never cleanse them, while all measures which tend to their happiness will necessarily lead to a higher moral tone and a consequent dislike to all uncleanliness of habits. We are strongly impressed with the belief that out-door recreations, however simple and childish, are far more conducive to the health, longevity, and well-being of a people than any other kind of pastime, whether billiards, news rooms, dog-fighting, ratting, cock-fighting, gambling, or any other of the long list of public-house amusements, so alluring and ensnaring to the working classes of the present generation.

Not that we sanction *all* out-door recreations. The statute fairs, with their excesses, must awaken an earnest desire for the reform or abolition of those gatherings. We would not rob the labouring man of his days of amusement and cessation from toil, but we would remove their prejudicial accompaniments, and substitute that which is cheerful and innocent for that which is coarse and demoralizing. In days when so much is done to soften, and refine, and educate, is every other improvement possible, save that which pertains to the morals of the people? In days when schools of art and design are aided from the public treasury as instruments of refinement—when exhibitions of the treasures of art are provided in our great towns as objects of interest to the excursionist, and are found so attractive to the humbler classes, can it be supposed that those classes will prove altogether insensible to the value of efforts made to infuse a better tone into their days of amusement, or that such endeavours must end in disappointment? In other cases, things pronounced impossible have become real achievements.

To move the masses to search for pleasure in a right direction is, undoubtedly, an arduous undertaking. In this attempt we have to battle with man's natural propensity to evil. To contend against moral evil is a great and difficult, but by no means a hopeless, undertaking, for in this case we are sure of the help of an Almighty arm. In lieu of these Martinmas debaucheries, we would institute in every parish throughout England simultaneous harvest festivals, to which should be invited rich and poor. The doings in the olden time may furnish valuable hints. An eloquent writer lately thus spoke of national festivals:—"When Julius Cæsar invaded Britain, Caswallon was the British king, a man beloved by his subjects. The ancient Britons rallied round the king they loved, and expelled the invader. Mighty was the triumph, intense the joy, grand the festival celebrated on the expulsion of the foe. An ancient bard says:—

> "Full twenty thousand beeves and deer
> Were slain to find the guests with cheer."

Such like general festivals, in which all within a parish should have a share, and do their part, is the real remedy for blots in our social system, not to say in our national Christianity, such as that of Martinmas." *

Having thus, in these last chapters, given a brief summary of the amusements, games, and various holidays, instituted and encouraged by the early citizens, we purpose, in our next, glancing at some of their habits and customs which we, their successors, have done well in denouncing and avoiding. The next will be on their fondness for dirt.

* *Yorkshire Gazette.*

CHAPTER XXVIII.

THEIR FONDNESS FOR DIRT IN THE OLDEN TIMES.

"Dirt is one of the grand antagonists of civilization. Once get a New Zealander to wash and shave, or a Hottentot to scrape his skin with a potsherd, and you have effected a master-movement against the stronghold of savagery."—THE RECTOR OF MELLIS.

THE early citizens were not only primitive in their tastes, but undoubtedly dirty in their habits. Not that this infirmity was peculiar to the gilds; the love of dirt pervaded all classes of society, and might be termed a national distemper. They did not learn their dirty ways from the Romans who settled here, for they were cleanly in their persons and habits, and great patrons of the bath. The balneum, or the balneolum, was inseparable from the house of every Roman. Neither could the Normans have instituted and established the reign of dirt in this realm, for they were too refined a race to have delighted in uncleanliness. Either, therefore, it must have been brought amongst our forefathers by the Saxons or the Danes, or it was indigenous to the soil. Indeed, the native Britons could hardly have been accustomed to cleanliness of habits, at a period in which, in cold weather, they were attired in no garments but the skins of beasts, and in which at all seasons their own skins were painted to prevent the necessity of personal ablutions. As the Irish historian remarks of them, "In those early days they wore no linen shirts next their skins, and never washed them; indeed, linen of any kind was unknown to them." If the old chroniclers speak truly respecting the residences of the Britons, that they burrowed in the earth like rats, and like rats abode therein, we can hardly wonder if they occasionally bore evidences of some contact with the earth, and if even their paint became hidden by an outer coverture of mud.

The Britons, no doubt, owed very much to the civilized Romans, who brought them out of their warrens, and taught them to live like men. Then came the Saxons, who taught us but little; if we may form an opinion from the small information we possess respecting the domestic history of our country during the existence of the Heptarchy, until its dissolution by Egbert, after having existed nearly four centuries. But the Danes were certainly in advance of the Saxons in many of the arts of civilization, and in fact great complaints are made by the British bards of the period of their luxurious and effeminate ways.

Nearly a century after the time of Alfred, the English were not greatly in advance of their ancestors of a much earlier date. From an old minstrel's ballad recited A.D. 1002, and quoted by Wallingford, we learn some curious particulars of those early days. The bard confesses that so superior were the Danish troops over the English, that Athelstan and Edgar had been accustomed to keep in pay large numbers of them for the purpose of training their own men to arms and discipline. The narrative informs us of the violence committed by these Danes, and of the wantonness indulged in by them; and specifies that to such a height of luxury had these mercenaries attained, that "they combed their hair once a day, bathed themselves once a week, changed their clothes frequently, and by all these arts of effeminacy, as well as by their military character, had rendered themselves so agreeable to the women, that the wives and daughters of the English were by no means safe in the company of such desperadoes."

We learn incidentally from this recital that the women were not such lovers of dirt as the men, and that if the latter never combed their hair or changed their clothes, it was not to please their wives but themselves. It was many ages before the profession of barber became greatly in request, and then surgery had to be united with it, in order that a living might be obtained by the professor. In fact, the services of the surgeon were as frequently required as those of the barber; or, in other words, people needed the services of the barber less frequently than they did those of the chirurgeon. In the reign of Edward I., so coarse were the people, and so dirty were these barber-surgeons, that the City ordinances of that period contain many enactments against their placing human blood in their windows to indicate that they practised phlebotomy. How utterly disgusting to make a show of such corrupt and poisonous matter as a sign of their trade. The "Liber Albus," under the date A.D. 1273,* has the following:—"Also that barbers shall not place blood in the windows."

Again, "of *barbers*":—"That no barbers shall be so bold or so daring as to put blood in their windows openly or in view of folks, but let them have it carried privily unto the Thames, under pain of paying two shillings unto the use of the Sheriffs."

In the same reign we find similar regulations respecting the perambulation of swine in the streets of the metropolis:—"Also that swine shall not wander about within the city."

Again, it is written of swine:—"And that no swine shall be found about the streets or about the lanes in the city, or in the suburbs, or in the fosses of the said city, from this time forward. And if swine shall be found in the places aforesaid, they shall be killed by those by whom they shall be found; and those who kill them shall have them freely and clearly, without any challenge thereof; or else the swine shall be bought back by him who owns it, at the price of *fourpence!* And he who shall wish to feed a pig *must feed it in his own house.*"†

From the same authority we learn that an ordi-

* Lib. iii. pt. 2.

† Ibid.

nance was enforced that "no leper shall be going about in the city, or make sojourn there by night or by day, under pain of imprisonment, but such persons shall have a common attorney for themselves to go each Sunday to the parish churches to collect alms for their sustenance.". The fishmongers, it seems, were great transgressors, throwing the offal of their trade into the streets. It is, therefore, ordained that "Fishmongers shall not throw their water into the streets or into the lanes, but shall cause the same to be carried into the Thames under penalty of two shillings."

At the same period (13 Edward I.) it is decreed "That no person shall rear swine, oxen, or cows in their houses within the franchise," also "of vendors of fish and flesh, that they shall not throw the water in which they wash the same upon the pavement, but shall have it carried to the Thames." Again comes up the subject "of dirt." "Item, that no person throw straw, dust, dung, or other refuse into the streets or lanes." In the next reign (Edward II.) it is curiously declared that dogs shall not wander about in the city. Also to avoid the noise, damage, and strife that used to arise therefrom (nothing is said of hydrophobia), it is forbidden that any person shall keep a dog accustomed to go at large out of his own enclosure without guard thereof by day or night within the franchise of the city, *genteel dogs excepted*, under pain of paying forty pence to the use of the chamber. And if any one shall make prayer for any person who shall do the contrary hereof, he shall pay forty pence unto the chamber for such his prayer."*

We must bear in mind that these several regulations were made by the Court of Common Council—the civic parliament—and from them we obtain a fair view of the habits of the times. Two or three additional extracts from these ordinances may throw further light upon the habits of the citizens at that period. In book iv., part 4, we read "That no one shall throw water, or other thing, from the windows, but shall carry the same *into the street.*" Juvenal's third satire exactly describes the dangers of those who traverse the streets at night, where, he says, there are as many dangers at night as there are open windows, and he is lucky who receives on his head only the contents of the basins, and not the vessels themselves. The keepers of swine again appear in the same book, where it is stated "That such pigstyes as are in the streets shall be removed, and if any swine shall be found in the streets they shall be forfeited; and four men are elected and sworn in to take and kill such swine as shall be found wandering within the city, to whomsoever they shall belong. The pigs belonging to the Priory and Hospital of St. Anthony, in Threadneedle Street, however, are specially exempted from this law; they had a free run at all times, hence the old saying "as fat as a Tantony pig."

A very gross evil, it appears, of which we in our day loudly complain, existed at a very early date, for

* Lib. iii. pt. 3.

in Edward II.'s reign many judgments are recorded, such as the following:—"Judgment of the pillory for selling a peck of stinking eels;"* also the like punishment "for selling a stinking pig;" the same for "selling a stinking partridge;" also for "putrid pigeons;" the like for selling "rotten fish, called conger, putrid herring and mackerel."

The same page contains a double offence; the offensive food was not only "stinking" but rotten, and, being pikes and eels, the vendor certainly deserved his elevation to the pillory. We here close our extracts from these ancient records with two or three very curious entries of cases in which the pillory was adjudged, one to a certain "woman because she was out at night after lawful hours," another for "being a common scold." Again, for "false dice," "for lies uttered against the mayor," "for false sacks of coal," "upon a person for pretending to be a physician," "for practising the art of magic," "for placing a certain piece of iron in a loaf of bread," "for stealing a leg of mutton;" also "upon one who feigned himself a holy hermit." The following was not the judgment of the pillory, but "judgment and penalty upon an alderman (name omitted in mercy) because that his mantle or cloak was single, and not trimmed with fur." "Robert Hurlebat and others" receive judgment "for giving a female orphan in marriage, without leave of the mayor;" and a subsequent entry declares "the value of the maritage of the orphan

* Lib. iv. pt. 4.

forfeited, such marriage being without leave." Another person (name not mentioned) is imprisoned for a year and a day, with the pillory each quarter for three hours, with a "whetstone" tied round the neck, for lies that were disproved. The origin of this custom is not known, but the whetstone was said to be the reward of one who told the greatest lie; we frequently meet, in old writers, with the expression, "Lying for the whetstone."

The habits of the citizens, no doubt, became greatly improved, and cleanliness had become much less rare in the reign of Henry VIII. than during the period of which we have hitherto treated; but even in the refined age of this monarch great advances were possible, as we learn from the following extract from a letter from Erasmus to Dr. Francis, in which he says—"The floors are commonly of clay, strewed with rushes; under which lies unmolested an ancient collection of beer, grease, fragments, bones, spittle, excrements of dogs and cats (*genteel* or house dogs above-mentioned), and everything that is nasty." The result of all this was frequent plagues and pestilence, which spread throughout the city and throughout the country, robbing England of her best and bravest sons, and followed by lamentation and woe—"Rachel weeping for her children, because they were not."

Plagues and pestilences were of far more frequent occurrence amongst us than is generally supposed, and an attentive perusal of the City records brings to light most melancholy pictures of the ravages of death. Such entries in the minutes of companies as the following are of frequent occurrence :—

From the Goldsmiths', quoted by Herbert :—
"A.D. 1350. Expenses :—because all the wardens before mentioned were dead,—expended on the poor,"—sum obliterated.

From the Carpenters' minutes, in reference to the preparations made by the City for the coronation of James I., under the date July, 1603 :—"By reason of God's visitation for our sinnes, the plague of pestilence then reigning in the City of London (the pageants and other shewes of triumph, in most sumptuous manner prepared, but not finished), the King roade not from the Tower through the Citie in royall manner, neither were the citizens permitted to come at Westminster, but forbidden by proclamation, for feare of infection to be by that meanes increased, for there dyed that weke in the City of London and suburbs of all diseases, 1103 ; of the plague, 857."*

The same year, "ye Lammas quarter-day was not held by reason of a pcept from the Lord Maior to the mr and wardens, commanding them to forbeare in respect of God's vistacon."†

In 1625, a more fatal visitation occurred, and interfered with the coronation of King Charles as the former one had that of his father, carrying away, it is computed, upwards of 40,000 souls, and, in consequence, all feastings and rejoicings were of

* Jupp, p. 68, also quoted by Howes from the City records.
† Ibid.

course suspended; and frequent entries occur in all the companies of noble contributions towards the wants of the sufferers. One entry this year in the Carpenters' books is curious:—"Paid for diett bred and wyne to carry in the coatch with vs, being an infeceous time, vj^{s} vj^{d}."*

The following item is very sad, which states that on the 27th July, 1665, the election of master and wardens shall be private, "in regard of the great increase of the plague, without a sermon, dinner, musicke, and other ceremonies; only a cup of wine and Naple biskate."†

From many similar entries in the minutes of the Leathersellers we extract the following, dated July, 1636:—"At this court, in regard of the precept directed from the Lord Mayor to this society to entreat them to forbear all general and public meetings and feasts during this year of God's visitation, it was ordered that, on the first Tuesday in August next, the M$^{r.}$ and wardens should make a reasonable dynner in their parlour for the assistants only, without any guests."

Notwithstanding the frequency of these visitations, no one seems to have hinted at the probability of dirt and insufficient drainage being the cause. Overcrowding the population was often suggested as a probable cause, and Queen Elizabeth forbad the building of any more houses as dangerous to the health of the people; but attempts to enforce cleanliness as a sanitary measure seem never to have

* Jupp, p. 84. Ibid., p. 128.

been made. This was the more surprising as the pestilence usually originated in the most dirty, as well as crowded, localities; and Lestrange, in his "Life of King Charles," says "these two plagues (1603 and 1625) were natives both of one parish (Whitechappel), under the same roof, and issued forth on the same day of the moneth."*

Terrific as was the remedy, the great fire of 1666, which was considered at the time the most awful dispensation of Providence, proved to be the greatest benefactor to the great City. Though Evelyn's noble plan for rebuilding was not adopted, yet the new City was a grand improvement upon the old one; and that disease which for many ages had, with short intervals, visited the metropolis, and decimated her population, seizing rich and poor with equal rapacity, has never since made even the faintest attack within the City walls.

In the continuation of the "Life of Lord Clarendon," a computation is made of the numbers destroyed in the last great plague, bringing a result of six months' ravages (which Lord Clarendon considered under the mark) of over 160,000.†

Dr. Hodges, in his book "De Peste," calculates the number at 68,596; De Foe at 100,000.‡ Whatever the number of victims may have been, no one can doubt that many of the survivors, of all classes,

* Jupp, note, p. 83.

† Octavo ed., viii. p. 620.

‡ "A dreadful plague in London was
In the year sixty-five,
Which swept an hundred thousand souls
Away—yet I alive!"—De Foe.

from the King to the City apprentice, acted under the circumstances with great generosity and good feeling. Many others were utterly lost and hardened by the shock, so much so, Pennant informs us, that fear of the disease seemed to have steeled the hearts of many, for, as soon as its nature was certainly known, above 40,000 servants were turned into the streets to perish; no one would receive them into their houses, and the villagers near London drove them away with pitchforks and firearms. But he adds, "We had in our capital, during this sad calamity, heroes that vie in piety even with Marseilles' good bishop. Sir John Laurence, Lord Mayor in the year of the plague, showed equal intrepidity, humanity, and charity. He took the wretched fugitives under his protection, and sustained them with his own fortune as long as it lasted, and then by subscription, which he solicited from all parts. The King contributed £1000 a week; in the whole the vast sum (much of which was subscribed by the City companies) of £100,000 was weekly distributed."*

The Duke of Albemarle and the good Archbishop Sheldon, each in his own sphere, acted a noble part. The latter, by pathetic appeals to his suffragans, says the same authority, procured large contributions in aid, and made a hospital of his palace at Lambeth for those sinking under disease and want.

Neither during the presence of this scourge, nor the intervals succeeding each visitation, do we meet

* Pennant, p. 328; also "London Remembrancer," p. 418.

with accounts of any great efforts made by the medical profession either to prevent or allay its virulence. Indeed it seems impossible that the state of medical knowledge could have been worse than it was in this country at that time, and up to the beginning of the eighteenth century. In Queen Elizabeth's reign, the most enlightened and educated, even of the nobility, were accustomed to place their lives in the hands of the veriest quacks and ignoramuses—old women, blacksmiths, and travelling conjurors being amongst the numbers of those known to have been consulted in matters of life and death; and only the more respectable of the profession, namely, the barber-surgeons, could lay claim to the smallest amount of training, and even they were accustomed to complain (hair-dyes not being then in request) that shaving was the most profitable branch of their profession.

From a rare and curious work, entitled "A General Description of all Trades, to which is prefixed an Essay on Divinity, Law, and Physic, London, A.D. 1747," we learn that at this time things were beginning to look up with these practitioners, and that the more ambitious of their number had long before designated themselves by the elegant name of apothecaries.

The author informs his readers that the "apothecary's is a very genteel business, and has been in great vogue of late years;" that the "attorney's is an employment worthy of a scholar and a gentleman;" that the "baker's is a very ancient as well as useful art;" and of "bellows-makers," he remarks, "this (the bellows) is an absolutely necessary article;" that "horse-milliners" are ironmongers, dealers in horse gear; and of "barber-surgeons," he informs us that they "are very much in use now-a-days." We cannot learn, however, from this erudite author, whether the improvement in trade, in which he seems to rejoice, was in regard to the shaving or the physicking department.

In the time of Charles II., no improvement had discovered itself, and than his life, we can conceive of nothing more sad than the "carrying off" of that most ungenerous, selfish, unprincipled of men. Upon his seizure by almost his first, but final illness, so personally beloved was he, that every one about the Court, his mistresses not excepted, sent in hot haste for his or her favourite mediciner, and it was said that his chambers were crowded with all the doctors in London. After having nearly bled the King to death, and used every remedy known, some applied mustard poultices and hot bricks to his feet and stomach, while others, perceiving no immediate improvement, applied "hot irons to his head, for they suspected it was an apoplexy." This, of course, was sufficient; no further experiments were needed; and "every thing having been done that man could do," as the chroniclers inform us, which most certainly was the case—we had almost said "and much more"—this poor King, in the prime of life, with as good a constitution as that of most men of his day, was thus ignorantly doctored to his death.

It is a happy thing for the present generation, that the practitioners of the medical art have established for themselves a reputation as high in public estimation as it is possible for any profession to attain, and that by their researches in the fields of science beyond the mere region of surgery and physic they have discovered the causes of diseases and epidemics, and have done as much to lengthen human life by their sanitary precautions to avert, as by their skilful treatment in arresting, disease. Nor should we forget the fact that the monarch just named, whose mode of death was so disgraceful to the medical profession of his own day, was himself one great instrument in bringing about the wondrous improvements which have taken place in these respects by founding the Royal Society, one of the first and greatest agencies for the encouragement of learning and science, amongst the most distinguished of whose associates have ever been conspicuous the members of the medical profession.

Upon the higher and more important question as to the extent of moral defilement resulting from the prevalence of dirt in all its varieties, how far the spiritual part of man becomes contaminated and polluted by continual contact with physical impurities, we do not now enter; but we do hold that "cleanliness is next to godliness," and we can hardly conceive of the possibility of the existence of a pure mind in an impure body. If, then, dirt be so efficient an instrument of national degradation, so "grand an antagonist of civilization," let our missionary efforts, both home and foreign, be directed to the extirpation of this monster evil, and to the teaching of the great truth that erroneous practice is as much to be deprecated as erroneous belief; and as dirt is found to be the prolific source of divers diseases and sundry kinds of death, and has ever proved itself in our great cities the great first cause of plagues and pestilences, the effect of which is wide-spread misery and desolation, let us hope that future historians may not have to speak of our generation, as we must of some former ones, as being ignorant of the dangers resulting from a general prevalence of this never-too-much-to-be-deprecated "fondness for dirt."

CHAPTER XXIX.

THE TWELVE.

"From the twelve companies the Lord Mayor was *exclusively* chosen for centuries. None of the lists of Lord Mayors, in our histories of London, afford a single instance to the contrary, from Fitz-Alwyn (A.D. 1189) to Sir Robert Wilmot (A.D. 1742).—HERBERT'S *History of the Twelve Great Companies.*

IT is sometimes a puzzle to the uninitiated to understand a term continually in use in civic parlance, viz., "the twelve." If the Lord Mayor entertains the masters of companies, it is generally mentioned that "the invitation included the masters of the twelve great companies." If a citizen speaks of "his company," it is usually asked if it is "one of the twelve." In any account of the City companies, amounting in number from eighty to ninety, it seems necessary to give some explanation of this distinction, and to state the reasons for the existence of this difference in rank or estimation.

So marked was the supposed superiority of "the twelve," that for many centuries no Lord Mayor was chosen from any company other than the twelve; and should a candidate for the mayoralty happen to be so unfortunate as not to be enrolled amongst the members of these honoured gilds, his election was always made conditionally that he would, before being sworn-in, exchange into one or other of them; in which case no difficulty occurred.

It is impossible now to ascertain the origin of this custom. That it was a mere custom, and not founded upon law, seems to be the general opinion of those who have written upon the point. Norton, in his "Commentaries," states that it was a mere usage founded upon ancient custom, and not upon prescription. "It even became a common impression that the Mayor must belong to one of the twelve great companies, as they are called, though it would be difficult to assign any ground for such a dogma." * He adds, in a note, that "There is a precedent, however, of the Lord Mayor being elected from the Coopers' Company, which is not one of the twelve chief companies, as early as 1742," giving Maitland as his authority.

Herbert affirms, that not only were the Lord Mayors, from the beginning, elected from the twelve great companies, but that the wardens of those great companies were the only ones allowed to attend the Lord Mayor as chief butler at coronations. The twelve alone had the honour of enrolling the sovereign amongst their members, and generally of entertaining foreign princes and ambassadors; they took precedence in all civil triumphs; they occupied the chief standings in all state processions through the City; they alone of the companies contributed to the repair of the City walls; and lastly, they were the companies most largely assessed in all levies for

* "Commentaries," p. 441.

the Government or the City. No wonder, therefore, that the common opinion prevailed, that no Lord Mayor could be elected but from one of these most distinguished gilds. Herbert remarks that this opinion was "indisputably founded on long prescriptive right and usage," and adds, "It was in 1742 that Sir Robert Wilmot, just mentioned, was sworn-in Lord Mayor, notwithstanding that he was not so qualified, and that upon the advice of counsel, who said there was no law for it. His lordship was of the Coopers' Company, and would have been translated to the Clothworkers' (which is one of the twelve), but his admission being carried only by a small majority, and they, at the same time, refusing him their hall, he resolved to give (them) no further trouble. It is now understood, that being free of one of the twelve companies is only necessary to qualify the Lord Mayor for president of the Irish Society. The Lord Mayor, it should be observed, if not free of the twelve, thus loses a privilege always appertaining of right to his office—that of the presidentship mentioned.*

That this custom was a very arbitrary one, considering the importance, wealth, and antiquity of many of the gilds not of the twelve, and a great indignity passed upon them by the implication that none of their livery, however distinguished, were worthy of the office of Lord Mayor, no one can doubt; and it is somewhat remarkable that an usage so obnoxious should have been submitted to so

* Herbert, vol. i. p. 37—quoting from Northouck, p. 348.

meekly for nearly five centuries. All our authorities, however, are at fault as to the period at which this custom was first broken through: and it is surprising that Maitland, so exact in all things; Norton, who quotes him as a final authority; Northouck, who is not often deceived in his facts or dates; and, above all, Herbert, so painstaking and erudite, whose minute search almost nothing has escaped—that they all, and all other writers on this subject, should have made a mistake of more than a hundred years in a matter of so deep interest to all the City gilds, and to their livery.

The distinction of breaking through this custom does not attach to Sir Robert Wilmot, cooper, A.D. 1742, who has hitherto always been named as the first Lord Mayor not a member of one of the twelve, but to Alderman Andrews,* leatherseller, who first put a veto upon an usage so obnoxious to the companies at large, and being supported by the Parliament, successfully carried his point, although not without considerable opposition (A.D. 1649).† It is to be supposed that the troubles of those rebellious times must have driven many important facts, such as this, from the memories of men; but it is nevertheless a fact, that in the year succeeding the death of Charles I., the then Lord Mayor, Sir Abraham Raynardson, was committed to the Tower (April 4, 1649), and Thomas Andrews, alderman and

* Sir Thomas Andrews, who was appointed one of Charles I.'s judges, but refused to act. Mayor a second time 1651.

† Ralph Dormer, Mayor 1529, refused to leave the Brewers', but *was imprisoned until he consented!*

leatherseller, was elected in his place. Herbert himself (vol. ii., p. 427, in a note) mentions the fact, that "Thomas Andrews, leatherseller, of Feltham, in Middlesex, succeeded Sir Abraham Raynardson during the residue of his mayoralty." As decisive upon the point, we quote the following entry, never before published, from the minutes of the Leathersellers' Company, under date 4th July, 1649:—

"Att this court it being related that Alderman Andrews, now Lord Mayor of the Citty, did Continue a member of this Company, which no other Lord Mayor ever did before, that was of any Company Inferior to the Twelve, but was alwaise Translated to one of the Twelve, before he tooke his oath of mayorallity, and that it might be a leading way of other Companies of the Citty to dyne with him which were willing so to do, but looking upon our Company to begin the work; in regard the Lord Mayor's Company did usually invite themselves first, and so consequently all or most of the other Companies of this Citty followed. It was therefore thought fitt, and thereupon fully agreed and ordered that the Master, Wardens, and Assistants, and so many of our Livery as would attend them, should invite themselves to dyne with the Lord Mayor as Benevolent guests, and thereupon also required our Beadles to repair to every man of our Livery to know his pleasure, that notice might be given to the Lord Mayor of the same, with as much conveniency as may bee."

We have already intimated, in the earlier portions of this work, that some of the gilds now existing, reported in 1837 by the Parliamentary Commissioners to amount to eighty-nine in number,* although not now the foremost in rank, are of far

* "The present municipal gilds number 89, though some few are practically extinct. In 1697 the Court of Aldermen ruled that a Liveryman of the twelve should possess £1000; of the inferior companies £500. So important was feasting deemed, that they now actually hold their banquets under their royal charters. Their annual feasts are legal and corporate franchises."—*Report of Parliamentary Commissioners*, 1837.

greater antiquity than many of the twelve, and that, therefore, the present order of precedency is not based in the slightest degree upon priority of foundation. We have shown that the Weavers stand by far the most pre-eminent in regard to antiquity; to whom may be added the Saddlers, and the Leathersellers, both which gilds, although it cannot be proved that their charters were much more ancient, existed as communities from a very early period, and the latter, the Leathersellers, so early as the Saxon era, are mentioned as traders in one of "the five staple commodities of the kingdom," which were wool, woolfels, leather, lead, and tin, and the locality of their market is designated, for "the sale of leather is to be kept on the outside of the ring at Smithfield." *

Neither does the present order of precedency rest upon mere wealth. Two or three of the twelve are poor, when compared with many others not included in that favoured number. Indeed, it is most difficult to say upon what principle the original selection could have been made. Herbert, the historian of "the twelve," can offer no solution of the difficulty. He candidly acknowledges, "that, notwithstanding the ancient rank of the twelve companies, many of the others are, on various accounts, of equal or superior importance. The Weavers, and Saddlers (and Leathersellers) claim a more remote antiquity; the Stationers, besides their growing wealth and extensive concerns, rank higher as a rich, commercial, and working company. The

* Herbert, vol. i. p. 397.

Dyers once took precedence of the Clothworkers. The Brewers are distinguished for their ancient and very curious records, and yield on that point perhaps only to the Leathersellers, who, at their elegant modern hall, in St. Helen's Place, have some matchless charters, as regards embellishment, and the most ornamentally-written 'wardens' accounts' of any we have yet inspected." *

A spirit of emulation, no doubt, existed at a very early period amongst the gilds, as to which should take priority of rank on state occasions; and the civic records afford ample evidence of the innumerable quarrels which occurred on this account. The "Chronicles of London," published 1827, printed from an original MS. in the British Museum, and which affords many curious items of intelligence concerning the early history of London, under the date 1375, has the following respecting one of these contentions for superiority:—"This yere at a wrestlynge, John Northwold, mercer, was sclayne at the black heth, where thorough aroos a gret discencion and debate among the craftes of London." Several similarly fatal encounters have been already noticed.

The City Records contain a very early list of the "number of persons chosen by the several mysteries to be the Common Council," from which we learn that above forty gilds were represented, and also the number sent by each. It will be observed that the Pouch-makers and the Leather-dressers, who properly formed a portion of the Leathersellers' Company,

* "Hist. of Twelve Great Companies," vol. i. p. 38.

are entered separately; the Tanners and the Curriers also as distinct gilds. It will be noted that this arrangement by no means corresponds with our present order. No Clothworkers are named, now one of the twelve; the Skinners are twenty-first, Haberdashers twenty-fifth, and the Ironmongers thirty-fifth—all now of the twelve. The following is the complete list:—

NUMBER OF PERSONS CHOSEN BY THE SEVERAL MYSTERIES TO BE OF THE COMMON COUNCIL, 50 EDWARD III., A.D 1368.*

Grossers	6	Stainers	4
Mercers	6	Cloth Measurers	2
Drapers	6	Haberdashers	2
Fishmongers	6	Brasiers	2
Goldsmiths	6	Salters	4
Vintners	6	Coppers	2
Tailors	6	Pewterers	2
Saddlers	4	Ale-brewers	2
Webbers	4	Hurriers (Hatters)	2
Tapistry Weavers	4	Smiths	6
Leathersellers ...... 2 }		Horners	2
Leatherdressers ... 4 } ...	8	Masons	4
Pouch-makers ...... 2 }		Ironmongers	4
Founders	2	Armourers	2
Joiners	2	Butchers	4
Chandlers	4	Cutlers	2
Fullers	4	Spurriers	2
Curriers	2	Plumbers	2
Freemasons	2	Waxchandlers	2
Brewers	5	Barbers	2
Flechers	2	Painters	2
Bakers	2	Tanners	2
Skinners	6	Woodmongers	2
Girdlers	4	Pinners	2

Giving a total of 148 members, or an average of three from each gild.

* "City Records," lib. ix. fol. 46.

The Common Council, thus constituted, no doubt was influenced, as all councils are, by certain leading spirits, and the gilds which sent as their representatives the ablest men, would consequently grasp to themselves, by their representatives, the chief authority, rank, and influence, and in process of time shut out the weaker companies from all participation in their good things. We can account for the singular anomaly in no other way, nor have we met with any writer upon civic matters who has ventured upon any explanation at all. This seems the more probable theory, from the fact that in the same year as that in which this council was selected "an ordinance was passed by the mayor, aldermen, and six, four, and two of the common council out of *thirteen* of the above mysteries (which were alone allowed this privilege) respecting the removal of any alderman or common councilman for misconduct."*

How the thirty-five gilds not included in this upper house, this select chamber, were bribed thus to allow their several fraternities to be left out in the cold, while the favoured thirteen were permitted by degrees to grasp all power and prestige to themselves, we know not, and probably never shall know; but no doubt they exhibited a preponderance of mean-spirited, unambitious citizens, who would consider the relief from their share in some paltry tax, such as that of repairing the City walls, ample compensation for being pushed into the background,

* Herbert, vol. i. p. 35.

and trampled upon by newer and less wealthy corporations.

Although for generations no definite arrangement had been decided upon, still twelve of the leading companies ruled, and appeared to claim to be representatives of the rest. At the burial of Elizabeth of York, queen of Henry VII., A.D. 1503, besides the mayor and aldermen, *certain crafts of London* were required to take part in the ceremony. The City records preserve the list of these *crafts*, and a description of the livery to be worn. The order directs "that the most worshipfull fealowships shall stand in Chepe" as follows, viz.:—

The Goldsmiths.	Skinners.
Grocers.	Haberdashers.
Drapers.	Salters.
Fishmongers.	Ironmongers.
Tailors.	

These nine were the only crafts named, although others were permitted to be present, but not in any post of honour. It will be remarked that these nine are to this day included in the twelve; but these chief companies were not always satisfied with their station, and fierce discussions were not unfrequent between them as to priority of rank. Thus, 10th April, A.D. 1483, 1 Richard III., is "an award made by the court of aldermen in a difference between the companies of Skinners and Tailors, respecting their precedency in processions, when it was (judiciously) determined that they shall take precedency of each other alternately every year." These bickerings were not finally put a stop to till 4 Henry VIII., A.D. 1513, when a court, specially summoned for the purpose, decreed "that all manner of fellawshippes shall keep the order of goyng in procession, and standyng as it was ordeyned in Mr. Shaa's daies."*

"Mr. Shaa's daies" were about thirty years before this date, viz., A.D. 1483, in which year Sir John Shaa was Lord Mayor. The City records have preserved this list, with the order thereof, "An. 1483, list of the companies having liveries (with their numbers), in temp. John Shaa, milit.," in which the first twelve stand thus:—

Mercers	66	Skinners	54
Grocers	84	Ironmongers	25
Drapers	80	Haberdashers ...	41
Fishmongers	76	Salters	30
Goldsmiths	51	Vintners	26
Tailors	84	Dyers	19

Between this date and the reign of James I., some alterations in this list took place, how we know not; but some of the above were displaced in the latter reign, and since that date no change has occurred. Historians inform us that this king, having determined to sell certain forfeited lands in the north of Ireland, and believing the citizens of London likely as any to carry out this Plantation, especially as they always provided the sovereigns of England with the necessary money to carry out their extravagances (which loans were never repaid), sent for the citizens—the Lord Mayor being Hum-

* Herbert, vol. i. p. 101.

phrey Weld—and explaining to them the scheme, they, after several interviews, finally agreed to accept the responsibilities, in November, 1611. To fully manage the great work, the corporation constituted a company, selected from members of the City companies, being aldermen and common councilmen. The members of these companies were applied to for the necessary funds for the purpose of the settlement, which at last exceeded the then princely sum of £60,000. A charter incorporated the Irish Society (otherwise this "company" of citizens) the 29th of March, 1613, and on the 28th of June another charter was granted to the annexed town of Coleraine. The society was then divided into twelve shares, in the names of the twelve great companies; and these had annexed to them the "minor" companies, in proportion to their payments. These minors numbering forty-three, it will be seen that fifty-five of the City companies became the undertakers for the Plantation scheme upon the Irish estates, embracing 300,000 acres.*

* Great reflections have at various times been cast upon the wisdom of committing large Irish estates to the government of the City companies, but, for my part, I believe that of all the wise acts committed by a sovereign who committed a great many foolish ones, there was none so statesmanlike in its foresight, and so happy in its results, as the Plantation of Ulster; and when people ask you what you have done during three hundred years with your power, your money, and your influence, you can point them proudly to the north of Ireland, where you have turned the wild rocks into springing waters, and made the barren wilderness of Ulster to flourish and blossom as the rose. If the other divisions of the sister isle were as prosperous, as contented, as loyal as Ulster is, we should have no need to suspend the Habeas Corpus Act in that country, no need to devise remedial

The twelve companies then selected are THE TWELVE, and thus we get at as much information as probably we shall ever obtain upon this question of precedency. We submit the final

LIST OF THE TWELVE GREAT COMPANIES.

The MERCERS.	MERCHANT TAYLORS.
GROCERS.	HABERDASHERS.
DRAPERS.	SALTERS.
FISHMONGERS.	IRONMONGERS.
GOLDSMITHS.	VINTNERS.
SKINNERS.	CLOTHWORKERS.

Were we required to give a definite answer as to the precise reign in which the present order of precedency of the companies was settled, we should say that of Henry VIII., but how, or upon what principle, we know not. No doubt a great deal depended upon the talent of the clerk for the time being, and even now much of the prestige and worldly eminence of a particular gild will depend upon the diplomacy and general ability of this high functionary; but much more would rest with the master for the time being, and one or two commanding spirits in his court, by whose counsels he might permit himself to be guided. Influence in high quarters was the magic spell by which certain of these crafts came out so high upon the list, while the want of this talent accounted for some of the wealthiest, most ancient, and most distinguished, being found

measures, and there would be no need, or rather no excuse, for bringing forward propositions that would overturn the foundations of society, and revolutionize the system of government.—*Gathorne Hardy, M.P.*

nowhere in the race. We have a suspicion, that in those days of universal bribery, when, from the King on the throne to the night watchman, gold was all-powerful, gifts and offerings were freely distributed by some of the companies. The great Cardinal Wolsey, we know, was in his day supreme, and to him more than to the King did all suitors bow. The accounts of some of the gilds look very suspicious just at this period. Item, "a compliment to his Excellency the Cardinal"—so much; another company enters "20 marks to my Lord Cardinall's Grace" "as a 'pleasure' for his services with the King."* In another entry the sum of £22 15*s.* is stated to have been paid "for 22 yards of crimson satten for my Lord Cardinall."† A very handsome present say we, and, no doubt, so noble a dress set off to much advantage the great cardinal's portly person.

We subjoin a very curious and laboriously prepared document, worked out by Dr. Hughson, and published in his "History of London," showing the relative position of fifty-six of the then chief companies, in 1665, with the number of chaldrons of coals required to be kept in store and retailed, to defeat the combination of the dealers who had entered into a confederacy to keep up the price of this necessary commodity. It will be noted that no *Coaldealers'* Company existed. All other trades were united in their gilds, and maintained "protection" to the greatest extent possible; but when a body of men,

* *Vide supra*, p. 276, and Herbert, vol. i. p. 412. † *Ibid.*

not incorporated, attempted to do the like, every "hall" in the City became a coal-shed, and the companies retailers of coal. The same had always been done in respect to corn, of which no monopoly was allowed, and to the great advantage of the community.

Companies.	Number of Chaldrons.	Incorporated.	Arms Granted.	Supporters Granted.
Mercers	488	1393	1568	none
Grocers	674	1345	1531	1531
Drapers	562	1439	1439	1561
Fishmongers	465	1363	1536	1575
Goldsmiths	525	1397	1571	1571
Skinners	315	1327	1551	1561
Merchant Taylors ...	750	1503	1481	1586
Haberdashers	578	1448	1570	1570
Salters	360	1530	1530	1587
Ironmongers	255	1351	1455	none
Vintners	375	1363	1442	none
Clothworkers	412	1365	1530	1587
Dyers	105	1471	—	—
Brewers	104	1438	—	none
Leathersellers ...	210	1354	1464	1531
Pewterers	52	1474	1533	—
Cutlers...	75	1455	1476	—
White Bakers	45	1503	—	—
Wax Chandlers ...	19	1483	1484	1563
Tallow Chandlers ...	97	1462	1456	1602
Armourers	19	1452	1556	none
Girdlers	105	1449	1454	none
Butchers	22	1605	—	—
Saddlers	90	1364	—	—
Carpenters	38	1477	1467	none
Cordwainers	60	1439	—	none
Barber-Surgeons ...	60	1462	1452	—
Painter Stainers ...	12	1581	—	—
Curriers	11	1606	—	—

Companies.	Number of Chaldrons.	Incorporated.	Arms Granted.	Supporters Granted.
Masons	22	1677	1474	none
Plumbers	19	1611	—	none
Innholders	7	1515	—	none
Founders	7	1614	1590	none
Poulterers	12	1504	—	—
Cooks	30	1482	—	—
Coopers	52	1501	1509	—
Tylers and Bricklayers	19	1568	—	none
Bowyers	3	1621	1489	none
Fletchers	3	—	1610	none
Blacksmiths	15	—	—	none
Apothecaries	43	—	—	—
Joiners...	22	1571	—	none
Weavers	27	1184	1487	—
Woolmen	3	—	—	none
Woodmongers ...	60	—	—	—
Scriveners	60	1616	1634	none
Fruiterers	7	1606	—	—
Plasterers	8	1501	1546	—
Brown Bakers ...	12	United to White Bakers 1569		
Stationers	75	1556	—	none
Embroiderers	30	1561	—	—
Upholders	9	1626	1465	—
Musicians	6	1604	—	—
Turners	13	1604	1634	—
Basket Makers ...	6	Founded by Mayor & Aldermen 1569		
Glaziers	6	1631	—	—

We have carefully tested the various dates of this table, and find them, as far as it is possible to ascertain, correct. One thing, however, seems curious; three or four gilds are named as having arms granted before the date of incorporation. Our only solution of this difficulty is, that the said companies possessed a charter earlier than we now know of, for it does not follow, because we can find no charter earlier than a given date, that therefore none had been conferred. We have ourselves added the list of companies entitled to supporters, as far as we can ascertain them, with the date of that grant. Dr. Hughson remarks of the following, that the Dyers were formerly of the twelve; but the Clothworkers obtained precedence, *temp.* Hen. VIII.; the Carpenters were founded in the thirteenth century; the Curriers A.D. 1367; the Masons, by prescription, about 1410; the Founders were enrolled 1365; and the Stationers were established 1403.

Not only is it contrary to all the rules of precedency for a past Lord Mayor to degrade to the rank of social knight, but as all London aldermen have undisputed precedency of all knights-bachelors, it would be opposed to custom and etiquette for even the youngest alderman to accept this inferior title. The aldermen have often had cause in the early times to appeal to authority, in order to preserve decorum on occasions of public ceremony, and on all such appeals it has been decided that a London alderman is of higher rank within the city than knight. The last instance of dispute which we now remember occurred in the reign of James I., when the order of precedence was settled at the Earl Marshal's Court, February 19th, 1611, by the following order, a copy of which was forwarded by direction of the Court of Aldermen to each of the City Companies, and which is recorded in the Earl Marshal's Book, I., 25, page 38 in the College of Arms.*

* *Vide* Jor. *Pemberton*, No. 28, fo. 307*b*.

"ORDER OF PRECEDENCY:

"Whereas, upon the humble petition of the Mayor, Knights, and Aldermen of the City of London, exhibited to the King's Most Excellent Majestie, complaining that divers citizens and commoners of the said City being knighted, did chalenge precedency of place before the aldermen at publique meetings within the City, it pleased his Majesty for the upholding of the auncient and seemelie orders of the said City, to referre the difference unto the Lords Commissioners, to the end that such order might be sett downe as might stand with the preservation of the creditt and reputation of such as under his Highness had authority in the government of the said City: whereas, the said Lords Commissioners haveing appoynted two severall dayes to both parties for the hearing and ending the said difference at both which dayes the said knights-commoners made defalte to attende with their councell at Whithall; * * * Forasmuch as the said knights-commoners did make defalte, and alledging that they would no longer stand in opposition in the premises, their lordships have thereupon ordered that the said aldermen shall have and take place and superiority in precedence within the said City before the said knights-commoners, and such as hereafter shall be made batchelor knights. * * * J. NORTHAMPTON, T. SUFFOLK, LENNOX, E. WORCESTER."
NOTTINGHAM,

It is difficult precisely to determine the period at which the twelve great companies first claimed their right to send an assistant each to the coronation to wait upon the Lord Mayor. Hoveden and Ralph de Diceto, Dean of St. Paul's, who is stated by Rapin * to have been an eye-witness of the second coronation of Richard I. (1194), both say that the citizens of London were his butlers, and those of Winchester served up the meat. Again, in the 20 Henry III. (1236), at the coronation of Queen Eleanor, it is recorded that "*Andrew*, Mayor of the City of London, came there to serve in the butlery, to help the chief butler, and claimed the place of standing before the King, but was repulsed by order of the King, and so gave way and served the two bishops on the King's right hand."† At the coronation of Richard II., the prudent citizens, not desiring to be publicly snubbed by his Majesty, took the precaution to feel their ground beforehand, and in the City Records is still extant their claim and the judgment thereon A.D. 1377, 1 Richard II.: "Be it remembered, that the Mayor and citizens of London * * * claimed that the same Mayor, by reason of his office, * * * in his own person may serve our lord the King on the day of his coronation, as well in the hall at his banquet as after the banquet in the chamber, from a *cup of gold* of the same King, and when he shall depart from the same feast he shall have the same cup, together with the ewer of gold, for his fee, and carry them away with him; and that *the other citizens*, who shall be chosen for this by the

* Rapin, p. 244, note 9.

† *Vide* "Liber Ordinationum," fo. 193*b*, and MS. "Cotton Vespasian," c. xiv., fo. 113.

aforesaid City, ought to serve at the same day in the office of butlership, to help the chief butler * * * as the mayors and citizens of the same City hitherto * * * have been accustomed to do," etc. "And the said lord the King, weighing well the great gratitude and succour which his progenitors before these times had abundantly experienced in the citizens of the City aforesaid, and hoping in future to find the like gratitude and succour in the aforesaid citizens, and that they may assume more cheerful hearts to render faithful service to our lord the King, and more eagerly succour him in his necessities, and heartily desiring to please the same citizens, hath willed and decreed that the citizens of the City aforesaid, should serve in the hall the office of butlership to help the chief butler, the King sitting at table on the day of his coronation; and when our same lord the King, after the banquet, having entered the chamber, shall ask for wine, the said Mayor shall serve the aforesaid lord the King from a golden cup, and should afterwards have that cup, together with the ewer to the same cup pertaining, of the King's gift. And so the same Mayor and the aforesaid citizens decently fulfilled the services aforesaid, and the aforesaid Mayor received the cup wherewith he served the lord the King, according to the will and decree of the same lord the King."* This right of the citizens was again granted at the coronation of Henry IV.,† also of Henry VI.;‡

* "Liber Custumarium," fo. 275-8, *b*. Quoted also in Strype's Stow, p. 153.

† Harl. MS., 714, fo. 28, 29.

‡ "Liber Dunthorne," fo. 61*b*.

again of Edward IV.* Hitherto the twelve companies had not been considered in the selection, nor had they all in the 4th of Edward IV. (1465) at the coronation of his queen, when eight citizens only were appointed to serve the chief butler.† At the coronation of Richard III. and his queen Anna, July 1483, "in the tyme of Mr. Shaa," it is stated that "as well Edmund Shaa, the Mayor, as the aldermen, and other citizens elected by the Common Council to wait upon the chief butler of England, as was the custom, were benignly and honourably treated;" and the cups and ewers were given to the Mayor as was the rule aforetime.‡ The number of "assistants" from the gilds was reduced to eight only, on the coronation of Elizabeth, Queen of Henry VII., but at succeeding coronations the "Twelve" again were represented, viz.:—

Henry VIII. and Catherine his queen, also Anne his queen.
Edward VI. (*vide* Rep. Hebthorn, No. 11, fo. 333*b*).
Mary (*vide* Rep. Barne, No. 13, fo. 76*b*, 77*b*).
Elizabeth (*vide* Rep. Leigh, No. 14, fo. 102*b*).
James I. and Anne his queen (*vide* Rep. Lee, No. 26, fo. 171).
Charles II. (*vide* Rep. Browne, No. 67, fo. 225).
James II. (*vide* Rep. Smith, No. 90, fo. 61).
William III. and Mary (*vide* Rep. Pilkington, No. 95, fo. 2).

* "Liber Dunthorne," fo. 62. † "Jor. Josscelyn," No. 7*b*-97.
‡ Lib. L., City Records, fo. 191, *a* and *b*, quoted in Strype's Stow, p. 153.

Anne (*vide* Rep. Gore, No. 106, fo. 253-5).
George I. (*vide* Rep. Stainer, No. 118, fo. 357, 382-3).
George II. (*vide* Rep. Becher, No. 132, fo. 45-48).
George III. (*vide* Rep. Blakston, No. 165, fo. 292).
George IV. (*vide* Rep. Thorp, No. 225, fo. 501).

In conclusion, we would observe that precedency is either of *courtesy* or *de jure*, of right. In the matter under consideration it is *of right*. The rank and order of these companies have been settled by authority. So the status of the Lord Mayor. When *past* Lord Mayor he loses not the rank of late the king's lieutenant, and it is not to be supposed that he would accept a lower rank, such, for instance, as a social knighthood. At the coronation of King James I., the Earl Marshal ruled that Alderman Craven, though no knight, had place, as senior, before all others who were knights. It has also been ruled in the Earl Marshal's court of honour, that all who have been Lord Mayors of London shall everywhere take place of all knights-bachelors, because they have been the king's lieutenants. All these details may appear very insignificant to some modern readers, but they are really possessed of great importance, and we should indeed be sorry to witness amongst the rulers of our ancient corporations either ignorance of the laws of honour, or negligence in those particulars of observance, ceremony, and precedence, which held so prominent a position in the estimation of the early rulers of the gilds.

CHAPTER XXX.

THE CITY CEREMONIALS.

"The sauce to meat is ceremony;
Meeting were bare without it."

SHAKESPEARE.

IN many parts of this work reference has been made to the large amount of ceremonial observed by the ancient citizens, and continued in many gilds to the present day. This work would not be complete, however, without a brief summary of the leading City ceremonials still observed by the Lord Mayor as chief magistrate.

We would premise that the election of Lord Mayor takes place on the 29th day of September. Anciently the election was held on the Feast of the Translation of St. Edward, 13th October, but was altered to Michaelmas Day by act of Common Council, 30 Henry VIII., 1546. A precept is issued from the Mayor's Court to the several livery companies, requiring their attendance at Guildhall in their livery gowns and hoods, to go thence to St. Laurence Jewry to attend divine service, thence to return to elect Lord Mayor. The Lord Mayor and sheriffs go from the Mansion House in FULL STATE to the Guildhall, and are received by the aldermen and officers. The

Lord Mayor, aldermen, recorder, and sheriffs are in black court suits and scarlet gowns. So important have the citizens ever deemed the matter of dress and observance, that at a court of the 20 Car. II., November 19th, 1668, the following order of Common Council was recorded:—"This court considering of what importance it is to the governours to maintain those forms of state and gravity which have been anciently observed amongst the aldermen of this City, did now for reviving thereof, in one particular of late being discontinued, agree and order that none of the MASTERS, the ALDERMEN, shall henceforth go to their parish churches, within the City and liberty, but in their gowns according to an order of the court of the 28th November, 3 Elizabeth, 1561;" and in more recent times, an order appears, dated 1777, 17 George III.:—"This court, taking into consideration that some of the chief magistrates have not appeared on court days with the *state coach*, doth desire that all future Lord Mayors do appear in the usual state on every public day."

At the election a nosegay is presented to each of the dignitaries just named by the hallkeeper. An imposing procession is then formed of all the chief officers and magistrates who proceed to church, *favente clementiâ Salvatoris*, where the aldermen and sheriffs divide on each side of the aisle to allow the Lord Mayor to pass to his proper seat. Formerly the Lord Mayor, aldermen, and sheriffs received the sacrament on this day. At the close of the ceremoney, the sword-bearer, in the name of the Lord

Mayor, invites the rector to dinner. Having returned to the hall, the common crier opens the business by the usual proclamation, when the recorder rises, and having made his obeisance to the Lord Mayor, goes to the front of the hustings and there makes his obeisance to the livery, and informs them of the occasion of their meeting. The Lord Mayor, aldermen, and recorder then retire to the aldermen's room to await the result. Thereupon the sheriffs, with the common-serjeant between them, advance to the front of the hustings, the common-serjeant announces the names of the aldermen below the chair who are eligible for Lord Mayor, from whom they are to return two "of the most sufficient and wisest citizens" for the choice of the Lord Mayor and aldermen. The livery having selected two, the sheriffs and common-serjeant proceed with the other officers, in solemn procession, to the aldermen's rooms. On entering, the sheriffs and common-serjeant make three obeisances to the court; the first at the entrance, the second in the middle of the court, and the third at the table; the Lord Mayor bows to each, at the third taking off his hat. Each alderman, beginning with the junior, then comes down to the table and declares for which of the two he votes, the recorder and common-serjeant overlooking the town clerk as he takes down the votes. The town clerk goes up to the Lord Mayor to know for whom his lordship votes, and the result of the election is then declared by the recorder.

The sword-bearer (in white gloves) hands the

Lord Mayor-elect to his place, which is on the left hand of the Lord Mayor, and having addressed the court, he receives the congratulations of each member according to seniority. In returning to the hall, the Lord Mayor-elect walks on the left hand of the Lord Mayor; his train as well as that of the Lord Mayor being supported. He declares to the livery his assent to serve, the sword-bearer places the chain upon his neck, the common hall is dissolved, and the Lord Mayor takes the Lord Mayor-elect to the Mansion House in his state coach, where the aldermen, etc., join them at dinner.

Very similar is the ceremonial on the election of sheriffs, which need not be here particularized.

Of the Lord Mayor's regalia, we may state that there are four swords belonging to the citizens of London:—

1. The *sword of state,* borne before the Lord Mayor as the emblem of that civic authority and power which has from time to time, by sundry charters of various kings, been granted by the crown to the citizens.

This is the sword which is surrendered to the sovereign at Temple Bar, when she comes within the City of London; and it is usually returned to the Lord Mayor, and by him borne before her Majesty. Excepting in processions, it is inverted with its point downwards in the presence of the Queen, or of her judges in her Court of Exchequer, but is borne before the Lord Mayor on all other occasions of authority, or judicial or executive proceedings.

2. Another is called the *pearl sword*, from the nature of its rich ornaments, and is carried before the Lord Mayor on all occasions of ceremony or festivity.

3. The third is a sword placed at the Central Criminal Court, above the Lord Mayor's chair.

4. The fourth is a *black sword*, to be used in Lent and on days of public fasts, and on the death of any of the Royal family.

In addition to the swords are the gold and silver maces, the sceptre, the cap of maintenance, etc.

Of the ceremonies before the Lord Chancellor in receiving her Majesty's approval of the citizens' choice and his presentation to the Barons of the Exchequer, the public are well informed by the public press. At the swearing-in of the new Lord Mayor, the outgoing Lord Mayor leaves the Mansion House in his private state carriage and six horses, attended by his sword-bearer, common-crier, and chaplain, for Guildhall, where the ceremonies are very elaborate and not dissimilar to those already described, but performed by a larger number of great officers. At the close the Lord Mayor and the late Lord Mayor proceed to the outer door, preceded by all the officers, and followed by the aldermen, recorder, sheriffs, and the two livery companies to which the said Lord Mayors belong, and return together in the late Lord Mayor's carriage to the Mansion House, the new Lord Mayor entering it first, and occupying the right-hand seat, the late Lord Mayor sitting on his left; the whole party meet at dinner, at which the late Lord Mayor's chaplain says grace before meat, and the chaplain to the new Lord Mayor after meat. This is a full dress dinner.

At the first Court of Aldermen, the Lord Mayor comes from the Mansion House in his state carriage with six horses, in his scarlet robe and collar of SS, and in the same manner to the first Court of Common Council; so also to the Central Criminal Court, of which his lordship is the first Commissioner; and in the commission takes place and precedence even of the Lord Chancellor.*

One of the most pleasant ceremonies, perhaps, in which the Lord Mayor takes part, is that of receiving from the royal parks his usual venison warrants.

In the month of December, the first warrants for venison from the royal forests are issued for the Lord Mayor, the sheriffs, and some of the officers of the corporation. Those in December are for does, and others in July for bucks.

The Lord Mayor receives warrants on or about the days in the following list, which was adopted in the mayoralty of Mr. Alderman Wilson.

* When the Central Criminal Court was about to be established, the Lord Chancellor's name was placed in the bill at the head of the commission, but Mr. Alderman Farebrother, Lord Mayor for the time being, protested against it as contrary to the ancient custom of the City, and *the bill was accordingly altered*, placing the Lord Mayor at the head of the commission. When the court was opened the Lord Mayor took his place accordingly, and appointed the clerk.—("Ceremonials of London," p. 56. Printed, 1850, for the use of the aldermen, sheriffs, and other officers, but not published.)

1. 1st December, for one doe	from Bushey Park.
2. 24th December, ditto	from ditto.
3. 3rd January, ditto	from the New Forest.
4. 19th January, ditto	from Richmond Forest.
5. 13th July, for one buck	from Waltham Forest.
6. 30th July, ditto	from the New Forest.
7. 15th August, ditto	from Windsor Great Park.
8. 12th September, ditto	from ditto.
9. 13th September, ditto	from Bushey Park.
10. 4th October, ditto	from the New Forest.
11. 4th October, ditto	from Waltham Forest.

The sheriffs also have four does and three brace of bucks; the recorder one doe and one brace of bucks; the chamberlain one doe and one buck; the town clerk one doe and one buck; the common-serjeant one doe and one buck; the remembrancer one doe and one buck, in the respective seasons.

In 1821, soon after the accession of King George IV. to the throne, this right to venison was called in question by his Majesty. The reply from the City was unanswerable. Numerous charters, from King Henry I. downwards, grant that "the citizens of London should have their chases to hunt as well and as fully as their ancestors had; that is to say, in Chiltre (in Hertfordshire), and in Middlesex and Surrey" (Charter of Henry I., A.D. 1101). Fitzstephen, A.D. 1174, expressly mentions the privilege of the citizens of London to hunt in Middlesex and Hertfordshire, and also in Kent as far as the river Cray:—"Plurimi civium delectantur ludentes in avibus cæli, nisis, accipitribus, et hujusmodi, et in canibus, militantibus in sylvis, habentes cives suum jus venandi in Middlexia, Hertfordsira, et tota Chiltra, et in Contiâ usque ad aquam Crayæ." *

Fabian, in his "Chronicles," gives the following account of a grand hunt, to which the citizens of London were invited by King Edward IV., in the twenty-first year of his reign (1481):—"In the month of Julet following, anno 1481, the kinge rode huntinge into the forest of Waltham, whither he comaunded the mayor, Sir William Heriot, draper, with a certayne of his brethren, to come and gyve attendaunce upon hym, with certayne commoners of the citye; where when they were comyn the kynge caused the game to be brought before them, so that they saw course after course, and many a dere, both rede and falowe, to be slayne before them; and after goodly dissport was passyed, the kynge comaunded his offycers to brynge the mayor and his company unto a pleasant lodge, made all of grene bowes and garniss with tables and other thinges necessary, where they were sit at diner, and servyd with many deyntie dysshes, and of dyverse wynes good plentye, as whyte, rede, and claret, and caused them to be sette to dyner, or he were servyd of his owne; and, over that, caused the lord chamberlayne, with other lordes to hym assygned, to chere the sayd mayor and his company sondry times whyle they were at dyner, and at their departynge gave unto them of venyson

* Many of the citizens take great delight in fowling with merlins, hawks, etc., as likewise in hunting; and they have a right and privilege of hunting in Middlesex, Hertford, and all the Chiltern country, and in Kent as far as the river Cray.—(Fitzst., p. 79, edit. Pegge.)

great plentie; and in the month of August fol-lowynge, the kinge, of his greate bounte, sent unto the mayoresse, and her systers aldermennes wyfes, two hartes and six bukkys, with a tonne of wyne to drynke with the sayde venyson, the whyche venyson and wyne was had unto the Drapers' halle, to whych place, at day assygned, the mayor desyred the aldermen and their wyfes, with sondry comoners," etc.*

The Lord Mayor, the Archbishop of Canterbury, and the Bishop of London are the auditors of the St. Paul's Cathedral Repair Fund. The Lord Mayor has the privilege of private audience with the Sovereign at all times; attends the levées and drawing-rooms by the privileged route along Pall Mall and Cleveland Row into the Ambassadors' Court to the entrée entrance. The Sheriffs, accompanying him, are likewise permitted to pass.†

* See p. 667, edit. Ellis.

† In 1839, Mr. Alderman Wilson, then Lord Mayor, had a correspondence with the Lord Steward, some question having arisen as to the Lord Mayor's right to this privilege. The Lord Mayor grounded his claim on immemorial usage, in consequence of his magisterial and public duties, which made it necessary for him to proceed by the shortest route. His lordship's carriage was ordered by the Lord Steward to be allowed to pass on that occasion by Pall Mall, subject to further consideration for the future; and on a further remonstrance by the Lord Mayor, the correspondence being laid before the Lord Steward for his further directions, a letter was sent from the Board of Green Cloth to the Commissioners of Police, with the orders of His Grace, that "when the Lord Mayor comes to Court, his lordship's progress may be facilitated through Pall Mall and Cleveland Row, instead of the usual route by Constitution Hill gate."

At the demise of the Crown, the Secretary of State communicates the fact to the Lord Mayor, who, with the aldermen and officers, attend at the palace. The Lord Mayor takes his seat as a Privy Councillor, and the aldermen and officers remain in the adjoining room. The Lord Mayor, aldermen, and officers sign the proclamation declaring the successor to the throne.

Whenever the Sovereign publicly passes through the City, he first communicates with the Lord Mayor; and before the passage of troops through the City, the Secretary of State for the Home Department writes to the Lord Mayor to inform him, and to request the sanction of the authorities of the City for the troops marching through. In reply to such a request the following is extant:—

"MANSION HOUSE, 31*st January*, 1839.

"MY LORD,—In reply to your lordship's request for the sanction of the City authorities to allow the first battalion of the Scotch Fusilier Guards to pass through the City on their way to the Tower, on the 1st and 2nd February, it is right I should state to your lordship that when troops pass through the City it is without their colours flying, drums beating, or bayonets fixed;* but I am informed that of late years it has been usual for the troops to pass to the Tower by a more circuitous route.

"Your lordship must be aware that troops passing through the City during certain hours of business would be attended with great

* There is one regiment of infantry, the 3rd, or "Buffs," which, in consequence of its having been originally formed from the trained bands of London, has the privilege to march through the City of London with bayonets fixed and colours flying. This right was exercised about 1821, and again in 1846, in the mayoralty of Alderman Johnson, when the City marshals had directions to receive and attend the regiment through the City.

inconvenience and confusion, and may lead to breaches of the peace.

"May I suggest that, if necessary for them to pass through, it should be before the hour of ten o'clock in the morning.

"If your lordship will let me know the hour, I will give directions to the police to render them every facility.

"I have the honour to be, my lord,

"Your lordship's obedient servant,

"SAMUEL WILSON, Lord Mayor.

"The Rt. Hon. Lord John Russell,
Secretary of State for the Home Department."

Of the Lady Mayoress we should add that her ladyship has the privilege of appointing maids of honour and a train-bearer; has her own private state carriage and four, with a master of ceremonies, and other important officials. At the Lord Mayor's procession, if she comes direct from her country residence, a guard of honour is sent to escort her, having with her two of her ladyship's maids of honour; the junior marshal attending, to receive her on her arrival within the City, and escorting her to join in the procession with her escort, who are placed by the chief marshal.

We close this chapter with what is undoubtedly one of the most agreeable ceremonies in which the Lord Mayor engages, viz., that of receiving, towards his heavy expenses, the following sums, which are to be found set forth, as his lordship's lawful sources of income for his year of office, in the valuable work already quoted from—"The Ceremonials of London," pp. 226, 227:—

PROFITS INCIDENTAL TO THE MAYORALTY.

From the Chamber.	£	s.	d.	£	s.	d.
In lieu of wines, etc.	80	0	0			
In lieu of newspapers . . .	31	10	0			
In lieu of stationery wares . . .	32	5	0			
In lieu of sales of alienations of several places and offices, by order of Common Council, 22nd Sept., 1749 . .	800	0	0			
In lieu of the sale of all officers' places of this city, by order of Common Council, 1st Nov., 1776	1000	0	0			
For the ten corn meters . . .	800	0	0			
In the room of Mr. Hyde, one of the fifteen coal meters, by order of Common Council	80	0	0			
Out of the profits of package and scavage .	173	6	1			
Out of the profits of the markets, by order of Common Council . . .	100	0	0			
In lieu of foreign taker's place, by order of Common Council, 17th July, 1744 .	40	0	0			
For the beams	100	0	0			
In lieu of artificers' places, by order of Common Council, 19th March, 1735 . .	120	0	0			
In lieu of wax, herring, and sturgeon, formerly rendered by the merchants of the Stillyard	5	6	8			
In lieu of pest-house . . .	10	0	0			
By order of Common Council, 20th May, 1800	1500	0	0			
Ditto ditto 4th April, 1811	1500	0	0			
In lieu of licensing the sessions papers, by order of Common Council, 9th Oct., 1778	100	0	0			
In lieu of the sum annually paid by the elders and ministers of the Dutch and French churches, as a compliment to the Lord Mayor for their protection, per order of Court of Aldermen, 3rd Dec., 1782	50	0	0			
In lieu of the gauger of oil and wine, per order of Common Council, 4th April, 1811	750	0	0			
Allowance for the prisoners before Christmas and Easter, by order of Common Council, 11th Dec., 1782 . . .	50	0	0			
				7322	8	4

	£ s. d.	£ s. d.
Brought forward		7322 8 4
Towards the expense of the several courts of Conservancy	300 0 0	
In lieu of furniture, on delivering over the same according to the inventory	100 0 0	
		400 0 0

N.B.—By order of Common Council of the 18th November, 1761, the said £100 is not to be paid till the General Purposes Committee have certified to the court that the purposes for which it was given have been complied with.

	£ s. d.	£ s. d.
For the loss of fees, by the abolition of the metage of coals, by order of Common Council of 28th March, 1832		500 0 0
From the Bridge House—		
Towards the feast		50 0 0
Of the Sheriffs—		
For presenting them at the Exchequer		13 6 8
For Freedoms—		
Three for Lord Mayor, by prerogative, and one for Lady Mayoress	100 0 0	
Two yearly given in lieu of Bartholomew Fair	50 0 0	
One for his coachman	25 0 0	
		175 0 0
From the Cocket Office—		
Profits estimated on an average of seven years, 1822 to 1828, both inclusive, to amount to per annum		900 0 0
		£9360 15 0

N.B.—The sum of £1500 to be deducted from the allowance to the Lord Mayor, by an order of the Court of Common Council of the 12th of April, 1821, in consequence of the abolition of the sword-bearer's table.

Note.—Besides the allowances above mentioned, the **Lord Mayor** also receives, for Cocket dues, from £1000 to £1200, and the bridgemasters pay, out of the funds of the Bridge House Estates, to the Lord Mayor for the time being, towards the cost of the Mayor's feast in the Guildhall, £50, and to the sheriffs £25 each. The first entry of these sums in the Bridge House accounts is as follows:—

Michaelmas 1556 *to Michaelmas* 1557.

"Paide this yere to Sir Thomas Offeleye, knight, lorde mayre, and unto Mr. Harp and Mr. White, sheriffs, as for and towarde the greate feaste within Guyldehalle called the mayre's feaste, by force of an Acte of Common Counsaill in that behalf made, and graunted to be paid oute of the chamber of London every yere, that is to saye, to the Lord Mayre £l. and to either of the said shireffs £xxv. . . . . . in th' ole . . . . . . £c."

CHAPTER XXXI.

THEIR RELATION TO TRADE.

"Whosoever commands the sea commands the trade; whosoever commands the trade of the world commands the riches of the world, and consequently the world itself."—RALEIGH.

IN a former chapter we have expressed our opinion that the cause of England's greatness was well guessed by Napoleon, and we think he displayed his discernment, when he called us, though with a sneer, a nation of shopkeepers. The shopkeepers of Old England for ever, say we! Verily, trade and commerce are the right things for a nation's ruler to encourage. A military monarch, like Napoleon, may enrich his coffers and extend his boundaries for a time by diplomacy and conquest, but all history teaches that, in order that a nation should endure and become increasingly great and powerful, her prosperity must be based, not upon the accessions of successful war, nor upon the trickeries of diplomacy, but upon a sound and wholesome system of commercial enterprise. The British power is felt on every shore and on every sea; for her merchant ships are there, and maintain her influence in every clime. Her wealth is mainly held by her rich landed nobles and her prosperous trading communities.

A large proportion of the wealth of the nobles, however, has been obtained from trade. There are not very many of the Norman barons who can be traced through their descendants to the present time; those who now possess the soil are to a large extent descended from our great bankers, goldsmiths, and other city traders.

The science of trade cannot be acquired by a people in a century—it must be fostered by the legislators, and deeply studied by its disciples, who must obey the current of its history, and maintain its traditions. England has ever honoured her traders as she has her warriors, statesmen, and lawyers. The traders have, perhaps, had rather more than their share of the good things of this life. The highest offices in the State are open to them, and the peerage is frequently strengthened by admissions from their ranks. It is a curious fact, to which we have already adverted, that more than two hundred peerages have been founded by Lord Mayors and other members of the London livery gilds since the time of Henry Fitz-Allyn (Mayor 1110), each of whom has been a trader of London.

One great cause of the prosperity of our British merchants in former times, we think, may be found to lie in the kindly solicitude with which the State has ever nourished the trading gilds or fraternities of which we have treated. It is an ancient patronage. The Saxon gilds were the first nurseries of trade in this country. Other countries have possessed their trade communities, but England alone has understood the principles upon which such societies should be based.

We think we have shown that in this country they were established for the purposes of trade, but, remembering that union is strength, they also perceived the difficulty there would be of securing a continuance of brotherhood amongst men united merely for trade purposes, and so those happy accessories were adopted—*feasting and religion.* There was much knowledge of human nature here. Men are never so amiable and forgiving as when enjoying the pleasures of good cheer, and never are they likely to be so successful as when impressed with the belief that they are doing their duty. Nothing of importance was ever done by our Saxon ancestors without the accompaniment of a good dinner, and their deep sense of religion is evident in basing their gilds upon a religious foundation, so that by reason of the employment of chaplains to pray for their souls, and the numerous works of devotion and charity in which they were bound by their rules to engage, the trade gilds may be said to have been in the early times, and even up to the Reformation, almost as much ecclesiastical as secular communities. But they were essentially colleges of trade.

There can be no cause of wonder, therefore, when we learn that many of the present wealthy livery gilds of London may claim an antiquity coeval with the Anglo-Saxon period; they have uninterruptedly cohered as fraternities to the present time throughout all the period intervening; sometimes, it is true, dwindling into insignificance and ready to collapse, and then, from the mere force of their vitality, springing into vigorous growth, and expanding through successive ages into the ample dimensions to which they have in the present day attained.

It is very true that "individuals may form communities, but institutions must found a nation." Our Saxon ancestors evidently appreciated the truth conveyed in this aphorism, and gave a fostering care to infant fraternities and gilds of commerce, and planted deep in a good soil the roots from which the great companies of the present day originally sprang. They have added strength to our empire; they have been the nurseries of enterprise and charity; by prudent management, and by the increase of the value of real property, they have become fabulously rich; and with age, manifest now, after many centuries of existence, instead of decrepitude, all the vigour of new institutions. A very little while since the announcement was made that one of these companies, the Merchant Taylors', had voted the munificent sum of £100,000, for the removal of their splendid school to a more convenient site, that of the Charterhouse. All honour to such men! They merit the prosperity awarded to their gild. The secret of the success with which these fraternities have been blessed lies, we repeat, in the religious and social features which form their distinguishing characteristics.

CHAPTER XXXII.

THEIR MODERN BANQUETS.

"Go, sirrah! Bid my Lord Chamberlain
Call in the banquet; usher the guests!
Let carking care give place.
Now is the time for jollity and ease,
Good fellowship, and love right brotherly.
Let him that hath no stomach for this feast
Fast him at home, alone!"—ANON.

IT was our good fortune one day to be invited to a dinner given by the Right Worshipful the Master and the Court of Assistants of one of the ancient Livery Companies of the City of London.

The celebrity of these banquets is well known; their fame is fully established; they have acquired, to use a hackneyed phrase, an European reputation. Nor have we one word to say against all this commendation. Cynics, no doubt, will profess to despise these hospitable *réunions*; they will throw in your face quotations by the handful from Juvenal's "Satires" down to Butler's "Hudibras," of course not forgetting Shakespeare, who, by the way, has some very unkind words against good dinners, such as—

"The mind shall banquet though the body pine:
Fat paunches make lean pates, and dainty bits
Make rich the ribs, but banker out the wits."

It is all very well to appeal to such an authority, but Shakespeare and other playwrights must adapt their thoughts to the persons who are supposed to speak them. Hence they put words of wisdom into the mouths of the wise, and they hesitate not to put the language of folly into the mouths of fools. Milton never puts gospel sentiments into the mouth of Satan, and so the above lines manifestly were made to be spoken by a fool, or, if they were not, they certainly ought to have been.

We have often wondered whether indigestion has had anything to do with these philippics; whether dyspepsia is the secret instigator of the horror entertained of turtle, turbot, merlins frits, anguilles à la Genoise, dory à la Hollandaise, cotelettes de mouton aux concombres, and even coté de bœuf se jardinière.

Locke says, "Many people would, with reason, prefer the griping of a hungry stomach to those dishes which are a feast to others." But let that pass. We confess that, having been invited to this dinner, we accepted the invitation, and went at the hour appointed.

Having been escorted with some ceremony into the *salle de réception*, very few minutes sufficed for the process of presentation. In truth, this little affair was well managed; it was a levée on a small scale, each guest being formally presented by the member by whom he had been invited, and receiving, if not a "royal" greeting, a hearty and dignified welcome. The Master was surprisingly *au fait;* he was the sovereign of the day surrounded by his court, his wardens being his cabinet ministers, while the ubiquitous clerk of the company approved himself a most efficient lord chamberlain and master of ceremonies. It is very curious and very pleasing to observe the reverence paid by the members of the "mysteries" to the office of their master, whose power is still allowed to be almost absolute during his term of office.

But the officer upon whom more than any other the master and the company depend for all things, either of business or pageantry, is the clerk. We know scarcely any position which requires so much power of adaptability in its occupier as that of a clerk of a City company. He is their steward, their legal adviser, their conveyancer. But this is not all. Each company has much of ceremony and pageantry to maintain, and much magnificent hospitality. They employ no chamberlain or gentleman usher to superintend their almost regal banquets. They boast of no earl marshal, no king of arms, either Garter, Clarencieux, or Norroy; no heralds, either Chester, Somerset, Richmond, Lancaster, Windsor, or York; neither pursuivants, portcullis, blue mantle, rouge dragon, or rouge croix. The clerk has to combine in his person the offices of them all, coaching up, as we may imagine, the new-made monarch for the year in all the bearings of his regality, and marshalling all comers, from the prince royal to the private trader, in due order according to the strictest rules of precedence. All this devolves upon the clerk of these corporations, and consequently much of their prestige and dignity depends upon his qualifications. It would be strange if all the companies were so fortunate as to possess an officer combining all these accomplishments; but, inasmuch as these gentlemen are educated specially for the post, and a knowledge of these official niceties and minutiæ is necessary for the efficient performance of their office, and forms a prominent portion of their training, we believe that as a rule they may be said to be of a far higher type than mere office drudges, and may rank among the higher class of educated and intelligent men.

The door being thrown wide open, an usher announced "Right Worshipful Master, Worshipful Wardens, and Court of Assistants, may it please you the dinner is on table." It appears that it did please them, for instanter a procession had formed itself for the dining saloon, all seeming to know their relative standing, and each stranger being escorted by the member whose guest he was for the day. The beadle in his ancient robes of office, similar to those of the Oxford and Cambridge esquire bedells, followed by the clerk, preceded the master to his chair of state; his chaplain in his robes following; the other officials in due order falling into their respective places. Upon the master taking his position the clerk retired, and, with the junior assistant, acted as vice-chairman. The musical gentlemen, chiefly from the Chapel Royal and the Abbey, with W. H. Cummings and Montem Smith and others, sat to the right and left of the clerk. Before each seat was a card, on which the guest's name was written, surmounted with the arms of the company beautifully engraven and emblazoned.

At the first glance round the table we were much impressed with the venerable appearance of the members of the court. They were indeed the *patres conscripti* of the gild. We, like old Homer, always turn poetical at the thought or sight of "hoary locks," and we enjoyed the spectacle amazingly. They formed rather a *fatherhood* than a *brotherhood*. More than one, we were informed, was in his eightieth year, and the youngest, to be eligible for a seat at the council, must have "worn the livery" about five-and-twenty years.

The next pleasing circumstance which attracted our observation was the affectionate and brotherly manner in which each greeted each, and the terms of harmony in which all their intercourse one with the other was conducted. There was something pleasing in the moral aspect of the scene. The association together of so many aged men in festive mood giving such strong evidence of mutual regard and esteem; friends, be it remembered, not of yesterday, but in no case of a less period than a quarter of a century; in some of forty or fifty, and in two or three instances of nearly sixty years' continuance. The master, as chairman, was effective, not dwelling on the routine business. The toastmaster likewise knew his work, and did it well. The use of the loving-cup—from the antiquity of the custom—was suggestive. "We liked it well." Sooth to say, like all after-dinner talk, the speeches were nothing worth. One or two "big-wigs" came out rather strong; but oratory seldom improves the flavour of pine-apple or olives, and it sounds somewhat harsh and rude at the very climax of a brilliant flight of impassioned eloquence to hear a walnut cracked. Of conversation, which we like better, there was much; all seemed lively and at ease, willing to please and be pleased. But one testimony we cannot omit, and it affords us pleasure to record it; during the four hours we "sat at meat, or passed the bowl," not one word did we hear which any Christian man in dying need regret having listened to or uttered. Profane expressions, too frequent in "the good old times," were not once heard, nor any light words or *double entendres*.

Of the singing we have little to remark. Performers so eminent as those named are not the men to execute any music badly, but there was upon the whole, we thought, a lack of novelty and appropriateness in the songs. Is there a deficiency of song-writers in these days? Our forefathers, if chroniclers speak truth, were richly served in many a varied strain by noble bards, whose harps would have refused to utter one note to so absurd a refrain as "Beautiful Star—beautiful sta-ar!"

The City gilds were famed for their liberality in olden times in the item of minstrelsy. Their records teem with entries of so many "minstrels to precede the master" to the feast, "dresses for the minstrels," and even "horses for the minstrels." John Bull is not, perhaps, the best judge of music in the world; but he prefers the sterling to the tinsel, and the appropriate to the sickly sentimental.

We do say that, amidst some dozen or fifteen pieces at a dinner, there might well be introduced one or two possessing either some touch of humour, or points specially suited to the occasion. If the company be fishmongers, something good might be said of fishes; or carpenters, something about hitting the nail, and so on through all the various crafts. We well remember, some years ago, being present at Richmond at one of the splendid summer feasts, for which the Worshipful Leathersellers' Company is so justly famous—at which good Richard Thornton—supposed to be the richest London merchant at that time, took so prominent a position, being a leather-seller of more than sixty years' standing, and the father of the company—quite a little excitement was created by the introduction of a simple but characteristic song about *leather*, written by one of the past masters. It displayed no particular amount of ability, yet each verse had some point, the last line being taken up in chorus by some eighty or ninety stentorian-voiced leathersellers, and the effect was "*stunning*."*

* Having obtained a copy of this song, we subjoin it for the edification of those who may think it worth a perusal:—

"Thirteen hundred and fifty-four, Edward the Third,
Found the Traders in Leather a motley herd;
So he chose from among them the worthiest fellows,
Whom he chartered and titled the prime leathersellers.

* * * * * * *

In closing our remarks upon this recent banquet we may add that we learned that these feasts were held monthly (large sums having been bequeathed

---

Our strength it increased as our fame did advance,
Which soon produced plenty of rivals from France;
With their kids and their chamois they made a great fuss,
But were always obliged to be leathered by us.

Prosperity joined us, and time gave us wealth,
Which our sick brethren shared to restore them to health.
When good works and charity bind us together,
I think we look finer than any gilt leather.

Civic honours we certainly have had our share,
We can boast of our aldermen, sheriffs, and mayor!
Thus may we go on to the length of our tether,
And prove the old adage, 'There's nothing like Leather.'

Whenever our country needed our aid,
The call was with cheerfulness always obeyed;
Plumes, helmets, spears, armour, and such foreign pride,
Were never yet equal to Johnny Bull's hide.

May our company flourish till Time's worn away!
And Justice and Truth in our council bear sway;
True friendship and harmony keep us together,
And long may we sing in the praises of leather!

May master and wardens, and courts of assistants
Preserve their authority while they've existence!
And as all our livery are such staunch fellows,
In a bumper we'll toast them, and all leathersellers!"

We have ventured to alter the first two lines, which, in the original, read thus:—

"Fourteen hundred and forty-two, Harry the Sixth,
Found the traders in leather most terribly mixt."

This division of companies occurred much earlier. Henry VI.'s charter to the Leathersellers, being not a grant, but a confirmation.

by generous brethren of the gild for purposes of hospitality and conviviality), besides a quarterly banquet on a large scale for the entire livery. Everything was of the best, plentiful, ornate, and liberal, but there was no extravagance or superfluity; and no gentleman or nobleman in England need to have wished for anything beyond it, even for his most ambitious entertainments.

These banquets are of a series which, without break or long interruption, has existed from the Anglo-Saxon era; through the troubles of the Danish and Norman times; through the many civil broils, the wars of York and Lancaster; through the fierce struggles of the Stewart and Cromwell factions; the great rebellion, and the revolution of 1688; they have contributed to form the character of the great London trading community, mitigating the almost necessary results of business competition, and encouraging mutual respect, confidence, and brotherly feeling. No wonder then that these time-honoured institutions now stand out in more than their original greatness, powerful, wealthy, and prosperous; patrons of learning and education, benefactors of hospitals and churches; bestowing their vast resources upon works alike of piety and of charity, and setting an example to the proprietors of the land which the best and noblest among them may do well to imitate.

All these and a thousand similar thoughts passed through our mind as we discreetly enjoyed the good things before us, and upon suggesting the inquiry to the ancient and courteous "gentleman on our right," how it came to pass that none of England's troubles, and none of her revolutions, or changes of dynasty, or other vicissitudes, had succeeded in destroying these valuable corporations, we received an answer, alike laconic, and to our mind satisfactory, in words "venerable and oracular in their unadorned gravity."—"THE DINNERS HAVE DONE IT."

CHAPTER XXXIII.

THEIR ARMORIAL BEARINGS.

"Grant her, besides, of noble blood that ran
In ancient veins, ere heraldry began."—DRYDEN.

WE mentioned in our last chapter, when describing the banquet, that each seat was provided with an engraving of the arms of the company; we may add that a very imposing affair indeed this engraving was.

This card, with its arms, is the text upon which we found the present discourse, claiming *in limine* for ourselves no profound acquaintance with the intricacies of this so occult science of heraldry. We do just know the difference between guttes d'or and guttes d'olive, tenny and purpure, the chief, the bend sinister, and the chevron; between a cross and saltire; between quarterly quartered, and cross snagged; in a word, we know the A B C of the language, and confess ourselves to be inquirers, rather than teachers, in the few remarks we have to offer upon City armorial bearings.

The study of the system of heraldry has been much neglected for the last two centuries. There is a philosophy even in heraldry. In truth, no one can be deemed fully educated who has not an acquaintance with at least the rudiments and broad outlines of the system.

Little is known with certainty of the origin of armorial bearings. Some consider that they were not unknown to the ancient Israelites in the wilderness, and that a divine sanction was there conferred upon them in the command that they should pitch their tents "by their own *standards*, according to the house of their fathers," and when Dan was directed to "go hindermost with their standards." David was certainly familiar with banners, for he sings, "In the name of our God we will set up our banners." Solomon, too, in the Canticles, in his impassioned apostrophe to the heavenly Bride, exclaims—

> "Thou art terrible as an army with banners."

Some claim them to have been in use in the old heroic age, and some affirm that Alexander the Great instituted the office of heralds. We know that the Roman soldiers were distinguished by Augustus by ornaments and devices on their shields, and many who have studied authorities and devoted research to this subject have ascribed to the Roman legions the custom of bearing emblazoned shields, banners, armours, crests, and other ensigns of nobility, at the pompous obsequies of the great.

Some ascribe to the Spaniards during their wars with the Moors, in the time of Julian the Apostate, the origin of armorial bearings; others to King

Arthur, to the Saxons, or to the Normans. We may safely claim, however, for Charlemagne the honour of regulating and systematizing armories; while the Crusades encouraged a love of heraldic devices, and increased the necessity for them. It would seem that the tournaments of the tenth century first brought heraldry into a science, which became more fully developed during the progress of the various expeditions to the Holy Land, and perfected in the succeeding period of chivalric jousts and feats of arms. Surcoats spread over the noblemen's coats of tournament, and over their horses, were not known till a much later period, no mention of such being discoverable earlier than the reign of King John.

Everybody knows that armorial bearings, duly conferred and borne, are indications of honour and dignity appropriated to communities and offices, or to individuals, as hereditary tokens whereby persons of ancient and exalted descent are not only distinguished among themselves, but from the common orders of the people who have no claim to such emblems of gentility. They bear the name of *arms* or *armories*, inasmuch as they were originally borne principally upon the bucklers, cuirasses, banners, and other habiliments of war. And because anciently they were embroidered upon the coats of the warriors, they came to bear the designation of *coats of arms* and *coat armour;* the custom arising, no doubt, from the practice among ancient knights of ornamenting their shields or helmets with some device, generally the favours of their mistress, to distinguish them one from another in their numerous jousts and tournaments.

From time immemorial these symbolic devices have been in use to distinguish friends from foes and different men in armies, and also as ornaments to the standards, ensigns, and shields. But these emblems were taken at the mere option of each chieftain, there being then no armories, such as those which we possess, recognized as the hereditary marks of the nobility of the house, and regulated according to the strict laws of that science which we designate heraldry.

Sir Walter Raleigh truly observes, "He that commands the wealth of the world commands the world;" and so it was that as trade and commerce advanced in this country, new men were found able to purchase the broad domains of many of the ancient lords, and with their possessions naturally coveted the usual accompaniment of nobility—a coat of arms. The claim seemed just, and was recognized; and wealth at length shared with valour these heraldic distinctions. But we always understood that in conferring arms some historical allusions or personal symbols were introduced, so that if his gentility had been won by commerce the receiver of the grants found ships, and bales of goods, prominent on his shield; if as a tallow-chandler a barrel of tallow might perhaps form the crest, while a candle *couchant* might be dexter chief. If a sweep had realized an estate, the crest no doubt would be a "broom," or "soot-bag," and an appropriate motto would be "Excelsior."

We cannot vouch for the truth of the statement, but it has been currently reported that when a Mr. Mutton applied for arms he had granted a *dead sheep, gules.* Mr. Smock had for his crest an article of female apparel, at which his dear wife took umbrage, saying "it was the most indelicatest thing to parade to the public;" but, poor lady, she knew little of the laws of arms, and was reconciled upon being assured that it was a most honourable distinction, being a "shirt of mail *imparfait.*" The family of Goose had that nutritious bird as their device. Mr. Quid, the fortunate tobacco-merchant, took the cigar as his emblem, and carried on his chariot's panels the suggestive motto, "*Quid rides.*" While for the well-known and estimable Mr. Moon, as he was rising from below the horizon to take a distinguished position in the eyes of men, eclipsing all lesser luminaries, Heralds' College selected with prophetic propriety the crescent. We forget the motto, but possibly it was Shakespeare's lines from Antony and Cleopatra—

> "My power's a crescent, and my auguring hope
> Says it will come to th' full."

That climax was honourably and worthily realized in a baronetcy.

It is more than probable that in some of these cases the authorities of Heralds' College were not consulted, for of course any man may *proprio motu* adopt arms or a motto; but as these are badges of honour and respect, they should not be assumable at pleasure, being considered a testimonial of merit, valour, or good services performed to the state, bestowed upon the holders by emperors and princes, who employ a marshal to take cognizance of the same, and expect all things connected with them to be done according to the laws of arms.

At the outset, when coats of arms were first instituted, the rules were few and simple. These arms were, in fact, a kind of livery composed of several bars, fillets, and colours; whence succeeded the fess, bend, pall, chevron, and lozenge. But the fundamental law of arms was that none but those who had taken part in a tournament were entitled to bear arms, however exalted their rank. During the progress of the Crusades, all who journeyed to the Holy Land as parties to the expedition, and were of the rank of noblemen and gentlemen, assumed these tokens of knightly dignity in order that they might be distinguished by their comrades in arms.

As the numbers of those entitled to armories increased, the various signs and symbols multiplied in like proportion; and as orders of nobility became established, the arms were distinguished by coronets and helmets of degrees. Thus a helmet, which was formerly worn as a defensive weapon, is now placed as the chief ornament over the coat of arms, and is allowed to be the true mark of gentility. The quality of the bearer may be known by the number of bars. The helmet of the king and the royal family is open-faced and grated; the dukes' and marquises' helmets, which are alike, differ from the king's by having a bar exactly in the middle, and two on each side (five bars in all); whereas the king's numbers six, three on each side. The helmets with four bars are common to all degrees of peerage under that of marquis. Baronets and knights possess the open-faced helmet. The closed helmet is for an esquire or gentleman. The grated helmet in front designates the sovereign prince. That in profile is common to all degrees of peerage. That standing direct, without bars and with the beaver a little open, denotes baronets and knights. The side-standing helmet closed signifies the rank of esquire or gentleman.

Another marked addition and honourable device is that of supporters, respecting which Ministriere lays down the following rules. They may be borne only by—

1st. Nobiles majores, viz., from dukes to barons.

2nd. All Knights of the Garter though under the degree of barons.

3rd. All Knights of the Bath who receive on their creation a grant of supporters.

4th. All such knights as the king chooses to bestow this honour upon.

Neither peeresses nor bishops have mottoes or crests; and the latter, though peers of Parliament, have no supporters.

With these simple rules of heraldry before them, people unacquainted with the history of London often wonder why in the world the trading corporations or livery companies,

> "The butchers, the bakers, the candlestick-makers,"

and a host more besides, should possess so gorgeous a blazonry of heroic and martial symbols, so many marks of honour and dignity, as those set forth in their armorial bearings, granted by royal authority, and duly enrolled according to the laws of arms. They wonder why these traders should be honoured with arms at all; and much more, that so many of them should glory in supporters, while the grocers, drapers, leathersellers, goldsmiths, merchant-taylors, and haberdashers actually place above their shield the helmet of an earl, in addition to supporters to the shield.

The City of London itself, the great parent and fosterer of trade, and the *alma mater* of all the companies, bears on her escutcheon no emblems whatever of trade. Her shield, quarterly quartered, bears the dagger as chief dexter. As if the personification of the genius of war and knightly valour, she holds forth no other device than the sword or dagger, and for a crest the cap of maintenance! The dagger to typify offensive, the cap of maintenance defensive warfare. These, with their warlike dragons as supporters, constitute the City's entire arms.

As it is usually understood that no system can be more exact than that of the Heralds, it may be important to inquire whether any inaccuracy has been committed in these various emblems, or whether the citizens (so often termed *peaceful citizens*) have at any period of their history manifested with their love of commerce any warlike proclivities to have entitled them to so distinguished grants from the fount of honour? We think, in our next chapter, we shall be enabled to satisfy our readers that, in respect to these arms and the granting thereof, all things have been well and correctly performed.

The engraved arms of the City gild, which so interested us at the banquet, set us upon inquiries respecting the arms of livery companies generally, and thanks to an antiquarian friend,* himself for nearly forty years the wearer of "*the liverie of companie*," as old Stow terms this privilege, we have now lying before us a most rare and choice old work, headed with the following quaint inscription on the frontispiece:—

"With his Majesty's Royal Pattent 1677.
The second edition, to which is added the City Arms,
HERALDRY DISPLAYED,
or LONDON'S ARMORY,
Accurately delineated in an Illustration of
All the ARMS, CRESTS, SUPPORTERS, and MOTTOS
of every distinct COMPANY and CORPORATE
SOCIETY in the honourable CITY OF LONDON,
Faithfully Collected from their several PATENTS,
approved and conformed by
DIVERS KINGS AT ARMS, in their Visitations.
A Work never till this exactly
performed, and will rectify many essential
mistakes, and manifest

---

* Martin Blackmore, Esq.

absurdities committed in PAINTING and
CARVING. To the Rt. Hon. Sir Robert
Godscall, Kt., Lord Mayor and the
Representative in Parliament for ye City
of London in 1742, together with
the Rt. Worshipfull the Court
of Aldermen.
Sold by S. Lyne, at the Globe in Newgate Street, London."

For the benefit of our curious readers, we will place before them the result of an analysis of this production. The entire series consists of ninety-eight coats of arms, very excellently engraved, eighty-one belonging to the livery companies of London, the Company of Physicians being the last, and seventeen to the Royal Society, the Royal Hospitals, Christ's Hospital, the East India Company, and other modern corporations.

Of the large number of eighty-one arms of livery companies, no fewer than forty have supporters (the Brewers' and Vintners', by the way, being imperfect, no legs being granted to the figures, which are of a type somewhat beneath the Centaur, and no doubt suggestive of the effects of strong drink unduly taken), ten bear the earl's helmet, two that of the baronet or knight, and forty-one that of esquire. The mottoes are very suggestive, chiefly from Holy Scripture. Nineteen either *hope in God* or *trust in Him*. Twenty-one have no motto; many of them being of trades the members of which could not perhaps with propriety be supposed to quote the sacred books—the Vintners to wit—vulgarly deemed an ungodly profession.

The Weavers' motto is—"Weave truth with trust."

The Clockmakers'—"Tempus rerum imperator" (Time the lord of events).

The Glaziers'—"Da nobis lucem, Domine" (Lord, grant us thy light).

The Fruiterers'—"Arbor vitæ Christus; fructus per fidem gustamus" (The tree of life is Christ: his fruit we taste by faith).

The Smiths'—"By hammer and hand all arts do stand."

The Saddlers'—"Hold fast, sit sure."

The Armorers'—"Make all sure."

The Salters'—"Sal sapit omnia" (Salt flavours all things).

The Haberdashers'—"Serve and obey."

The Wax Chandlers'—"The truth is the light."

The Tallow Chandlers'—"Quæ arguuntur a lumine manifestantur" (Things which are reproved are made manifest by the light).

The Butchers'—"Omnia subiecisti sub pedibus oves et boves"—(Thou hast put all things under his feet; all sheep and oxen).

The Distillers'—"Drop as rain, distil as dew."

With our knowledge of modern London, the idea of a Company of Gardeners in the City is curious, even though their haunts might have been in Hatton Garden, or Baldwin's Gardens, in Moorfields, or St. Giles-in-the-Fields, or even in Doctors' Commons. It must have been long since this trade flourished in the great metropolis; such "craftsmen" now seldom show themselves there; the only recollection we have of such being in the seasons of frost and snow, when the city is overrun with migratory hordes of men from Spitalfields and Bethnal Green, glorying in the designation of "*frozen-out gardeners.*" This craft, however, was at one time powerful. It was deemed a laborious calling, as is evident from the fact that on their shield the only emblem is a naked man (apparently intended for our first common progenitor) digging with prodigious effort; a basket of fruit forms their crest, and for a motto—

"In the swet of thy brow's (*sic*) shalt thou eat thy bread."

The most curious circumstance we remark throughout this series is the fact that the Mercers' Company, the first and most honourable in rank of all the companies, claims neither supporters, helmet, nor crest. We profess ourselves at a loss here. A corporation so distinguished, numbering, says Stow, "several kings, princes, and nobility, and ninety-eight lord mayors amongst the brethren;" a company of which Richard II. and Queen Elizabeth were enthusiastic members, with Richard Whittington, that "*flos mercatorum*," as he is designated in his epitaph, with the three Greshams, those "kings of trade," and an innumerable host of distinguished names, nine at least of whom became founders of noble families; and one of whom, Sir Baptist Hicks, was promoted directly from his shop in Cheapside to the House of Lords, by the title of Lord Campden; —that this craft, A 1 among the City gilds, should be so little honoured by the heralds is to us an inexplicable enigma.

Heraldry appears to have stood high at all times in the estimation of the rulers of the gilds. Many of the most eminent of the citizens were carried to their tombs with knightly honours, their armour and helmet being placed upon their graves. All the companies possessed most gorgeous and costly palls or hearse-clothes of cloth of gold, of exquisite workmanship, to be used at the funerals of the livery. Heraldry was studied here, as in all their pageants and ceremonials. ,The Lancaster herald was employed to direct the embroiderer in the decoration of these splendid works of art. Even a trade so unambitious as that of the Carpenters, as we have already seen, expended in the year of our Lord 1513, 5 Henry VIII., the large sum of £15 12*s.* 9*d.* upon the manufacture of one of their palls. One item we extract from the Records of that worshipful Company, as follows :—

"Paid to the brotherer (embroiderer) for hyss workman schypp viiil.

"Spent upon Mastyr Lankestyr, the herrad (herald) of armys, for ovyrsyght of your cloth, 2*s.* viii."

If the Lancaster heralds in all ages were equally moderate in their fees, as in the case before us, we think no complaint whatever need be made of them on the score of extravagant charges. "Two shillings and eightpence" in the reign of Bluff King Hal to a wealthy City corporation, for overseeing the emblazoning of a pall, was far from extortionate.

We would add a few words, before leaving this subject of arms, respecting the popular notion that the dagger as dexter chief on the City escutcheon, was granted to the citizens by Richard II. in consequence of the valour of Sir William Walworth, in slaying the rebel, Wat Tyler, at Smithfield. The truth is that the dagger or sword was conferred upon the citizens previously to this period. In evidence of this we refer to the ancient seal still used by the Lord Mayor for the ward precepts, which is certified to have been in use nearly 500 years, it being upon record that in the second year of Richard II. (A.D. 1381), in consequence "of the old seale of the office of the maioralty of the citie being very small, old, inapt, and uncomely for the honour of the citie," this present one was made.

Equally unfounded was the theory of Stow, who, in narrating the destruction of the "olde seale" in 1381, which, like the present one, bore the dagger, describes it as "bearing the sword and crosse of St. Paul, who died by the sword." The citizens, though their grand cathedral was consecrated by the name of St. Paul, the universal bishop of the Gentiles, were not very likely to claim any special honour from his martyrdom; nor is it probable, even though his effigy might appear upon certain of their ecclesiastical seals or documents, that their grant of arms would make any reference to the great apostle. But in very truth the arms possess, properly speaking, no "crosse." The shield is, indeed, quarterly quartered, and this process involves the figure of a cross to divide the shield, but the heraldic device is the dagger or sword, to indicate valour and bravery in the field. The crest, too, is a most honourable distinction, being the ducal cap of maintenance. When John of Gaunt, son of King Edward III., was created Duke of Lancaster by the same monarch, the king girded him with the sword, and put on him a cap of fur. Richard II. similarly invested the Duke of Hereford and others, and from that time until the present mode of creation by patent obtained, this honourable investiture continued. We know not of any higher tokens of honour which a monarch could confer upon his favoured citizens than those which the early kings of England have bestowed upon their faithful subjects within the City; and in the next chapter we shall endeavour to show that the loftiest distinctions which should attach exclusively to knightly valour and military eminence have been fully merited by the generous and warlike citizens of London.

CHAPTER XXXIV.

THEIR TRAINING TO ARMS.

"Follow the drum;
With man's blood paint the ground; gules, gules;
Religious canons, civil wars are cruel;
Then what should war be?"—SHAKESPEARE'S "*Timon.*"

OUR old chroniclers delight in recording the deeds of valour performed long ago by London's citizens. Some may be credited—some may not. That good old monk who wrote seven centuries ago, called Geoffrey of Monmouth, said strange things and told strange stories.

Yet men have believed this worthy, and the well-known "Liber Horne," that able compilation by a Chamberlain of London of that name, written in the reign of Edward II., is prefaced by the insertion of old Geoffrey's account of the foundation of London, which he ascribes to Brute, a descendant of Æneas, about half a century after the destruction of Troy; he being succeeded by seventy kings who reigned successively before the arrival of Julius Cæsar! Ludgate was built, according to his theory, by King Lud; and we are not sure whether some other great works are not by him ascribed to that glorious monarch old King Cole. The reveries of Geoffrey have been adopted by many of our historians, and I dare say he has his disciples to this very day.

Even the steady-going and learned Coke quotes Geoffrey's account of the colonization of Britain with great respect, and he endeavours to prove thereby that the common law of England is of Greek origin. For ourselves, we are free to confess, with all reverence for the great Lord Coke, that as to our ancestors or their laws being Grecian, all we can say is—*we don't believe it.*

But *qu'il importe?* Anyhow we know that from an early date the London citizens have been worthy, honest, and brave. We should think none the better of them even could it be proved that a hero was their first father, "*Miserum est alienæ incumbere famæ.*"

> "Worth makes the man, the want of it the fellow;
> The rest is all but leather and prunello."

No one doubts that Boadicea made a noble stand against the Romans, and that she was ably supported by the British under the very walls of London. The Romans felt the force of the British weapons, too, at Verulam. Tacitus affirms that the professed design of the Britons was to extirpate the Roman colony. As this effort failed, however, the next best thing for them to do was to learn of their conquerors. And so they did. But unfortunately they learned of them bad things as well as good. Their gladiatorial encounters were succeeded by our prize fights. Their Floralia and other Pagan rites resulted in our May games with their queens of May. And no doubt our brave Britons learned something of the military art from those who were the conquerors of the world, although they were at all times the equals of the Romans in warlike spirit and masculine energy.

Whatever their individual prowess might have been, until the time of the Normans they knew no generalship; and the Saxons, and after them the Danes, made easy conquests, not because the men were weak or effeminate, but because the centralizing power was unknown—the power of marshalling armies. Braver men as individuals never fought; but before an army with trained officers and leaders they were powerless. They managed trade affairs far better. The London merchants survived every conquest and every civil convulsion. The trade gilds were organized gradually but surely; they never were out-generalled, and to the present day remain as evidence in favour of building one's house upon a rock.

The first trade gilds in England enrolled or chartered were semi-military institutions. All their rights and privileges were held upon military service, or at any rate by military deeds. In a former page we referred to Stow's description of this *Cnighten Gild*, which consisted of thirteen individuals to whom certain customs and privileges were granted in the "merrie days of King Edgar." They besought the king to have certain land on the east side of the City conferred upon them with the liberty of a gild for ever. The king granted their request with the conditions following, namely, that each of them should victoriously accomplish three combats, one above ground, one underground, and the third in the water; and after this that they should run with spears against all comers. All which we learn they most gloriously fulfilled, and the same day the king named them the *Cnighten Gild*, and thus originated the Ward of Portsoken.

Fitzstephen * describes the excellent training in arms which the youth of London in his day were accustomed to receive. He speaks of the citizens as the most efficient soldiers in the kingdom, mustering 80,000 troops. Although we can place little dependence on these numbers, yet we may collect from the statement that the military strength of the citizens was great, and their character as soldiers established. We must also bear in mind that those were warlike times, and that even the laws were sometimes enforced not according to right, but strength or valour. The Normans introduced that cruel custom *the trial by battle*, and although by King Alfred's code the Londoners were specially exempt from this law, and William by his charters confirmed all their privileges, yet there can be little doubt that what was a universal rule elsewhere had even in London many who would have deemed it cowardly to take protection under an exemption. Justice Blackstone, indeed, attributes this exemption of the citizens from *trial by battle* to the opinion that "fighting was foreign to their education and employ-

* "Descriptio Nobillissim. Civit. Lond."

ment," but we think there is ample evidence to show that fighting was not foreign to their education, and that it was their besetting sin, and that even although exempted from this inhuman custom, such was their pugnacity and hardihood that succeeding monarchs were necessitated to discountenance the habit; as may be seen from the charter of King Henry I. to the citizens, one item of which expressly enjoins "*that they shall not wage battle.*"

This is so different to a mere granting the privilege of exemption, that we see no reason to doubt that the usage had become injurious to the interests of the citizens and of trade, and consequently they were forbidden to continue it.

It may not be out of place to explain briefly the nature of this barbarous ordeal. Of the trial by combat, or judicial duel, Selden has treated at large in his "Duello." The Lombards, he tell us, introduced it into Italy, from whence it spread throughout Europe. The Normans introduced it into England, and it was resorted to both in civil and criminal suits. If any one charged another with treason, murder, felony, or other capital offence, he was said to *appeal* him, and was termed an appellant, and the party charged was at liberty either to put himself upon his country for trial, or to *defend himself by his body*. If the defendant chose the latter mode of defence, the appellant was bound to meet him on an appointed day in marshalled lists; and the parties fought armed with sticks shod with horn. The vanquished one was adiudged to death, either as a false accuser or as guilty of the charge. If the defendant could maintain his ground until the stars appeared, the appellant was deemed vanquished: if the defendant called for quarter, or was slain, judgment of death was equally passed upon him. It was a necessity, therefore, for men who lived in such times as those not only to be possessed of good courage, but to be well skilled in the art of defence. In civil suits the combats differed by plain sticks only being used, and the vanquished being doomed to perpetual infamy instead of death. For a full and faithful illustration of this mediæval passage of arms, we refer our readers to Sir Walter Scott's "Fair Maid of Perth."

About half a century ago a revival of this barbarous process was attempted in the case of a man acquitted by a jury of the charge of murder, being *appealed* by the next of kin, but it resulted in the immediate abolition of *the trial by battle* by the Act 59 George III., c. 46.

In the beginning of the fourteenth century the London citizens appear to have established a surpassing reputation for military prowess. So highly were their exploits valued that the second charter of King Edward II. was conferred expressly on that ground. In the preamble it recapitulates the great services rendered to the Crown by the citizens in besieging the Castle of Leeds in Kent, and achieving other successful operations in divers parts of the kingdom: and it expressly enjoins that such services by them performed shall not be drawn into precedent.

From this we learn that the citizens acted as volunteers on these occasions; and that nothwithstanding the king's behest, their enlisting was optional, since by ancient privilege they were not required to go to war beyond their own boundaries. This must have been a great boon to men of trade in an age when a state of war was almost continuous, and when nearly every man was under a necessity to appear in arms at his lord's demand. The real origin of the exemption of the citizens of London from this service outside their own domains was, no doubt, that by the condition of *burgage tenure* according to the feudal system they were bound only to defend their own walls.

As London consisted chiefly of the trading gilds, who vindicated to themselves all the power and wealth of the City, with them lay the responsibility of ruling the metropolis, and, in many instances, guiding the State. They felt that their influence lay in the warlike front they were enabled to maintain in times of civil war, and whether expected to fight or not, they were fully determined at all times to be prepared. Before the institution of a standing army the companies furnished the sovereigns with large supplies of men and arms for foreign service. For this purpose their members were well trained; not only did each gild possess its distinctive armorial bearings, its stand of arms, its banners, and its standards, but amongst its other officials a professional armorer was maintained and constantly employed in its service.

Even a company so humble as that of the Carpenters took a share in such preparations, and their accounts contain many quaint entries of the cost of equipping soldiers for the wars in the time of King Edward VI. Not only do the wardens charge vis. viiid. for a "standyng at hys crownacion," but they particularize many items for "sodyars in the monythe of Octobre for the wags (wages) and preste (priest) money and abylments of war in the thyrde yere of King Edward the Sixt." Then follow items for "swerdes," "daggers," "swerde-gyrdylls," "cotton to make their cotts" (qy. tents?), etc. Good and brave carpenters! No doubt, like other men of your time, ye "served God in your generation." Peace be to your ashes!

CHAPTER XXXV.

THEIR WARRIORS.

" Against whose fury and unmatched force
The awless lion could not wage the fight."—SHAKESPEARE.

LET us not imagine that the prowess of the liverymen was hid in a corner in those days of disquiet and unrest. Each company boasted many martial sons, some of whom had, no doubt, seen foreign service in their wild days; some, perchance, like the father of Thomas à Beckett, who, after fighting in the Holy Land against the Saracens, opened shop in Cheapside and wore the Mercers' livery, were looked up to as proved heroes by their *confrères;* whilst others who had never quitted England could wield the sword with skill, and could display a courage equal to that of the most chivalrous warriors. Near the cross in Cheapside, in the year A.D. 1331, stood a building, not very ornate, but rather a stage of Thespian simplicity, whereon were accommodated certain lookers-on at tournaments and jousts. Herefrom were to be witnessed most notable exhibitions of skill, for close at hand the City knights challenged all comers to single combat, or to trial of numbers against numbers. Stow describes some scenes held this year which possessed more than usual interest, and which lasted throughout three days. A scaffold of wood had been erected for Queen Philippa and "her beautiful ladies, all most richly attired," to witness this national spectacle. We cannot learn any particulars of the several combatants, who, no doubt, were worthy of their city and of the occasion; but this we do learn, that, in the midst of the final encounter, the ladies' scaffold "brake in sunder, whereby they were (with some shame) forced to fall downe," and many knights and others were much hurt. It is pleasing to learn, however, that, owing to the intercession of the queen, the "carpenters were not put to death;" and that a building of stone was soon after erected near to the church of St. Mary-le-Bow, for the king, the queen, and other states, to see the gallant spectacles in safety.

Whatever the character of the trade practised by the several gilds, the members appear to have been almost universally men of arms. Some very remarkable instances occur of individual members rising to great eminence as soldiers. Who would have expected to meet with a *warrior tailor*? And yet the company of Merchant Taylors have supplied their own and other countries with noble specimens.

The name of Sir John Hawkwood may be mentioned in illustration. Fuller says of him very drily that he turned his needle into a sword and his thimble into a shield. His usual cognomen was Joannes Acutus, from the sharpness of his sword or his needle. The son of a tanner, he was apprenticed to a tailor in the City, was pressed for a soldier, and, by his valour and ability, rose to the highest commands in foreign parts. Having once tasted blood and the pleasures of glorious war, he had no heart for the tamer avocations of the board and the scissors, and, throwing away for ever the tape measure and French chalk, became famous as the leader of armies.

For his bravery under King Edward III., he received from that monarch the honour of knighthood on the field. By extraordinary valour at the battle of Poictiers, he gained the friendship of his heroic general, the Black Prince. At the peace between England and France, he persuaded five thousand horsemen and fifteen hundred foot, mostly English, to follow him to assist the Marquis of Montserrat against Galleazzo, Duke of Milan. He next joined the Duke of Milan, was equally successful, and subsequently married Domitia, a niece of the duke, with whom he received a large fortune. In 1394, after a long life of renown and uninterrupted success, he died, full of years and crowned with honour, at Florence, where his figure on horseback, painted *al fresco* on the walls of the cathedral by the celebrated Paolo Uccelli, is still to be seen. Beneath is the following inscription:—

"*Johannes Acutus, eques Britannicus, ætatis suæ cautissimus et rei militaris peritissimus habitus est.—Pauli Uccelli opus.*"

This inscription is published in the early works

of the Society of Antiquaries, with the date added of 1436. It is a circumstance worthy of record that Sir John Hawkwood's fellow apprentice, though he remained true to his craft and to their grand Merchant Taylors' Hall in Threadneedle Street, was also greatly distinguished as a warrior, having for his great valour been dubbed on the field Sir Ralf Blackwell by King Edward III.

Throughout the reigns of Edward III., Richard II., and Henry IV., the citizens of London were not only a most powerful and wealthy party in the State, but they furnished some of the best and the most skilful soldiers in the realm. Where could a more heroic knight be found than the unfortunate Sir Nicholas Brambre, thrice Lord Mayor? Old Holinshed, Froissart, and the other chroniclers of the time, abound with such expressions as "the then Mayor of London was a man of arms;" "the aldermen of London in their armour led on the onslaught;" and the like. Sometimes we find the citizens opposed to the reigning monarch, driven into revolt by tyranny. When the Dukes of York and Gloucester, the King's uncles, took arms professedly in the name of the King (Richard II.), the Londoners fought at Oxford against them, where Sir N. Brambre was taken prisoner after the battle, and brought to London. The King's uncles were glad he was taken, and declared he should suffer like the rest. He was accordingly beheaded without London, displaying no more fear in his death than he had done in his life. Froissart says he once did the King good service when he slew Lister with his own hands, whereby all the rebels were discomfited, for which the King knighted him; but he was at last beheaded by reason of his adherence to the Duke of Ireland.

When Queen Isabella besieged her tyrant husband, Edward II., at Bristol, and succeeded in obtaining the crown for her son, Edward III. (A.D. 1327), how much she owed to the bravery of "the citizens of London, who were rich, and lived by their merchandise, which commerce was carried on both by land and sea, and by means of which they were in great prosperity," may be gathered from Froissart; who, moreover, informs us that when the Queen heard the message from the people of London, she and her son arrived there, and "by their assistance became successful in her enterprise," for without their aid "she would have found considerable difficulty in attaining to her desires; and so the said King (Edward II.) was taken to Bristol, and was imprisoned in the castle of Berkeley, and Edward his son was crowned at Westminster."

Similar things occurred to Richard II., who held his crown by force, and not by the love of his people. The same chronicler says, "he kept 10,000 archers night and day to protect him;" but the people of London remembered all that had been done to Edward II., "and said one to another, if the King Richard is suffered to tyrannize, there is no hope for prosperity for England," and they sent to France for the Earl of Derby, and put Richard of

Bordeaux into the Tower. "Thus the Londoners communed together," says he, and adds that there were in London 24,000 men in complete armour, and 30,000 archers, and "they were hardy and possessed of high courage." What followed we all remember. Henry IV. entered London with a noble procession, "*all the burgesses and merchants of London of every craft in their own peculiar livery and device.*"

But then for the coronation! and the banquet. That was, indeed, a grand day for the gilds. We have not space for the details, but the mere order of precedence will suffice to indicate how far the throne was prepared to pay honour to the men of London.

At the magnificent coronation banquet the following was the order:—

I. Table.—The King.
II. Table.—Five peers of the realm.
III. Table.—The valiant men of London.
IV. Table.—The new Knights of the Bath.
V. Table.—Knights and squires.*

During the many troubles of this reign, the good citizens remained true to the man of their choice. Early in the reign an insurrection, headed by the first noblemen of the land, was suppressed almost

* We may remind our readers that on this occasion the custom at coronations of creating Knights of the Bath, an order first introduced into England by the Saxons, was instituted, and was usually followed until the reign of Charles II., from which time till it was revived by George I., the custom lay dormant. It is to be observed that the "valiant men of London" took precedence even of Knights of the Bath.

entirely by the citizens, who, at a moment's notice, supplied Henry with 20,000 men.

The records of the several livery companies explain the mode of raising large forces in cases of emergency. On the occasion of the rising of the "Kentish men" after the coronation of Richard III. and his Queen Ann Nevil, we learn from the books of the Mercers', Taylors', and Drapers' Companies, that each furnished 200 men, and the minutes of the Goldsmiths' bear the following entry:—"1484. A genl marche in the citie, made in the time of Mr. Shaa, Knight, maior, for confermacon of the said citie, when the Kentishe men aroos ayenst the Kyng and the Quene, after the coronacon of the Kyng and Quene." Fifty-six persons are named who had to find from one to five men each, "in jackets of one sute and defensibly armyd," amounting to eighty-nine in number; the "yonge men oute of the lyvery" of the company were seventy-three in number. A similar grand muster was made a few months later upon the march of "the Northern men" upon the City. The Goldsmiths' books have the following entry on the occasion:—"A marche made at the coronacon of King Richard III., at the comyng of the Northern menne into this citie, wher they had mustered in Fynesbery Felds, the Kyng and hys lords then beyng there presente." As recently as the reign of Henry VIII., the same Company records, A.D. 1536, Oct. 26, that at a general assembly held this day "Mr. Hayes opened and declared before all the assistants, that the

King's grace had sent a letter unto my lorde the mayre, and to my masters the aldermen, his brethren, to provide and send unto his grace in all the haste possible CCL. men of armes, well harnessed on horseback, the one halfe townsmen, and the other halfe byllmen. Of whiche sayd CCL. men, my lord mayre assygned this fellyshippe to prepare and make good provyson for XII. men of armes on horsebacke, VI. bowemen, and VI. byllmen. Whereupon yt was agreed by all the sayd assistants that provysyon should be made for the sayd XIJ. men at the costs and charges of thys house."

In the reign of Queen Mary, 1553-4, the Kentish men again rose in rebellion (their leader on this occasion being Sir Thomas Wiat), to oppose the proposed marriage of Philip of Spain with the Queen, and further to advance the cause of the unfortunate Lady Jane Grey, whose untimely end they thus expedited. The Carpenters' records (as quoted by Jupp, p. 50) contain some curious particulars of the share which they took in defence of authority, and which verify the statement given by Stow, to the minutest details, and show the military spirit which was encouraged by the City gilds.

The number of warlike mayors and aldermen is something very great. We may select a few names (out of many) of mayors knighted on the field:—

Nicholas Brembre, 1377.
John Philpot, 1378.
Nicholas Exton, fishmonger, mayor, 1387.
Nicholas Twyford, 1388.

Sir Matthew Philips, goldsmith, mayor, 1463, created Knight of the Bath for bravery on the field.

Bartholomew James, draper, mayor, 1479, by Edward IV.

William Horne, 1487.

Ralph Astrie, 1493.

The celebrated Lord Mayor Walworth.

The most eminent batch of loyal aldermen we remember is the celebrated twelve immortalized by Maitland. The occasion was the attempt of Falconbridge to force the City. Alderman Basset, the commanding officer at the bridge, sallied out to meet the invader. Earl Rivers, with a strong force, likewise took the field, but Falconbridge was repulsed "by that gallant citizen Ralph Joscelin, late Lord Mayor, and pursued with great slaughter as far as Redriff" (Rotherhithe).

"The King, Edward IV., hurried off to the City in pursuit of the rebels, staying no longer than while he knighted the twelve following aldermen for their gallant behaviour on the field":—Sirs John Stockton, Ralph Varney, John Young, William Taylor, Richard Lee, Matthew Philips, George Ireland, William Stoker, William Hampton, Thomas Stallbrooke, John Crosby (of Crosby Hall), and Bartholomew James.

Let it not be forgotten that these heroes were one and all followers of trade, and Masters of their several gilds. Can it be wondered that the highest distinctions and privileges should have been conferred, not only upon the individuals, but upon the communities by whom they had been bred? No honours from the Crown could be too exalted for men of such a stamp, or for communities made of such. We think that "*the wars of the citizens*," and the valour of those brave men wearing "*the liveries of companies*," who were willing to give of their wealth and to shed their blood in the cause of justice and of right, have surrounded the memory of those generations with honour, and have demonstrated that such citizens were worthy of their knightly and chivalric escutcheons, which the blot of cowardice or treachery has never defiled.

We now close our review of the history of the City of London and of the Livery Companies. We trust that those who may have taken the trouble to peruse these sketches, will have found in our unadorned and unpretending pages many particulars with which they had never before met, some of them useful in elucidating periods of our country's history least familiar to us, and affording frequent glances behind the scenes, and pictures of the manners and customs of the early citizens within doors and without, such as no formal history supplies.

We trust that the future may be as prosperous as the present is honourable to the representatives of these great corporations. When we consider their vast responsibility, as patrons of livings, as governors of some of the greatest foundations in the kingdom, and as proprietors of estates of fabulous extent and wealth; and when we remember the manner in which hitherto each of these duties has been performed; we readily acknowledge that we know of no better wish than that their future may be as satisfactory as the past and the present; that they may continue to be generous and just; that their noble recollections of times gone by may stimulate to noble conduct in times to come; that the reputations of the corporations, over which the various courts severally bear rule, may be as near to them as their own individual honour; that they may continue for ever, as now, firm friends of education, of religion, and of our Protestant Church; that their love of hospitality may continue; their vast charity be maintained with unabated liberality; and such foundations as that of St. Paul's School (supported by the Mercers), Merchant Taylors' (maintained by the company of that name), the Leathersellers' School at Lewisham, with those at Tonbridge, Stockport, etc., and similar eminent schools attached to others of the companies, may continue to flourish as nurseries of our greatest and best men, redounding alike to the honour of the great livery companies, by whom funds for their support have been so munificently provided, and to the country which enrols amongst her citizens such patriots and benefactors.

We trust also that the mighty city, under whose protection these great gilds have been reared and fostered, may long continue the pride of Englishmen and the model of local self-government. Considering the complicated nature and vast extent of the business devolving upon the members of this powerful corporation, the marvel is that men can be found possessing sufficient knowledge, energy, and leisure to keep machinery so extensive in motion, and with so excellent a result. For many ages a succession of mayors, aldermen, common-councilmen, and other officials, has been maintained ready and able to administer justice, and to uphold their privileges and immunities. "Dynasties have changed during this long term; governments have fallen; but the municipal constitution of the City of London remains the same. What inexhaustible resources have the City rulers ever found; how equal have they been to every emergency; how much munificence have they displayed; how faithful have they been to their trust; how irreproachable in conduct! With what unstinting hands have they dispensed the City charities; how strictly administered its justice! By an honourable course like this—pursued for centuries—has the Corporation of London advanced our city to its present greatness. Long may it continue in such good hands! Long may it be governed so wisely and so well."

APPENDIX.

A COMPLETE LIST OF MAYORS, FROM A.D. 1189 TO A.D. 1869.

THE names from 1189 to 1419 are extracted from Riley's "Liber Albus;" the remainder from various sources; but chiefly from Herbert's lists of Mayors of the TWELVE GREAT COMPANIES.

1189 to 1212	Henry Fitz-Alwyn
1213	Roger Fitz-Alwyn
1214	Serlo le Mercer
1215	William Hardel
1216	James Alderman (*deposed*); Solomon de Basing
1217 to 1222	Serlo le Mercer
1223 to 1226	Richard Renger
1227 to 1230	Roger le Duc
1231 to 1236	Andrew Bukerel
1237	Richard Renger
1238	William Joynier
1239	Gerard Bat
1240	Reginald de Bungay
1241 to 1243	Ralph Eswy
1244	Michael Tovy
1245	John Gizors
1246	Peter Fitz-Alwyn
1247 to 1248	Michael Tovy
1249	Roger Fitz-Roger
1250	John Norman
1251	Adam de Basing
1252	John Tulesan
1253	Nicholas Bat
1254 to 1257	Ralph Hardel
1258	John Gizors
1259 to 1260	Wm. Fitz-Richard
1261 to 1264	Thos. Fitz-Thomas
1265	Hugh Fitz-Otho; Wm. Fitz-Richard
1266	Alan la Suche
1267	Thos. de Eppegrave; Stephen de Edde-worthe
1268	Hugh Fitz-Otho
1269 to 1270	John Adrien
1271 to 1272	Walter Hervey
1273	Henry Waleys
1274 to 1280	Gregory de Rokesley
1281 to 1283	Henry Waleys
1284	Gregory de Rokesley
1285	Ralph de Sandwich
1286	John Bretone

1287 to 1292	Ralph de Sandwich	1347	Thomas Legge
1293 to 1296	John Bretone	1348	John Lovekyn
1297 to 1298	Henry Waleys	1349	Walter Turke
1299 to 1300	Elias Russel	1350	Richd. Kislingbury
1301 to 1307	John le Blount	1351	Andrew Aubrey
1308	Nicholas de Farndone	1352 to 1353	Adam Fraunceys
1309	Thomas Romeyn	1354	Thomas Legge
1310	Richard de Refham	1355	Simon Fraunceys
1311 to 1312	John Gizors	1356	Henry Picard
1313	Nicholas de Farndone	1357	John Stody
1314	John Gizors	1358	John Lovekyn
1315	Stephen de Abingdon	1359	Simon Dolseley
1316 to 1318	John de Wengrave	1360	John Wroth
1319	Hamo de Chiggewelle	1361	John Peeche
1320	Nicholas de Farndone	1362	Stephen Cavendish
1321 to 1322	Hamo de Chiggewelle	1363	John Notte
1323	Nicholas de Farndone	1364	Adam de Bury
1324	Hamo de Chiggewelle	1365 to 1366	John Lovekyn
1325	Hamo de Chiggewelle (*deposed*) Richard de Betoigne	1367	James Andrew
		1368	Simon Morden
		1369	John Chichester
1326	Richard de Betoigne	1370 to 1371	John Bernes
1327	Hamo de Chiggewelle	1372	John Pyel
1328	John de Grantham	1373	Adam de Bury
1329	Simon Swanlond	1374	William Walworth
1330 to 1331	John de Pounteney	1375	John Warde
1332	John de Prestone	1376	Adam Stable (*deposed*) Nicholas Brembre
1333	John de Pounteney		
1334	Reginald de Conduit		
1335	Nicholas Wotton	1377	Nicholas Brembre
1336	John de Pounteney	1378	John Philpot
1337 to 1338	Henry Darcy	1379	John Hadley
1339 to 1340	Andrew Aubrey	1380	William Walworth
1341	John Oxenford (*died*) Simon Fraunceys	1381 to 1382	John Northampton
		1383 to 1385	Nicholas Brembre
		1386 to 1387	Nicholas Exton
1342	Simon Fraunceys	1388	Nicholas Twyford
1343 to 1344	John Hamond	1389	William Venour
1345	Richard Lucere	1390	Adam Bamme
1346	Geoffrey Wichyngham	1391	John Hende
		1392	William Staundon

1393 John Hadley
1394 John Fresshe
1395 William More
1396 Adam Bamme
1397 Richard Whittington
1398 Drew Barentyn
1399 Thomas Knolles
1400 John Fraunceys
1401 John Shadworth
1402 John Walcot
1403 William Askham
1404 John Hende
1405 John Woodcock
1406 Richard Whittington
1407 William Staundon
1408 Drew Barentyn
1409 Richard Merlawe
1410 Thomas Knolles
1411 Robert Chichele
1412 William Walderne
1413 William Crowmer
1414 Thomas Fauconer
1415 Nicholas Wotton
1416 Henry Barton
1417 Richard Merlawe
1418 William Sevenoke
1419 Richard Whittington
1420 William de Cambridge
1421 Robert Chichele
1422 William de Walderne
1423 William Cromar
1424 John Michelle
1425 John de Coventry
1426 John Rainewelle
1427 John Godney
1428 Henry Bartone
1429 William Eastfielde
1430 Nicholas Wotton
1431 John Wells
1432 John Pervis
1433 John Brokle
1434 Roger Otley
1435 Henry Frowicke
1436 John Michelle
1437 William Eastfielde
1438 Stephen Browne
1439 Robert Large
1440 John Paddesley
1441 Robert de Cloptone
1442 John Hatherley
1443 Thomas Catworthe
1444 Henry Frowicke
1445 Simon Eyre
1446 John Olney
1447 John Godney
1448 Stephen Browne
1449 Thomas Chalton
1450 Nicholas Wilford
1451 William Gregorie
1452 Godrey Fielding
1453 John Norman
1454 Stephen Foster
1455 William Marrowe
1456 Thomas Cannyng
1457 Geoffrey Boleyne
1458 Thomas Scott
1459 William Hulin
1460 Richard Lee
1461 Hugh Wyche
1462 Thomas Coke
1463 Matthew Philips
1464 Ralph Joscelyne
1465 Ralph Varney
1465 John Young
1467 Thomas Oldgrave
1468 William Taylor
1469 Richard Lee
1470 John Stockton
1471 William Edwardes
1472 William Hampton
1473 John Tate
1474 Robert Drope

1475 Robert Bassette
1476 Ralph Joscelyne
1477 Humphry Heyford
1478 Richard Gardiner
1479 Bartholomew James
1480 John de Werks
1481 William Harriott
1482 Edmund Shaa
1483 Robert Billesdon
1484 { Thomas Hill (*died*)
William Stocker (*died*)
John Ward }
1485 Hugh Bryce
1486 Henry Colet
1487 William Horne
1488 Robert Tate
1489 William White
1490 John Mathew
1491 Hugh Clopton
1492 William Martin
1493 Ralph Astrie
1494 Richard Chawrey
1495 Henry Colet
1496 John Tate
1497 William Purchase
1498 John Percival
1499 Nicholas Alwyn
1500 William Remington
1501 John Shaa
1502 Bartholomew Read
1503 William Capell
1504 John Winger
1505 Thomas Kneesworth
1506 Richard Haddon
1507 William Browne (*died*)
Lawrence Aylmer
1508 Stephen Lennyngs
1509 { Thomas Bradbury (*died*)
William Capell }
1510 Henry Kebble
1511 Roger Acheley
1512 { William Coppinger
Richard Haddon }
1513 { William Browne, jun. (*died*)
John Tate }
1514 George Monoux
1515 William Butler
1516 John Rest
1517 Thomas Exmewe
1518 Thomas Myrfine
1519 James Yarford
1520 John Brugges
1521 John Milborne
1522 John Mundy
1523 Thomas Baldrie
1524 William Bailey
1525 John Allen
1526 Thomas Seymer
1527 James Spencer
1528 John Rudstone
1529 Ralph Dormer
1530 Thomas Pargitor
1531 Nicholas Lambert
1532 Stephen Peacock
1533 Christopher Askew
1534 John Champneys
1535 John Allen
1536 Ralph Warren
1537 Richard Gresham
1538 William Forman
1539 William Holles
1540 William Roche
1541 Michael Dormer
1542 John Coates
1543 { William Bowyer (*died*)
Ralph Warren }
1544 William Laxton
1545 Martin Bowes
1546 Henry Hubberthorne
1547 John Gresham
1548 Henry Amcotes
1549 Rowland Hill

1550 Andrew Judd
1551 Richard Dobbes
1552 George Barnes
1553 Thomas White
1554 John Lyon
1555 William Garrard
1556 Thomas Offley
1557 Thomas Curteis
1558 Thomas Leigh
1559 William Hewett
1560 William Chester
1561 William Harper
1562 Thomas Lodge
1563 John White
1564 Richard Mallory
1565 Richard Campion
1566 Christopher Draper
1567 Roger Martin
1568 Thomas Rowe
1569 Alexander Avenon
1570 Rowland Heyward
1571 William Allen
1572 Lionel Ducket
1573 John Rivers
1574 James Hawes
1575 Ambrose Nicholas
1576 John Langley
1577 Thomas Ramsey
1578 Richard Pipe
1579 Nicholas Woodroffe
1580 John Brouche
1581 James Harvey
1582 Thomas Blanke
1583 Edward Osborne
1584 Thomas Pullison
1585 Wolstan Dixie
1586 George Barne
1587 George Bond
1588 { Martin Calthorp (*died*) / Richard Martin }
1589 John Hart
1590 { John Allot (*died*) / Rowland Heyward }
1591 William Webb
1592 William Rowe
1593 { Cuthbert Buckle (*died*) / Richard Martin }
1594 John Spencer
1595 Stephen Slaney
1596 { Thomas Skynner (*died*) / Henry Billingsley }
1597 Richard Saltonstall
1598 Stephen Soames
1599 Nicholas Moseley
1600 William Ryder
1601 John Garrard
1602 Robert Lee
1603 Thomas Bennet
1604 Thomas Lowe
1605 Leonard Halliday
1606 John Watts
1607 Henry Rowe
1608 Humphrey Welde
1609 Thomas Campbell
1610 William Craven
1611 John Pemberton
1612 John Swinnerton
1613 Thomas Middleton
1614 Thomas Hayes
1615 John Jolles
1616 John Leman
1617 George Bolles
1618 Sebastian Harvey
1619 William Cockaine
1620 Fran. Jones
1621 Edward Barkham
1622 Peter Proby
1623 Martin Lumley
1624 John Gore
1625 Allen Cotton
1626 Cuthbert Hacket
1627 Hugh Hammersley

1628 Richard Dean
1629 James Campbell
1630 Robert Ducie
1631 George Whitmore
1632 Nicholas Rainton
1633 { Ralph Freemen (*died*)
Thomas Moulson }
1634 Robert Parkhurst
1635 Christopher Cletherow
1636 Edward Bromfield
1637 Richard Fenn
1638 Maurice Abbott
1639 Henry Garraway
1640 { William Acton (*deposed*)
Edmund Wright }
1641 { Richard Gurney (*deposed*)
Isaac Pennington }
1642 The same
1643 John Wollaston
1644 Thomas Atkin
1645 Thomas Adams
1646 John Gayer
1647 John Warner
1648 { A. Raynardson (*deposed*)
Thomas Andrews }
1649 Thomas Foot
1650 Thomas Andrews
1651 John Kendrick
1652 John Fowke
1653 Thomas Viner
1654 Christopher Packe
1655 John Dethick
1656 Robert Tichborne
1657 Richard Chiverton
1658 John Ireton
1659 Thomas Alleyne
1660 Richard Browne
1661 John Frederick
1662 John Robinson
1663 Anthony Rateman
1664 John Lawrence
1665 Thomas Bludworth
1666 William Bolton
1667 William Peake
1668 William Turner
1669 Samuel Starling
1670 Richard Ford
1671 George Waterman
1672 Robert Hanson
1673 William Hooker
1674 Robert Viner
1675 Joseph Sheldon
1676 Thomas Davies
1677 Francis Chaplin
1678 James Edwards
1679 Robert Clayton
1680 Patience Ward
1681 John Moore
1682 William Pritchard
1683 Henry Tulse
1684 J. Smith
1685 Robert Geffery
1686 John Peake
1687 { John Shorter (*died*)
John Eyles }
1688 { John Chapman (*died*)
Thomas Pilkington }
1689 to 1690 the same
1691 Thomas Stamp
1692 John Fleet
1693 William Ashurst
1694 Thomas Lane
1695 John Houblon
1696 Edward Clarke
1697 Humphrey Edwin
1698 Francis Child
1699 Richard Levett
1700 Thomas Abney
1701 William Gore
1702 Samuel Dashwood
1703 John Parsons
1704 Owen Buckingham

1705 Thomas Rawlinson
1706 Robert Bedingfield
1707 William Withers
1708 Charles Duncombe
1709 Samuel Garrard
1710 Gilbert Heathcote
1711 Robert Beachcroft
1712 Richard Hoare
1713 Samuel Stanier
1714 William Humphreys
1715 Charles Peers
1716 James Bateman
1717 William Lewen
1718 John Ward
1719 George Thorold
1720 John Fryers
1721 William Stewart
1722 Gerard Conyers
1723 Peter Dolmé
1724 George Merttins
1725 Francis Forbes
1726 John Eyles
1727 Edward Becher
1728 Robert Baylis
1729 Richard Brocas
1730 Humphrey Parsons
1731 Francis Child
1732 John Barber
1733 William Billers
1734 Edward Bellamy
1735 John Williams
1736 John Thompson
1737 John Barnard
1738 Micajah Perry
1739 John Salter
1740 { Humphrey Parsons (*died*) / Daniel Lambert }
1741 { Robert Godschall (*died*) / George Heathcote }
1742 Robert Willimott
1743 Robert Westley
1744 Henry Marshall
1745 Richard Hoare
1746 William Benn
1747 Robert Ladbroke
1748 William Calvert
1749 { Samuel Pennant (*died*) / John Blachford }
1750 Francis Cockaine
1751 { Thos. Winterbottom (*died*) / Robert Alsop }
1752 Christopher Gascoyne
1753 { Edward Ironside (*died*) / Thomas Rawlinson }
1754 Stephen Janssen
1755 Slingsby Bethell
1756 Marshe Dickinson
1757 Charles Asgill
1758 Richard Glynn
1759 Thomas Chitty
1760 Matthew Blakiston
1761 Samuel Fludyer
1762 William Beckford
1763 William Bridgen
1764 William Stephenson
1765 George Nelson
1766 Robert Kite
1767 Thomas Harley
1768 Samuel Turner
1769 { William Beckford (*died*) / Barlow Trecothick }
1770 Brass Crosby
1771 William Nash
1772 J. Townsend
1773 Frederick Bull
1774 John Wilkes
1775 John Sawbridge
1776 Thomas Halifax
1777 James Esdaile
1778 Samuel Plumbe
1779 Brackley Kennett
1780 Watkin Lewes

1781 William Plomer
1782 Nathaniel Newnham
1783 Robert Peckham
1784 Richard Clarke
1785 Thomas Wright
1786 Thomas Sainsbury
1787 John Burnell
1788 William Gill
1789 William Pickett
1790 John Boydell
1791 John Hopkins
1792 James Sanderson
1793 Paul Le Mesurier
1794 Thomas Skinner
1795 William Curtis
1796 Brook Watson
1797 John Anderson
1798 Richard Carr Glynn
1799 Harvey Combe

*** From A.D. 1400 to A.D. 1800 there were but fifty Mayors who were not either knights or baronets. From this date we add their rank.

1800 Sir William Staines
1801 Sir John Eamer
1802 Sir C. Price, Bart., M.P.
1803 Sir John Perring, Bart.
1804 Peter Perchard
1805 Sir J. Shaw, Bart., M.P.
1806 Sir William Leighton
1807 John Ansley
1808 Sir Charles Flower, Bart.
1809 Thomas Smith
1810 Joshua Smith
1811 Sir C. S. Hunter, Bart.
1812 George Scholey
1813 Sir Wm. Domville, Bart.
1814 Samuel Birch
1815 Sir M. Wood, Bart., M.P.
1816 The same
1817 Christopher Smith
1818 John Atkins, M.P.
1819 George Bridges, M.P.
1820 John Thorp, M.P.
1821 Christopher Magnay
1822 Sir W. Heygate, Bt, M.P.
1823 Robert Waithman, M.P.
1824 John Garratt
1825 William Venables, M.P
1826 Anthony Brown
1827 Matthias Lucas
1828 William Thompson, M P.
1829 John Crowder
1830 Sir John Key, Bart., M.P.
1831 The same
1832 Sir Peter Laurie
1833 Charles Farebrother
1834 Henry Winchester, M P.
1835 William Copeland, M.P.
1836 Thomas Kelly
1837 Sir John Cowan, Bart.
1838 Samuel Wilson
1839 Sir Chapman Marshall
1840 Thomas Johnson
1841 Sir John Pirie, Bart.
1842 John Humphrey, M.P.
1843 Sir William Magnay, Bart.
1844 Michael Gibbs
1845 John Johnson
1846 Sir George Carroll
1847 John Hooper
1848 Sir J. Duke, Bart., M.P.
1849 Thomas Farncombe
1850 Sir John Musgrove, Bart.
1851 William Hunter
1852 Thomas Challis, M.P.
1853 Thomas Sidney, M.P.
1854 Sir Francis Moon, Bart.
1855 David Salomons, M.P.

1856 Thomas Finnis
1857 Sir Robert Carden
1858 David Wire
1859 John Carter
1860 William Cubitt, M.P.
1861 The same
1862 William Rose, M.P.*
1863 William Lawrence, M.P.
1864 Warren Hale
1865 Benjamin Phillips†
1866 Thomas Gabriel‡
1867 William Allen
1868 James Lawrence, M.P.

* Accepted a knighthood 1867.
† Also accepted a knighthood 1866.
‡ Created a baronet.

LORD MAYORS OF LONDON MEMBERS FOR THE CITY DURING THEIR MAYORALTY.*

We find that during the last two centuries the following Lord Mayors were Members of Parliament for the City during the period of their Chief Magistracy:—Sir John Moore, 1681, Alderman of Walbrook Ward; Sir John Houblon, 1695, Alderman of Cornhill Ward; Sir Francis Child, 1698, Alderman of Farringdon Without; Sir William Withers, 1707, Alderman of Farringdon Within; Sir Gilbert Heathcote, 1710, Alderman of Lime Street Ward; Sir Robert Beachcroft, 1711, Alderman of Portsoken Ward; Sir Richard Hoare, 1712, Alderman of Bread Street Ward; Sir John Eyles, 1726, Alderman of Vintry Ward; Humphry Parsons, Esq., 1730, Alderman of Portsoken Ward (he was Lord Mayor a second time in the years 1740-41); Sir John Barnard, 1737, Alderman of Dowgate Ward; Micajah Perry, 1738, Alderman of Aldgate Ward; Sir Daniel Lambert, 1740, Alderman of the Ward of Tower; Sir Robert Godsschall, 1741, Alderman of Bishopsgate Ward (died in his Mayoralty); George Heathcote, Esq., 1741, Alderman of Walbrook; Sir Robert Willimott, 1742, Alderman of Lime Street Ward; Sir Robert Ladbroke, 1747, Alderman of Castle Baynard Ward; Sir William Calvert, 1748, Alderman of Portsoken; Sir Stephen Theodore Janssen, 1754, Alderman of Bread Street Ward; Slingsby Bethell, Esq., 1755, Alderman of Walbrook; William Beckford, Esq., 1762 (Lord Mayor again in 1769-70), Alderman of Billingsgate Ward; Right Hon. Thomas Harley, 1767 (a son of the Earl of Oxford), Alderman of Portsoken Ward; Barton Trecothick, 1769, Alderman of Vintry Ward; Frederick Bull, Esq., 1773, Alderman of Queenhithe; John Sawbridge, Esq., 1775, Alderman of Langbourn Ward; Sir Watkin Lewes, 1780, Alderman of Lime Street Ward; Nathaniel Newnham, Esq., 1782, Alderman of Vintry; Richard Clark, Esq., 1784, Alderman of Broad Street Ward; Sir William Curtis, 1795, Alderman of Tower Ward; Sir Brook Watson, 1796, Alderman of Cordwainer

* Extracted from the *City Press* with the kind permission of the Proprietors.

Ward; Sir John William Anderson, 1797, Alderman of Aldersgate Ward; Harvey Christian Combe, 1799, Alderman of Aldgate Ward; Sir James Shaw, 1805, Alderman of Portsoken; Sir Matthew Wood, 1815-16, Alderman of Cripplegate Ward; John Atkins, Esq., 1818, Alderman of the Ward of Walbrook; George Bridges, Esq., 1819, Alderman of the Ward of Lime Street; John Thomas Thorp, Esq., 1820, Alderman of Aldgate (this Lord Mayor was Chief Butler at the coronation of George IV., and received as his fee the gold cup out of which his Majesty drank); Robert Waithman, Esq., 1823, Alderman of Farringdon Within; William Venables, Esq., 1825, Alderman of Queenhithe Ward; Sir John Key, 1830 and 1831, Alderman of the Ward of Langbourn; William Lawrence, 1863, Alderman of the Ward of Bread Street. [FORTY IN ALL.]

It may here be noted, as an historical fact well worth knowing, that the first Mayor who was Member for the City of London during the period of his mayoralty was Nicholas Farindon, A.D. 1308. This gentleman was the son of William Farindon, who (A.D. 1281) is said to have purchased the Aldermanry between Ludgate and Newgate for twenty marks. The date of his will is 1361, fifty-three years after his first mayoralty. He was again Mayor of the City, A.D. 1313-14.

LORD MAYORS OF THE CITY, M.P.'S FOR THE PROVINCES DURING THEIR MAYORALTY.

SUBJOINED is a list of Lord Mayors of the City of London who represented the undermentioned cities and boroughs in Parliament during their Chief Magistracy. As above, the period embraces the before-named two centuries:—The first Lord Mayor we have upon record as having represented other than the City of London in Parliament during the period of his Chief Magistracy, is Sir Thomas Bludworth, in 1665, when it is said he was returned for the City of Westminster. He was Alderman of the Ward of Aldersgate; Sir John Parsons (1703), M.P. for Reigate, Alderman of Bassishaw; Sir James Bateman (1716), M.P. for Ilchester, Alderman of Coleman Street Ward; Sir William Lewen (1717), M.P. for Poole, Alderman of Castle Baynard Ward; Sir George Thorold (1719), M.P. for Grantham, Alderman of Cordwainer Ward; Sir Richard Glyn (1758),

M.P. for Coventry, Alderman of Dowgate Ward; Sir Samuel Fludyer (1761), M.P. for Chippenham, Alderman of Cheap Ward; William Beckford, Esq. (1762), Alderman of Billingsgate Ward. This gentleman was returned both by the City of London and the borough of Petersfield. He sat, however, for the City, and is said to have sent £400 to Petersfield "to pave the streets of the town" in lieu of his becoming their representative. Brass Crosby, Esq. (1770-71), M.P. for Honiton, Alderman of Bread Street Ward;* Paul le Mesurier, Esq. (1793), M.P. for Southwark, Alderman of Dowgate Ward; Sir William Heygate (1822), M.P. for Sudbury, Alderman of Coleman Street Ward; Henry Winchester, Esq. (1834), M.P. for Maidstone, Alderman of Vintry Ward; Sir James Duke (1848), M.P. for Boston (subsequently for the City of London), Alderman of Farringdon Ward Without; David Salomons, Esq., M.P. for Greenwich (the first Jewish Sheriff of London), Alderman of the Ward of Cordwainer; William Cubitt, Esq. (1860-61), M.P. for Andover, Alderman for the Ward of Langbourn; William Anderson Rose (1862), M.P. for Southampton, Alderman of Queenhithe Ward; and James Clarke Lawrence (1868), M.P. for Lambeth, Alderman of Walbrook Ward.

* Brass Crosby was the Lord Mayor who was imprisoned in the Tower of London, in 1770, for "refusing to back the Press warrant" against the printers of the *Middlesex Journal*, the *Gazetteer*, and the *Evening Post*, for publishing the parliamentary debates. In consequence of the bold and noble stand he and his City coadjutors made, and by his having fearlessly asserted the rights of the Chief Magistrate of the City in "regard to the matter in his place in Parliament" as Member for Honiton, from that day to the present the House of Commons have not ventured to assail the liberty of the Press, or to attempt the prevention of the publication of the debates in either of the Houses of Parliament.

LIST OF CITY CHARTERS WITH NOTES OF CONTENTS.*

MAGNA CHARTA.—"Quod Civitas Londoniensis habeat omnes libertates suas antiquas et consuetudines suas." (That the City of London have all its ancient liberties or franchises and its customs.)

WILLIAM THE CONQUEROR (began reign A.D. 1066).—To the Bishop and Portreve. Citizens to be law-worthy, their children to be entitled to heirship.

HENRY I. (began reign A.D. 1087).—Grants the Sheriffwick of Middlesex and the farm of Royal revenues arising therefrom. Citizens to appoint their own Justiciar, and not to be obliged to plead in Courts beyond the walls. To be exempt from "Scot," "Danegelt," and the "Murder" (*i. e.*, from the payment then required to be made by the inhabitants of the same frankpledge or district implicated in a murder). Also from waging battel; but purgation in pleas of the Crown to be allowed by the Oaths of Compurgators, *i.e.*, witnesses swearing that they believe the party entitled to credit in his denial of an offence, and deem him innocent of it, otherwise, "waging law." Exemption from providing lodgings for the King's household, and from toll (every kind of payment on goods in transit), passage (payment for passing over ferries), and lastage (payment on every last of leather exported). Citizens to enjoy the privileges and profits of their own "sokes" (districts analogous to manors, the country being divided into socs or sokes, or manors, the City Wards appearing to be comprehended by this term), and not to be amerced beyond their "weres" (*i. e.*, the amount a man was accounted worth in law, according to his rank). Lawsuits in City Courts not to be lost for formal defects in pleas. Citizens to be allowed to have Attachments against boroughs taking toll of them and for debts.

HENRY II. (began reign A.D. 1154).—Recital and confirmation of Henry I.'s Charter. Citizens to be free from bridtoll (bridge-toll, for passing over bridges), childwite (fine for child begotten of a female

* Extracted from the *City Press*, with the kind permission of the proprietors.

bond slave), jeresgive (probably the same as heriot), and scotale (probably same as scot, that is, King's-tax). But Jacob's "Law Dictionary," sixteenth edition, 1802, says that it is where an officer of the forest keeps an alehouse and exacts custom for fear of his displeasure. Although they were to be free, as stated in former Charter, from pleading beyond the City walls, yet this was not to apply to pleas as to tenures outside, or by the King's officers or moneyers of the Mint.

RICHARD I. (began reign A.D. 1189).—1st Charter, 5th year. Recapitulates Henry II.

2nd Charter (8th year). Kiddles (wears) in the Thames to be removed.

JOHN (began reign A.D. 1199).—1st year, 7th June. Same as Henry II.'s Charter.

2nd Charter (11th June, 1st year). Grants and confirms the Sheriffwick of Middlesex for the rent of £300 "blank" money (*i. e.*, full weight of metal to the pound weight). Citizens allowed to "amove" the Sheriffs "when they will." Sheriffs to be presented to the Justices of the Exchequer to account with the King. If the Sheriffs do not make satisfaction in accounting, the citizens must do so; but for the personal offences of the Sheriffs the citizens not to be punished.

3rd Charter (17th June, 1st year). Same as 2nd Charter of Richard I.

4th Charter (20th May, 3rd year). Weavers' Gild expelled.

5th Charter (9th May, 16th year). *Right to choose their own Mayor granted.* Mayor to be presented to the King's Justiciar. Payments to the Sovereign as to his Royal Chamberlainship reserved.

HENRY III. (began reign 1216).—1st Charter (18th February, 11th year). Recapitulates 2nd Charter of King John.

2nd Charter (query, same date as first). Mayoralty granted on same terms as 5th Charter of King John.

3rd Charter. Kiddles (wears) in the Thames prohibited.

4th Charter (16th March, 11th year). Same as Henry II.'s and first of King John.

5th Charter (18th August, 11th year). Rights granted to the citizens in the disafforested Warren of Staines.

6th Charter (26th February, 31st year). Said to be the first that mentions Mayor, and Commonalty, and Common Seal. Mayor to be presented to the Barons of Exchequer to be "admitted Mayor;" (previously he was presented to the King.) Sanctions transfer of

Queenhithe by Earl of Cornwall, and makes over the dues claimed by him to the City.

7th Charter (18th June, 37th year). This charter refers to the Liberty of St. Paul's, according to Norton. Luffman calls it a Charter of Remission.

8th Charter (11th January, 51st year). Trading immunities throughout the kingdom granted to the citizens.

9th Charter (26th March, 52nd year). Grants the right of pleading in the King's courts by attorneys for things done against the King's peace. Pleas of merchandise to be decided by the law merchant in the boroughs and fairs concerned therein; citizens not to be called upon to swear upon the graves of the dead; citizens to be subject to prisage of wines to the King; attorneys may be appointed by foreigners suing in the City courts; as to weighing at the King's trone or beam; debts of citizens may be enrolled in the Exchequer. (This was to afford the citizens the benefit of a judgment in the superior courts.)

Edward I.*—1st Charter (18th April, 26th year). Mayor to be presented to the Constable of the Tower, if the King or the Barons of the Exchequer are absent from London or Westminster.

2nd Charter (17th April, 27th year). Recital by Inspeximus of the last Charter of Henry III.

Edward II.—1st Charter (18th June, 13th year, A.D. 1318). That the keeping of the bridge be committed to others of the City than Aldermen, to be chosen by the Commonalty, to whom they shall be responsible. Mayor to remain in office one year; Sheriffs to have two clerks and two serjeants or bailiffs; Mayor to hold no other civic office, and not to draw suits before him belonging to the Sheriffs' Courts, or otherwise; the Aldermen to serve but one year; the tallages or rates, after being assessed in each Ward, not to be increased by the Mayor, and the amounts thereof to be paid to four of the Commonalty, who shall account for the disposal thereof; strangers to be admitted to the Freedom in the Hustings Court; that those who have the full privileges of the City be in Scot and Lot; City Seal to be in the custody of two Aldermen and two Commoners, to be chosen by the Commoners; none to be brokers but those chosen by the merchants of the mysteries of their vocation; the Chamberlain, Common (Town) Clerk, and the Common Serjeant, to be chosen by the Commonalty; rights of exclusive trade granted to freemen.

* Luffman (p. 67) says of the Charter of Edward I., that the citizens are to be of some certain mystery, or admitted by the Commonalty.

2nd Charter (15th December, 12th year). Military services of citizens in besieging the Castle of Leeds, in Kent, recited, and grant made that those services be not construed into a precedent.

Edward III.—1st Charter (6th year, 1st March). Grants to the citizens the rights of Infangthef (jurisdiction over those within the walls who committed theft), and Outfangthef (jurisdiction over persons belonging to the City taken for theft outside the walls). Also *Power to bequeath in Mortmain.* Sheriff to be amerced one hundred shillings for the escape of a prisoner. City to be chargeable with those who flee to sanctuaries within the City. (This was to provide for the sustenance of felons and others in sanctuary for forty days, who might abjure the realm before the King's Coroner or Bailiff, at the church door, and then go into exile, but were not supplied with food after the forty days were ended). Mayor to be escheator. The Constable of the Tower to take no prisage of victuals or wines. Lands of citizens without the City to be liable to indemnify the citizens with regard to offices held by citizens. One writ to suffice for allowance of the City Charters by the Justices in Eyre in each King's reign.

2nd Charter (1st year, query). Grant of farm of Southwark, as regards the Shrievalty or Bailiwick thereof.

3rd Charter (26th March, 11th year). Exclusive right of trading within the City confirmed to the citizens, notwithstanding an Act of Parliament, 9 Edward III., cap. 1, which allowed all merchant strangers to trade freely in the kingdom.

4th Charter A.D. 1341, (query 15th year, 26th May). Bye-Laws may be made by Mayor and Aldermen, with assent of Commonalty.

5th Charter (28th year, 10th June). City maces to be of silver instead of copper. Luffman (p. 102) refers to a 6th Charter (Office of Aldermen to be annual); and (p. 115) to a 7th Charter referring to Brokers.

Richard II.—1st Charter. Inspeximus Confirmation. The exclusive trading privileges of the City confirmed. Inquisitions of Office, etc., to be taken by the citizens themselves for all customs and impositions, and for all purprestures (interferences with property for improvements), the custody of orphans granted to the Mayor and Chamberlain, King's protections against suits not to avail against citizens.

2nd Charter (7th year). Inspeximus Confirmation.

Henry IV. (began reign 1399).—1st Charter. Newgate, Ludgate, and other gates granted to the City, and tronage or weighing goods, for collection of customs, etc.

2nd Charter. Privileges to Merchant Strangers, by allowing them to sell in gross to all the King's subjects by Act 7th Henry IV., cap. 9, not to authorize within the City such Merchants buying and selling to others, but only for their own use.

HENRY V. (began reign 1413).—2nd year, 1st and 2nd mere confirmations.

HENRY VI.—(7th year). Purprestures, encroachments on property for improvements, provided for.

EDWARD IV. (began reign 1461).—1st Charter (2nd year, 9th Nov.) *Certifying City Customs by the Recorder* provided for; Aldermen not to be called upon to serve as jurymen, controllers, or collectors, of King's taxes, or subsidies, beyond the City, although having landed property outside the walls. Southwark re-granted with the right to all estrays, treasure-trove, and other revenues for £10 per annum.

2nd Charter (27th August, 3rd year). Tronage, *i. e.*, weighing of customable or taxable articles at the King's beam, to be in the hands of the citizens.

3rd Charter (20th June, 18th year). Purchases in mortmain allowed to the extent of 200 marks per annum. (Consideration for this Charter was the payment of £1,923 9*s.* 8*d.*) (Norton, p. 490.)

4th Charter (20th June, 18th year). Refers to Scavage (searching or surveying customable articles); Package (packing goods requiring to be packed, *quæ.*, after being customed); Picking (sorting and rejecting improper substances mixed with goods); Portage (moving goods); and Garbling (sorting of spices). City Coroner not to be appointed by King's Chief Butler, but by the City. The exclusive trading privileges of the City confirmed against Merchant Strangers. The office of Gauger granted.

HENRY VII.—(23rd July, 20th year). Confirmation of Henry IV.'s second Charter as to Tronage.

HENRY VIII. (began reign 1509). (1st year, 12th July). Confirmation.

2nd Charter (16th June, 10th year). Inquisitions, heretofore taken at St. Martin's-le-Grand, to be taken at Guildhall.

3rd Charter. Tronage confirmed and absolutely granted to the City.

EDWARD VI. (began reign 1547).—(23rd April, 4th year). Lands, tenements, etc., in Southwark, which Henry VIII. had purchased of Charles (Brandon), Duke of Suffolk, granted to the "Commonalty."

Also the manor as late possessed by the Archbishop of Canterbury, for £647 2*s.* 1*d.* Norton (p. 510, in note) says this valuable estate has been considered applicable to the maintenance of London Bridge.

James I.—1st Charter (3rd year, 26th August). 25th year, per Quo Warranto Case, Conservancy of Thames confirmed to the City.

2nd Charter (6th year, 20th September). Confirmation of Charter. City boundaries enlarged by the addition of certain extra-municipal districts, viz.:—Duke's Place, Great and Little Saint Bartholomew's, Blackfriars, Whitefriars, and Coleharbour.

3rd Charter (12th year, 15th September). Confirmation.

Charles I. (began reign 1625).—1st Charter. Inspeximus and Confirmation of City Charters and Customs.

2nd Charter. Scavage and Waterbailage.

Charles II.—(24th June, 15th year). Per Quo Warranto Case, it is *January*. The Grand Inspeximus Charter. The Quo Warranto Case was 35th Charles II.

William and Mary (began reign 1689).—(28th July, 4th year). Confirmation.

George II. (began reign 1727).—Confirmation. By the two preceding Charters, *all* the Aldermen are made Justices of Peace, and those who have passed the chair of the Quorum.

The Act restoring the City Charters and Privileges, after the Judgment in Quo Warranto (35 Charles II.), William and Mary (Sess. 1, cap. 8) mentions as to rents on leases—The "Chamber," "Bridge House," "Hospitals," as distinct.

George III.—(2nd year, cap. 18). Upon all elections of Mayor, Sheriffs, Chamberlain, Bridgemasters, and Auditors of Bridgemasters' and Chamberlain's Accounts, to be chosen by Liverymen, no one to poll who does not take the prescribed oath as Liveryman.

INDEX.

THE END.

F. BENTLEY AND CO., PRINTERS, SHOE LANE, FLEET STREET.

840844

Printed in Great Britain by
Amazon.co.uk, Ltd.,
Marston Gate.